Physical Punishment in Childhood

Physical Punishment in Childhood

The Rights of the Child

Bernadette J. Saunders and Chris Goddard

(W)WILEY-BLACKWELL

A John Wiley & Sons, Ltd., Publication

This edition first published 2010
© 2010 John Wiley & Sons Ltd.

Wiley-Blackwell is an imprint of John Wiley & Sons, formed by the merger of Wiley's global Scientific, Technical, and Medical business with Blackwell Publishing.

Registered Office
John Wiley & Sons Ltd, The Atrium, Southern Gate, Chichester, West Sussex, PO19 8SQ, UK

Editorial Offices
The Atrium, Southern Gate, Chichester, West Sussex, PO19 8SQ, UK
9600 Garsington Road, Oxford, OX4 2DQ, UK
350 Main Street, Malden, MA 02148-5020, USA

For details of our global editorial offices, for customer services, and for information about how to apply for permission to reuse the copyright material in this book please see our website at www.wiley.com/wiley-blackwell.

The right of the author to be identified as the author of this work has been asserted in accordance with the Copyright, Designs and Patents Act 1988.

Library of Congress Cataloging-in-Publication Data

Saunders, Bernadette J.
    Physical punishment in childhood : the rights of the child / Bernadette J. Saunders and Chris Goddard.
        p. cm.
    Includes bibliographical references and index.
    ISBN 978-0-470-68256-2 (cloth) – ISBN 978-0-470-72706-5 (pbk.)   1. Corporal punishment of children.   2. Child abuse–Prevention.   3. Children's rights.
I. Goddard, Chris (Christopher)   II. Title.
    HQ770.4.S28 2010
    362.76–dc22

                                                                                      2009033753

A catalogue record for this book is available from the British Library.

Set in 10.5 on 13 pt Minion by Toppan Best-set Premedia Limited
Printed in Singapore by Markono Print Media Pte Ltd

1   2010

This book is about the rights of the child, and recognizing that children are important people whose voices should be heard and respected.

We dedicate this book to the children who inspired us through their insights and ideas in this research, and to our own children who have enriched our lives, and brought us so much joy.

Christopher, Lachlan and Elyshia
Tom, Alex, Michael and Julia

Contents

Acknowledgements

This book relied upon the willingness of children, parents, grandparents and professionals to reflect upon their experiences and thoughts about physical punishment – a sensitive and controversial issue. We sincerely thank all of the participants, particularly the children, for allowing us to reproduce their insights and ideas. Children's contributions were especially important to us. Their voices motivated us to write this book with a view to influencing parenting practices and societal attitudes. As one eight-year-old said in a focus group:

> If adults heard the conversations that we're having I think that they'd be able to see why smacking is bad and why we shouldn't smack.

The Australian Research Council and the Australian Childhood Foundation (ACF) supported the research financially. The ACF also provided support in many other ways; special thanks are extended to the Chief Executive Officer Dr Joe Tucci, and to Dr Neerosh Mudaly, a Senior Counsellor at the ACF and a Senior Research Fellow at Child Abuse Prevention Research Australia. They provided guidance, support and encouragement. We also thank the Faculty of Medicine, Nursing and Health Sciences, and the Department of Social Work at Monash University. We acknowledge the role of the Board of Child Abuse Prevention Research Australia, which provides support for research at our Centre. We also thank Wiley/Blackwell Publishers for their patience during the writing process.

Thank you to our colleagues Lillian De Bortoli, Dr Janet Stanley, Dr Jan Coles and Joy Karton for their support and encouragement. Special thanks also to Dr John Frederick and Dr Bronwyn Naylor for their time and comments. Last, but by no means least, we owe sincere appreciation to our families and friends. In particular, Bernadette extends heartfelt thanks to her husband Chris, for his constant support and understanding, and to her wonderful children. She also expresses much gratitude to her mother Josephine and late father Kevin O'Toole. Chris would like to thank his wife Lydia for reading almost every word he writes, and their children for their patience.

1

Introduction

You shouldn't hit people ... because there's a better way than hurting someone. (12-year-old)

This book is about the rights of children to live in environments where they are loved, nurtured and valued as people with important insights. We contend that children must be recognized as individuals with human rights as well as special needs for protection (Goddard, 1993). In complex, adult-centric, materialistic societies, children may be viewed as appendages of adults, and their feelings and experiences minimized. Children's smaller stature and evolving competencies distance them from adults, who perceive themselves to be more advanced and more important. It is 20 years since the United Nations Convention on the Rights of the Child (UNCRC) (1989) was drafted, and perhaps adult–child relationships have changed (Jenks, 1996). Children may now be more visible and audible, but too many children continue to be hurt and silenced by the abuse of adults (Mudaly and Goddard, 2006), and children may still be 'afraid to speak because they fear physical punishment' (Saunders and Goddard, 2007, p. 36).

It is 30 years since Sweden prohibited physical punishment, recognizing children's rights to the same protection from assault as adults. Twenty-four countries have since followed Sweden's example. The rest of the world, however, continues to tolerate physical punishment to some degree. In this

Physical Punishment in Childhood: The Rights of the Child, by Bernadette J. Saunders and Chris Goddard
Copyright © 2010 John Wiley & Sons, Ltd.

context, physical punishment may dampen children's curiosity and spontaneity, and enhance their vulnerability to abuse:

> The silencing and powerlessness of children who suffer degrading and unjust treatment by adults responsible for their care and protection is a characteristic of childhood often maintained by sanctioned physical punishment. (Saunders and Goddard, 2008, p. 415)

Defining physical punishment

Defining physical punishment is challenging. The impact on children may be inconsequential or catastrophic. Some researchers differentiate between what they term 'normative' physical punishment, such as a painful slap on the child's backside, and more severe physical punishment. Others argue that 'normative' physical punishment includes severe responses, including the use of implements to hit children (Gershoff, 2002b). For those who do not consider mild physical punishment to be abusive, deciding a threshold of when 'acceptable' physical punishment ends and child abuse begins is both difficult and value-laden: 'the line between legitimate corporal punishment and child abuse is, at best, fuzzy' (Freeman, 1994, p. 21).

Differentiating physical punishment and physical abuse

Definitions of words that may be associated with physical punishment also create confusion. For example, definitions of physical abuse, such as those put forward by the World Health Organization and by the International Society for the Prevention of Child Abuse and Neglect (Butchart *et al.*, 2006) and definitions of corporal or physical punishment, such as those proposed by the End Physical Punishment of Children organization (Nilsson, 2003 and Pinheiro, 2006), suggest a subtle, or non-existent, differentiation between these two responses to children. Yet physical punishment is not consistently defined, either legally or colloquially, as physical abuse. 'Physical abuse' is

> the intentional use of physical force against a child that results in – or has a high likelihood of resulting in – harm for the child's health, survival, development or dignity. This includes hitting, beating, kicking, shaking, biting, strangling, scalding, burning, poisoning and suffocating. Much physical violence against children in the home is inflicted with the object of punishing. (Butchart *et al.*, 2006, p. 10)

'Physical punishment' is

> any punishment in which physical force is intended to cause some degree of pain or discomfort: hitting children with a hand, or with a cane, strap or other object, kicking, shaking or throwing children, scratching, pinching, biting or pulling their hair, forcing them to stay in uncomfortable positions, locking or tying them up, burning, scalding or forced ingestion – for example washing mouths out with soap. (Nilsson, 2003, p. 3)

Pinheiro, in the *World Report on Violence against Children*, maintains that

> corporal punishment involves hitting ('smacking', 'slapping', 'spanking') children, with the hand or with an implement – whip, stick, belt, shoe, wooden spoon, etc. But it can also involve, for example, kicking, shaking or throwing children, scratching, pinching, biting, pulling hair or boxing ears, forcing children to stay in uncomfortable positions, burning, scalding or forced ingestion (for example, washing children's mouths out with soap or forcing them to swallow hot spices). (2006, pp. 52–3)

Actions included in Nilsson's (2003) and Pinheiro's (2006) definitions of physical and corporal punishment may well result in injuries which would be condemned as physical abuse if they were not inflicted upon children for disciplinary reasons.

The report by the International Society for the Prevention of Child Abuse (Daro, 2006), which drew on a survey of key informants from 72 countries across Africa, the Americas, Asia, Europe and Oceania, revealed that only 48.6% of all informants felt that physical punishment is considered abusive in their countries:

> [P]hysical discipline, although often cited in the research as being potentially harmful to a child's emotional and physical well-being, remains normative practice within many countries and is not considered, in and of itself, synonymous with child abuse. (Daro, 2006, p. 14)

While injury to a child may differentiate sanctioned physical punishment from illegal physical abuse, common law in countries such as the UK, the US, Canada, and Australia makes clear that even severe injury to a child may be successfully defended as reasonable physical chastisement (Bailey, 2003; Bitensky, 2006; Cashmore and de Haas, 1995; Freeman, 1999; Pollard, 2003; Turner, 2002). The legal notion of 'reasonableness' allows the courts to apply standards prevalent in society (Department of Health, 2000), but definitions vary:

Words such as 'due', 'moderate', 'necessary' and 'reasonable' as applied to chastisement are ever changing, according to the ideas prevailing in our minds during the period and conditions in which we live. (Carpenter v. Commonwealth, 186 Va. 851, 44 S.E.2d 419, 424, (Va. 1947))

Straus and Gelles define physical punishment as 'a legally permissible violent act (or acts) carried out as part of the parenting role' (1990, p. 137). In this context, physical punishment and child abuse may be linked as forms of aggression, distinguished only by where they sit on a possible continuum (Rodriguez and Sutherland, 1999). In some cases the mild 'smack' or 'tap' on a child's hand or bottom escalates into severe and some- times criminal abuse. Even fatal abuse has been linked to physical punish- ment (see for example Nielssen *et al.*, 2009; Wilczynski, 1995; 1997b), and definitions of fatal abuse (such as this one from Somander and Rammer, 1991) may reflect this:

[T]he killing of a child by one or a series of assaults by a parent or a person with the status of a parent to eliminate a disturbing behaviour of a child without the intention to kill. (p. 47)

'Corporal punishment', physical punishment and 'lawful correction'

The term 'corporal punishment' is typically used in association with physi- cal punishment legally inflicted in schools and children's institutions (Human Rights Watch, 2008). The terms 'physical chastisement' and 'lawful correction' are frequently used in legal documents and the writings of legal researchers. However, the terms 'physical punishment', 'physical discipline', 'physical chastisement', 'lawful correction' and 'corporal punishment' are often used interchangeably. Definitions of these terms typically emphasize the perpetrator's intent to cause pain or discomfort but not to injure the child:

Corporal punishment is the use of physical force with the intention of causing a child pain, but not injury, for the purposes of correction or control of the child's behaviour ... this definition includes the phrase 'but not injury' in order to distinguish corporal punishment from physical abuse [but] causing pain is intentional. (Straus, 1994, pp. 4–5)

Tenuous distinctions and preconditions appear in Straus's (1994) defini- tion. Of significance, Straus (1996) observes that parental self-control may be absent from incidents of physical punishment, and the child may be unintentionally injured as a result. Moreover, a parent's reason for physically punishing a child may have more to do with the parent's emotional state and living conditions, particularly in situations of domestic violence, than with the inappropriateness of the child's behaviour (Cohen, 1996; Silverstein *et al.*, 2009). Bitensky, subtly modifying Straus's (1994) definition, defines 'corporal punishment' as 'the use of physical force upon a child's body with the intention of causing the child to experience bodily pain so as to correct or punish the child's behavior' (Bitensky, 2006, p. xix). The Committee on the Rights of the Child defines 'corporal punishment' as 'any punishment in which physical force is used and intended to cause some degree of discomfort, however light' (Bitensky, 2006, p. 4).

Defining 'discipline'

Greven (1990) attempts to distinguish physical discipline from corporal punishment by maintaining that the former is a positive and necessary aspect of parenting, while the latter is an infliction of pain on a child both for retribution and parental power assertion. However, punishment of children, especially physical punishment, is not an essential element of discipline. Carey defines 'punishment' as 'one of a variety of strategies a person may choose to use when disciplining' (1994, p. 1006). He defines 'discipline' as 'correcting, shaping or refining the mental facilities or moral character of an individual' (Carey, 1994, p. 1006).

The distinction between punishment and discipline is significant because all children need discipline. McCord (1996) contends that painful punishment actually detracts from discipline as it communicates to children that it is acceptable to inflict pain on others.

Defining 'violence'

Another word associated with physical punishment is violence, variously defined with emphasis either on causing pain/injury or on legality. 'Violence' has been defined in the following ways: 'behaviour' which involves 'physical force' with the intention of hurting, damaging or killing 'someone or something' (Pearsall, 1998, p. 2063), 'an act carried out with the intention, or perceived intention, of causing pain or injury to another person' (Straus, 1994, p. 7), and 'the use of force in a social situation in a way that those in power define as illegitimate' (Dartington Social Research Unit, 1983, in Bullock, 1989, p. 18).

The Dartington definition suggests that physical force such as the lawful chastisement of children may not be violence, whereas the former definitions of violence would include all types and degrees of physical punishment. Physical punishment's broad manifestations and community approval led Graziano *et al.* (1996) to suggest a continuum of violence beginning with 'sub-abusive' violence. 'Sub-abusive' violence includes 'appropriate' well-meaning disciplinary responses such as 'spanking, hitting, whipping and so forth, at all levels of violence too low to be considered abusive' (Graziano *et al.*, 1996, p. 413). Other writers refer to 'child rearing violence' (Hemenway *et al.*, 1994, p. 1011), 'ordinary violence' (Straus, 1983, p. 213), 'normal violence' (Gelles and Cornell, 1990, p. 21) and 'primordial violence' (Straus, 2009, p. 1314). Indeed, Steinmetz and Straus refer to the family as the 'cradle of violence' (1973, p. 50). Almost two-thirds of children in Mullender *et al.*'s study perceived 'threats to hurt' and physical aggression as equally violent (2002, p. 47).

Physical punishment and 'domestic violence'

A related term, not usually associated with physical punishment, is 'domestic violence', generally defined as 'violence between adults in the home' (Mullender *et al.*, 2002, p. 36). 'Domestic violence' is usually perpetrated by a man against a woman with whom he has some relationship (McGee, 1997). The so-called 'witnessing' of 'domestic violence' is considered a form of child abuse (see, for example, Bedi and Goddard, 2007). However, the term 'domestic violence' does not typically incorporate adults' violent responses to children (Lansdown, 2000).

In the study by Mullender *et al.* (2002), 95% of children understood 'violence/hitting', 'fighting' and 'arguing' to be constituents of 'domestic violence', with a small percentage of children also including child abuse in their definition. McGee (1997) describes children witnessing, over-hearing, feeling responsible for, and seeing the effects of adult-to-adult violence occurring in their homes. Children who have lived in violent families predominantly express sadness and fear, though they may simultaneously feel anger, distress, fear and confusion (Mullender *et al.*, 2002). Parental physical punishment is a form of domestic violence requiring recognition and research. Lansdown states that 'violence involves a lack of respect for the victim, and a belief that the perpetrator is entitled to behave in ways that are not reciprocal'. We have started, she observes, to challenge 'these assumptions in respect of violence against women' but they persistently influence 'the large majority of parents in the upbringing of children' (2000, p. 417).

Colloquialisms

Pollock (1983, pp. 200–201) reveals that prior to the 19th century, when the euphemisms 'spanking' and 'smacking' appeared in the diaries of Louisa Alcott and Frances Shelley, the word 'whipping' was probably an umbrella term for various means of physical punishment, with or without an implement. Primary sources indicate that children were 'whipped' with a parent's 'palm' and with a 'stick'; a 'whipping' may not have described parental brutality (Pollock, 1983, p. 200). The nature of the physical punishment to which children were subjected historically may therefore be unclear. Words may be misleading and 'ambiguous' (Straus, 1994, p. 5). In the US, Straus observes, many people in poorer communities refer to all physical punishment as 'beating', although some of these people would use 'spanking' to refer to hitting the child on an exposed bottom. In contrast, middle-income Americans 'spank' their children by 'slapping or hitting any part of the child' (Straus, 1994, p. 5). In Canada, Turner defines 'punitive spanking' as

> the bringing down of the hand or an object once or more than once on the clothed or bare buttocks of another with a degree of force to convey the spanker's real disapproval or anger with some aspect of the other's behaviour or character ... to be an effective punishment, the degree of force used must cause the other pain. (2002, p. 194)

In Australia and the UK, parents commonly refer to physical punishment as 'smacking'. When parents' views on 'smacking' are sought in polls, a range of responses may be included and understood, such as 'single smacks, spanking, beating with a slipper or wooden spoon or whipping with a belt' (Leach, 1999, p. 4).

The *New Oxford Dictionary of English* (Pearsall, 1998, p. 1756) and *The Australian Pocket Oxford Dictionary* (Moore, 2002, p. 1040) define a 'smack' as 'a sharp slap or blow'. Pearsall suggests that a 'smack' is characteristically applied 'with the palm of the hand' (Pearsall, 1998, p. 1756). Children have defined a 'smack' as 'a hard or very hard hit ... usually on the bottom, arm or head [and] smacking hurts' (Willow and Hyder, 1998, p. 11). Willow and Hyder assert that children's perspectives refute adults' contentions that 'smacking' is not the same as hitting. They maintain that adults prefer to equate 'smacking' with a 'gentle tap' or a 'loving slap' yet 'in all group discussions children said 'smacking' was hitting' (Willow and Hyder, 1998, p. 89). Indeed, one child observed, 'A smack is parents trying to hit you, [but] instead of calling it a hit they call it a "smack"' (Willow and Hyder, 1998, p. 27).

The significance of sanctioned physical punishment

It seems clear that 'much violence is learnt at home, home therefore is surely where we should begin to arrest the process' (Goddard, 1994, p. 12). Physical punishment was permitted in all Australian schools until 1983 (Ware, 1983). It was banned in UK state schools in 1986 and in private schools a decade later. Although schools prohibit corporal punishment, common law and statute still permits parents to punish children physically, even with an implement, such as a belt, a wooden spoon or a stick. While the acceptability of hitting children is increasingly questioned (see, for example, Tucci *et al.*, 2002; 2006), attitudinal changes are not reflected in, or encouraged by, current laws. Parents are expected to discipline their children, even physically, with forethought and self-control. Many children, however, have been seriously injured, or even killed, in the name of discipline (Korbin, 1989; Nielssen *et al.*, 2009; Wilczynski, 1995; 1997b), and when charged with assault, parents may sometimes defend their actions as lawful correction.

Questions about what is and what is not acceptable behaviour towards children, and when physical punishment ends and child abuse begins, elicit considerable public and professional controversy. Child protection professionals struggle when confronted with conflicts between children's rights and parents' rights. Yet, legally permitted physical punishment exposes children to a physically threatening environment, violates children's rights to physical integrity and to protection from harm, promotes violence as an acceptable means of resolving conflict, and reinforces the misconception that physical punishment is an effective form of discipline. Countries such as Australia, the US, the UK and Canada lag behind many other countries that have taken positive steps to enhance the status and human rights of children by prohibiting physical punishment.

An overview of this book

In Chapter 2 we discuss the literature on children, childhood and parenting with a particular focus on the part physical punishment and child abuse have played in silencing children and denying them rights as human beings. Chapter 3 explores some legal perspectives on physical discipline of children, and reviews differing common law and legislative responses to physical punishment. Chapter 4 briefly outlines the practical and ethical process undertaken to gather, analyse and report the contributions of the children and adults who participated in the research upon which this book is based.

Chapter 5 begins with reference to research that indicates the current nature and incidence of physical punishment in the US, the UK, Canada and Australia. We then extend our analysis of language, exploring the different meanings attributed to words commonly associated with physical punishment and discipline and highlighting differences between them. This analysis serves to enhance understanding of the descriptions that follow of participants' physical punishment at school, at home and in public. In Chapter 6 we extend our exploration of the meaning given to words associated with physical punishment, particularly the descriptors 'violent', 'violence' and 'child abuse'. We then explore participants' understanding of these and whether they associate them with parents' disciplinary responses to children. Professionals' concerns about physical punishment are then presented in the context of differing perceptions of its effectiveness.

Chapter 7 completes our language analysis through an exploration of language associated with children's sanctioned physical punishment, and language used to refer to children and to characterize childhood. Attention is focused on the power of words both to minimize and challenge violent actions directed at children. Some adults' and children's perceptions of children's status in contexts that sanction physical punishment are then documented. Chapter 8 explores some of the literature on the effects of physical punishment. The insights of the children and adults in this research are then presented.

In Chapter 9 we ask what motivates parents to punish children physically and, in contexts where physical punishment continues from one generation to the next, how it is explained and justified. Discussion focuses on different parenting styles as well as some theoretical understandings of the reasons why physical punishment persists. We then present the perspectives of the adults, families, and children from this research.

Chapter 10 focuses on arguments about the morality of physically punishing children. We present participants' views on current legal responses and law reform, along with children's comments on alternatives to physical punishment and their ideas about channels through which children's feelings and views could be communicated. Finally, Chapter 11 briefly considers what needs to change in order for children to be granted the right to the physical integrity that they deserve.

2

Childhood and physical punishment in historical perspective

Introduction

Parents have always been dissatisfied with the extent of children's compliance with their wishes and demands, and they have resorted to various means to encourage obedience. An early inscription found in Mesopotamia suggests that parents were concerned about children's disobedience (Sommerville, 1990). Later, Plato observes that a 'child in his present helplessness loves and is loved by his parents, though he is likely to be at odds with them at some future time' (Laws, 6, 754E, cited in Hamilton and Cairns, 1961). Aristotle similarly suggests that children's obedience to parents is short-lived: 'Children start with natural affections and disposition to obey' (Nicomachean Ethics, Bk. 10, 1180b, cited in Barnes, 1984).

More recently, Hood-Williams remarks that parents still expect children 'to respect, honour and, above all, to obey' (1990, p. 158). Freeman argues, however, that whilst in the past children typically deferred to adults' wisdom, today 'there is little ... of what earlier generations would have recognised as respect' (1983, p. 16). Nevertheless, he contends, perceptions of children as property rather than people and the pre-eminence of family autonomy remain strong, even if parental power over children is weakening.

Physical Punishment in Childhood: The Rights of the Child, by Bernadette J. Saunders and Chris Goddard
Copyright © 2010 John Wiley & Sons, Ltd.

Parents and children: a brief historical overview

Childhood has characteristically been a time of dependence, subordination and vulnerability. The childhoods of very young children in particular have largely been determined by the perspectives and behaviours of the adults responsible for their nurture. The status and capabilities accorded to children change across time and place.

Documentation of these childhoods is a relatively recent phenomenon arising within the field of sociology (James and Prout, 1997; Jenks, 1996; Qvortrup *et al.*, 1994). Increasingly, adults are recognizing children's existing as well as developing capabilities and insights. However, historically derived perceptions of children continue to affect the way in which children are treated today. The history of parent–child relations and children's rights is therefore integral to a discussion about children's current position as recipients of sanctioned physical punishment. As Mayall suggests, when thinking about 'any social group which is subordinated within the social order' it appears fundamental to reflect upon 'the past bearing down on the group's social position and its ability to negotiate, improve or transform' (2002, p. 39).

Parent–child relations

In *Centuries of Childhood*, Philippe Ariès (1962) contends that childhood, as we know it, was non-existent in medieval times. Once children developed independence from their parents, around the age of seven, they became individuals not differentiated from older people. He did not contend that children were 'neglected, forsaken or despised', just that childhood as a category appeared to extend only to about the age of seven (Ariès, 1962, p. 266). Ariès arrived at this conclusion by studying medieval literature, art and artefacts. Children in medieval paintings were depicted as smaller in size than adults but their clothing and other physical features were not dissimilar to those of adults. Infants, in contrast, were depicted wearing baby clothes. Ariès further maintains that parents' emotional ties to children were fragile. As serious illness and death in childhood were common, emotional detachment served to lessen parental distress. In contrast, Ariès observes that 17th century paintings began to depict children in a different way than adults. Paintings portrayed children behaving frivolously and requiring adult protection, and deceased children were also depicted. These changes, Aries suggests, reflect significant changes in children's status and adults' feelings toward children. Childhood became a longer, separate phase in human development, reinforced with the intro-duction of schools for children. A perception of children 'as fragile crea-tures of God who needed to be both safeguarded and reformed' (Ariès, 1962, p. 133) began to emerge. With the introduction of education came 'a kind of "quarantine" period for children' (Clarke, 2004, p. 5), between birth and adulthood, during which time children were disciplined, often physically.

Like Ariès, other researchers have traced the history of childhood and arrived at their own conclusions about adults' attitudes toward children, and children's experiences of childhood. Pollock (1983) observes that several researchers, including de Mause (1976), documented the murder, abandonment and ill-treatment of children in classical civilizations through to the 18th century. Swaddling, for example, was perceived as convenient for adults who were then free to ignore their babies (de Mause, 1976). As mentioned, adult indifference towards children may reflect a lack of paren-tal investment in children likely to succumb to fatal illness or injury in childhood (Ariès, 1962). On the other hand, inadequate childcare and a lack of parental affection for individual children have been offered as part explanation for the high mortality rates; some children may have been intentionally neglected and cruelly treated (Pinchbeck and Hewitt, 1969). Indeed, as child survival rates improved prior to the widespread adoption of modern hygiene and medical practices, Trumbach (1978) suggests that a contributing factor may have been positive changes in societal and paren-tal attitudes toward children.

Various writers have linked harsh treatment of children in later histori-cal periods to one or more of the following: the development of an educa-tion system; 'the concept of Original Sin' and 'inherent sinfulness'; 'state policies'; 'the law'; 'employment'; and the development of 'the closed nuclear family' (Pollock, 1983, pp. 26–7). Researchers disagree about when the concept of childhood emerged and whether it resulted in an increase or a decrease in the harshness and extent of physical punishment experi-enced by children. However, most researchers claim that severe physical punishment was very common, and numerous authors contend that chil-dren were 'systematically abused' (Pollock, 1983, p. 33). De Mause main-tains that 'century after century of battered children grew up and in turn battered their own children' (1976, p. 41).

Stone observes that in 16th- and 17th-century homes 'whipping' was commonplace and 'the prime aim' was to break the child's 'will' (1977, p. 167). Pollock (1983), however, refutes much of the research cited above, suggesting that the sources of information on which assertions were made about the characteristic harshness of childhood, or the non-existence of childhood, are unreliable or unrepresentative. She suggests that Ariès blindly researched medieval times for modern conceptions of children. He thus failed to see age-determined social and task-oriented groupings in medieval societies. Children may have been viewed differently from the way they are perceived now, but they maintained a unique status. Moreover, Pollock suggests that de Mause wrote a history of child abuse, not an account of childhood. Swaddling, for example, may be viewed as a protective measure to shield babies from harm and keep them warm, and parents who anticipated the loss of a child may have invested more rather than less in their child's care in an effort to beat the odds. Influenced by sociobiological theory (Dawkins, 1976), Pollock maintains that mothers were deeply attached to their children, and 'parents were grief stricken at the loss of a child' (1983, p. 51).

Pollock drew on diverse primary historical sources, including parents' and children's diaries, to argue that child abuse was not as common as some claim, and physical punishment occurred infrequently and as a last resort. She cites Alcott (1799–1888), who documented using physical punishment as a means of discipline when his children were under the age of seven. He then used reasoning and other means of discipline. Alcott's daughter's diaries, begun when she was 10 years old, recorded only that her father scolded her. Physical punishment was not mentioned (Pollock, 1983).

Pollock suggests that in the 19th century parents and educators demanded 'total obedience', which resulted in more frequent use of physical discipline and, for some children, subjection to extreme cruelty (1983, p. 199). However, she contends that parents throughout history have attempted to 'control' or 'regulate' a child's behaviour by using not only physical means of discipline but 'deprivation of privileges, advice, lectures, making the child feel ashamed, and remonstrations' (1983, p. 199). Pollock observes that the nature of the parent–child relationship is more significant in determining the type of discipline that was used than the period of time in which the parenting took place. The 19th century, she suggests, may have been an exception to this as it appears to have been a notably cruel time for children. However, parents who were strict and parents who indulged their children may be found in every historical period. It also appears that parents were probably more inclined to punish younger children physically and to use reason to guide the behaviour of older children (Pollock, 1983).

Pollock also presents evidence that parents' attitudes toward children did not always predict their behaviour. She cites three primary sources in the 17th century, all of whom believed children were 'full of original sin' yet none of whom documented physical punishment of their children (1983, p. 199). One of the sources condemned it. In the 18th century, two sources documented their intention 'to take great care of their off-spring' yet one of the sources whipped her children to ensure obedience while the other appeared 'less concerned with obedience and did not mention inflicting any whippings' (Pollock, 1983, p. 199). Three sources from the 19th century 'viewed their offspring as depraved', yet only two of the sources physically punished their children (Pollock, 1983, p. 199). Pollock concludes that the history of childhood, well into the 20th century, suggests the 'unique emotional relationship between parent and child is a crucial determinant of disciplinary methods'. Indeed, she continues, 'the protective nature of parental care inhibits most parents from enforcing their authority with brutality' (Pollock, 1983, p. 202). Hendrick criticizes Pollock's history of childhood, claiming that she 'trawls through diaries and autobiographies' to confirm her opinion about parents' altruism, and parents' anxieties about their children's emotions (1997, p. 27).

Clearly, diverse histories of childhood reveal variations in parent–child relations at any point in time along with variations in the economic and social circumstances in which children lived. Variation is also apparent in adults' opinions about the nature of children and their capabilities.

Adults' opinions about the nature of children

Adults' opinions about, and interactions with, children are influenced by the 'cultural mores' and 'practised values' of the communities of which both adults and children are a part (Lloyd-Smith and Tarr, 2000, p. 62). As Smart *et al.* (2001) observe, the following quotes highlight the wide disparity that may exist in adults' thoughts about, and expectations of, children. Durkheim emphasizes the notion of children as less than adults; children are portrayed as incomplete but developing human beings. Childhood, he contends, is 'the period in which the individual, in both the physical and moral sense, does not yet exist ... The educationalist is presented with a becoming, an incipient being, a person in the process of formation' (Durkheim, 1979, p. 150, originally published in 1911). Waksler, in contrast, recognizes children 'as fully social beings' who are capable during childhood, and whose 'actions constrain, facilitate, encourage and in a myriad of ways have implications for others, adults in particular' (1991, pp. 23, 68).

At least four perceptions of children: as demonic, as 'noble savages', as angelic, and as 'developing beings', have arguably had an enduring influence on parents', professionals' and policy makers' thoughts and actions (Jamrozik and Sweeney, 1996, pp. 19–31; Smart, Neale and Wade, 2001). These perceptions of children may co-exist in adults' thoughts, creating an 'uneasy tension with each other' (Smart *et al.*, 2001, p. 15).

'Little devils' or demons

Stemming from the Christian belief that babies are born with 'original sin', children may be perceived as innately bad. Consequently, adults may believe that they have a duty to rid children of their evil and wilful tendencies. Strict physical discipline may be considered necessary to teach children to be good and to beat the devil out of them (Straus, 1994). In the 16th and 17th centuries, in the nonconformist Christian tradition, for example, 'good habits' were formed through 'controlled sleeping, fasting between meals, whispered requests for food at table, regular family prayers, and the judicious application of corporal punishment' (Cleverley and Philips, 1987, p. 29).

Children perceived as 'headstrong and stubborn' were beaten into submission 'for their own good' (Jenks, 1996, p. 71). This Christian belief in a child's innate tendency to be tempted by the devil is said by some to have persisted into the 21st century and continues to influence some parent–child relationships (Hendrick, 1997; Smart *et al.*, 2001) (see also Chapter 7).

'Noble savages'

Around the end of the 17th century, the philosopher John Locke (1632–1704) challenged perceptions of the child as innately bad. He proposed that the child's moral character was shaped by experience. Locke describes the child's intellectual state as a *tabula rasa* or blank tablet upon which adults could make their imprint as the child matured. From Locke's perspective, children begin life with equal potential so adult inequality stems from the environments in which they are raised (Cleverley and Philips, 1987).

While few may now consider that children need to be beaten to rid them of the devil, adults may still contend that teaching children morals and civilized behaviour requires heavy-handed, or implement-assisted, persuasion. Indeed, in current policy and practice, children's lives may be adversely affected by a perception of them as 'incomplete vulnerable beings' who need to be turned, sometimes by physical coercion, 'into mature adults' (Mayall, 1994, p. 3).

'Little angels' or 'innocent beings'

In the 18th century, in his fictional story *Emile* (see Foxley, 1974), Rousseau (1712–78) put forward the idea that children are essentially good and innocent but may become corrupted by the world into which they are born.

In view of this, he suggests that childhood should be a special time in which children's innate goodness ought to be nurtured and developed away from the depraved world of adults. Before Rousseau, childhood theorists had been concerned about society's difficulty in curbing children's wilfulness and encouraging children to be polite and diligent. Rousseau emphasizes the opposite. He warns adults that children's wills can indeed be broken and their 'natural curiosity' destroyed (Sommerville, 1990, p. 150). Rousseau's ideas demonstrate recognition of, and respect for, children as children rather than subordinate 'adults in the making' (James and Prout, 1997, p. 37). Indeed, Rousseau perceives children to possess qualities which adults could benefit from adopting. While Rousseau's ideas were welcomed by the 'enlightened aristocracy and the new middle classes', the majority of Western European children at the time were impoverished and subjected to hard labour and exploitation (Clarke, 2004, p. 8). This context, Clarke contends, exposed an inconsistency which stimulated thought and literature related to childhood throughout the 19th and into the 20th century. Rousseau's recognition of children as persons deserving adults' respect is currently advocated by the new sociology of childhood (see, for example, James *et al.*, 1998).

Smart *et al.* (2001) assert that perceptions of children as 'devils', 'savages', or 'angels' co-exist in current adult thinking, reflecting an entrenched contradiction about the reality of childhood. Indeed, in the English-speaking world today:

> Attitudes of caring and concern towards children appear to coexist comfortably with attitudes of indifference and even disdain towards them. Adults entertain ideas about children's rights, and international agreements on human and children's rights are ratified, yet the treatment and respect afforded to children are in many ways deficient. (Saunders and Goddard, 2001, p. 443)

Children are afforded a low, predominantly 'exclusionary status' (Hood-Williams, 1990, p. 56), which is perpetuated by socialization methods that include violence and degradation (Taylor, 1998). Even social scientists, Hood-Williams contends, either ignore children or perceive children as 'incompetent' others (1990, p. 157).

Children as 'embryonic adults'

A fourth way of seeing children that continues to have an impact on adult/child relations (Jamrozik and Sweeney, 1996; Smart *et al.*, 2001) stems from the realm of science and thinkers such as Darwin, Freud, Watson, Piaget and Bowlby. Children's minds and bodies were subjected to close scrutiny until predictable developmental stages were identified (Smart *et al.*, 2001). Described as 'pre-cognitive, non-verbal, immature [and] developmentally delayed', children's inadequacies were emphasized above recognition of their capacities (Waksler, 1991, p. 69). The descriptive term 'childish' could thus be interpreted as insulting (Waksler, 1991). Children are seen as 'potential persons' valued as the adult that they may become and thus tolerated through incremental stages of child development (Smart *et al.*, 2001, p. 4). Scarre maintains that a primary perception of children 'as weak, ignorant, irrational, incompetent, unrestrained and uncivilised' hampers concern about their treatment and encourages complacency in relation to 'social, educational and political arrangements' designed to manage them (1989, p. x).

As 'embryonic' beings children may be viewed as subordinate and not quite human (Smart *et al.*, 2001, p. 8). As 'projects' belonging to their parents and compelled to attend institutions such as churches and schools, children may be disciplined, punished and tamed 'for their own good and the good of others'; hence the origins of the 'loving "smack"' (Smart *et al.*, 2001, p. 7). Indeed, we contend that the unquestioned assault of children may stem from disrespectful attitudes toward children that emanate from images of the child as 'a genderless object, less than a subject, not human and not a person' (Saunders and Goddard, 2001, p. 457).

More recent comment about the nature of children

> While children may have different competencies to adults, this no longer means that their knowledge and achievements are inferior …
>
> There is a growing recognition that adults are life-long learners and that, no less than children, their competencies change according to their experiences through the life course. Nor are adults self-sufficient, they have dependencies just as children do. (Smart *et al.*, 2001, pp. 13, 14)

Recent theoretical perspectives on childhood and the nature of children recognize the ideas espoused by Rousseau, outlined above. Childhood is perceived as a social construction, unique to each individual child, but affected by the economic, political and cultural conditions within which that childhood is lived, and children are perceived as people whose human rights and perspectives on issues that affect them should be respected. From this theoretical perspective, it becomes important for children's views to be actively sought and documented with a view to 'the improvement of childhood conditions' (McGillivray, 1997b, p. 16). In contemporary society some aspects of past childhoods have arguably disappeared (Postman, 1982; Winn, 1983). Children, through media and technology, are increasingly exposed to issues and experiences that were previously restricted to adults; and children, both at home and at school, may more readily interact with adults on a more equal footing. In this context, Postman (1982) contentiously maintains that conceptions of well-behaved children, in 'deference to adults', and of children intent on 'learning skills essential for the adult world' are disappearing from contemporary childhood (Cunningham, 1995, p. 180).

Joseph (1995, p. 2) highlights four aspects of life that, he contends, continue to define childhood and deny children essential human rights: disenfranchisement, financial dependence, an 'essentially 'passive' legal status' as parents' belongings, and the receipt of adult discipline. Given children's current status, Waksler draws an insightful analogy between the positioning of children and the inferior status that used to be afforded to tribal groups. He suggests that '[j]ust as it turned out that tribal societies are not "child-like", it may be that children themselves are not either. Rather, the idea may be an adult stereotype of children, a stereotype that facilitates adult control and an adult assumption of superiority' (Waksler, 1991, p. 235).

Despite some progress in raising the status of children, children's rights may continue to be overlooked in deference to those of adults. Indeed, children may perceive themselves to be oppressed especially when 'adult power over children and young people is institutionalised' in some families by practices such as lawful physical punishment (Mason and Falloon, 1999, p. 12) (see also Chapter 7).

The child as a possession

While some argue that children are 'no longer property as they were in the Puritan or Victorian eras', children are 'not yet fully persons' (Freeman, 1983, pp. 17–18). In Australia, a parent may no longer claim to legally own his or her child. While Australian Family Court proceedings used to determine 'guardianship', 'custody' and 'access' to children these terms were replaced in the *Family Law Amendment (Shared Parent Responsibility) Act* 2006 with 'lives with', 'spends time with', and 'communicates with'. The concept that 'parents do not have rights in or to their children, but have *responsibilities*' was paramount in the drafting of the *Family Law Reform Act* 1995 (Chisholm, 2005, p. 11). Parents are expected to do what is best for their child, however distressing or disruptive that may be for the parent

(Foster and Gingell, 1999). Nevertheless, perceptions persist of children as objects that parents own. Archard, for example, observes that the parent 'has rights over something, the child, which the non-parent lacks. But then again, the latter may have rights of ownership over other objects which the parent does not' (1993, p. 84).

Given persisting perceptions of ownership and associated control of children, it has been suggested that Article 5 of the UNCRC (1989) might be interpreted by adults entrusted with the care of children as entitling them to physically punish the children (Boss, 1994). Article 5 states that:

> States Parties shall respect the responsibilities, rights and duties of parents or, where applicable, the members of the extended family or community as provided for by local custom, legal guardians or other persons legally responsible for the child, to provide, in a manner consistent with the evolving capacities of the child, appropriate direction and guidance in the exercise by the child of the rights recognized in the present Convention. (UNCRC, 1989)

The 'paradox' of protecting children is the 'tension' between the circumstances required to maintain children's safety and the reality that small children may be most vulnerable when in their parents' care (Turner, 2002, p. 119). Rayner's (1992) response to this dilemma is that parents' powers cannot be exercised where parents and children have conflicting interests. Parents have a responsibility to guide children but in a context that recognizes children's rights.

In this context, Garbarino suggests that the following questions need to be answered when defining 'risk' to a child:

> Are children disposable private property of parents? Or, are children endowed with 'certain inalienable rights' as human beings? Is violence a 'normal' and desirable method of social control [or] an aberration? Are children a private matter of parents? Or do parents hold children 'in trust' (for God, state or clan)? (1994, p. 51)

As Freeman contends, 'children are persons, not property; subjects, not objects of social concern or control' and children ought to be perceived as 'participants in social processes, not social problems' (1998, p. 436).

The rights of the child

People have long argued about children and children's rights (Smith, 2000). Indispensable to discourses about a commitment to children's rights is recognition of the fundamental personhood of the child who without rights is powerless (Preston, 1990). It is the child's humanity, together with the dignity and the respect that belonging to humanity demands, which appears to be missing in many adult policies and practices in relation to children. Rights 'is the language of equality', and claims to rights 'are about dignity, respect, liberty, opportunity, access to and protection from the law, and participation in one's own fate' (McGillivray, 1994, p. 252). Without rights, children may be subjected to the whims of adults, and every day children's human rights are ignored and violated.

Children's rights movements began in the late 19th century, growing from concern for children who were being abused and exploited through employment and living conditions, deprived of an education, and suffering physically and emotionally. Child welfare and child protection laws were eventually introduced (Edgar, 1994) (See also Chapter 3). Belonging to the 'category of children', as opposed to the 'counter-category of adults', results in marked differences in access to 'activities, opportunities, experiences, relationships and identities available for children across a number of insti-tutions and domains of social activity' (Alanen, 2003, p. 33). Cunningham maintains that for the first half of the 20th century children's 'powerless-ness' and 'dependence' on parents were emphasized, and 'good parenting' consisted of maintaining and extending this (1995, p. 185). He, like Postman (1982), suggests that in the second half of the 20th century the authority of parents diminished, with children demanding and receiving early entry into the adult world.

However, children's low status and unrecognized capacity to claim their rights and voice their opinions were highlighted by the need for the UNCRC (1989), which followed two Declarations of Children's Rights, dated 1924 and 1959. The differentiation between adults' rights and children's rights is fundamentally an artificial one stemming from children's apparent exclu-sion from the '"everyone" entitled to human rights' (Burdekin, 1994, p. 8). This occurred 'in much the same way as the term "he" was supposed to incorporate "she" but in fact served ... to exclude and marginalize women' (Lansdown, 1995, p. 25).

Women, critically perceived as more child-like than men, had to work toward recognition of their rights as human beings who are not male (Oakley, 1994). Excluded and marginalized as less than adult and not quite human, children living in countries that ratified the UNCRC (1989) were theoretically accorded special recognition both as persons and as children. It is a sobering fact, however, that children were not consulted when the UNCRC was drafted. Freeman argues that if children had been consulted some 'significant additions and amendments' would probably be unneces-sary (1998, p. 439). Article 19(1) for example, states that:

> States Parties shall take all appropriate legislative, administrative, social and educational measures to protect the child from all forms of physical or mental violence, injury or abuse, neglect or negligent treatment, maltreatment or exploitation, including sexual abuse, while in the care of parent(s), legal guardian(s) or any other person who has the care of the child.

Article 19 could have more clearly prohibited physical punishment (Freeman, 1998).

The professional 'discovery' of child abuse and the silencing of children

> To the casual reader of history with an interest in children and childhood, two impressions are soon gained: firstly, children do not feature prominently in historical texts; and, secondly, it is clear that where they are referred to, children have frequently suffered at the hands of adults. (Goddard, 1996, p. 7)

Indeed, 'children have suffered at the hands of adults throughout time' (Goddard, 1996, p. 8). Some have catalogued the horrors of exposure and infanticide (see, for example, Radbill, 1980). Sexual offences against children were also recorded (Corby, 2006).

Child abuse was also common in the early years of white settlement in Australia. Gandevia (1978) documents the history of infanticide in his review of child health and welfare in Australia from 1788. In approximately one-quarter of inquests on children less than three years of age in Melbourne in 1863, deaths were due to abuse, neglect and ignorance. Gandevia suggests that infanticide was a major concern but juries in criminal cases were 'reluctant to bring a verdict of infanticide against mothers' (1978, p. 104).

The murder of children was common and is reflected in newspaper headlines. A search of *The Argus*, Melbourne's quality paper of the time, shows 332 stories about infanticide in the 1870s alone. Headlines such as 'Body of infant girl found', 'Body of strangled newborn infant found', and 'Murder of child' appeared regularly (The Argus Index, 2005). It is clear that the media and the public were interested in the issue, but it was almost another 100 years before professional interest was awakened.

Early research into child abuse in Australia followed an article by Kempe *et al.* (1962), published in the *Journal of the American Medical Association*. As Mudaly and Goddard (2006) note, the early research was concerned with child abuse as a medical condition. Kempe *et al.* describe the 'emotional unwillingness' of doctors 'to consider abuse as the cause of the child's difficulty' (1962, p. 18). It is interesting to observe the echoes of Gandevia's observations on the reluctance of juries in criminal trials, noted above.

Mudaly and Goddard (2006) examine some of the seminal Australian papers in the context of Kempe's assertion that, in severe abuse cases, 'the bones tell a story that the child is too young or frightened to tell' (1962, p.18). They suggest, however, that 'it is too easy to assume … that the children were too young to tell of their experiences' (2006, p. 20). Birrell and Birrell (1966) wrote one of the earliest Australian papers on the subject. Mudaly and Goddard point out that one of the victims in the Birrells' paper was nine years of age. Another girl, aged three, is described as screaming and running whenever her father visited her in hospital, where she was recovering from her injuries (Birrell and Birrell, 1966). The child's screams were 'rendered inaudible' for, in spite of her obvious fear of her father, she was returned to him and seriously re-abused (Mudaly and Goddard, 2006, p. 21).

Mudaly and Goddard examine child deaths where children have asked for help before they died, and observe that the 'failure to talk to and listen to these children casts a long shadow over their deaths' (2006, p. 25). They argue that the silencing of children has a 'long and effective history' (Mudaly and Goddard, 2006, p. 32). Just as the definition of child abuse 'broadened over time' (Corby, 2006, p. 40), so the silencing of children extended to other forms of abuse. Mudaly and Goddard cite a number of myths that have been used to minimize the problem of child sexual abuse: children were said to lie, to fantasize, and to be seductive. These myths, they observe, have been used by organizations such as churches 'seeking to protect themselves' rather than protect children (2006, p. 32). Catholic churches do not have a monopoly of such behaviour. The former Governor-General of Australia, Peter Hollingworth (also a former Anglican Archbishop) resigned after apparently accusing a young girl of 'leading a priest on', and stating that he did not condone a bishop's sex with a young girl 'regardless of whether or not the girl was a willing participant' (Goddard, 2003, p. 17).

The courts also continue to play a role in the silencing of children, according to Mudaly and Goddard (2006). They examine the recent case in the Victorian Supreme Court where a 17-year-old victim 'AB' was allowed to be cross-examined by her stepfather, who had already been convicted of raping her repeatedly when she was a young child (see also Goddard, 2000). Continuing research at Monash University suggests that such treatment of children is not confined to sexual abuse.

In 2007, in the County Court of Victoria, a father who had shaken his baby daughter so violently that she was left with severe disabilities was given only a suspended jail sentence (Hodgson, 2007). The girl, aged six weeks at the time of the abuse, now has 'cerebral palsy, spasticity, vision impairment, seizure disorder and quadriparesis, or weakness in all limbs' (Goddard and Tucci, 2007, p. 25). The judge justified the suspended sentence on the grounds that the father was 'the best person' to care for the girl (Goddard and Tucci, 2007, p. 25).

These cases underline the continuing vulnerability of children in spite of the professional 'discovery' of child abuse. As Mudaly and Goddard emphasize, there are many forces that continue to silence children. Children who have been abused contend with 'deep-seated and long-standing' problems, and professionals' responses 'are part of those problems and are equally entrenched' (2006, p. 32). The legal system continues in many cases to treat children cruelly. The law on physical punishment is 'still ambiguous' (Corby, 2006, p. 90), so that it allows further cruelties (see Chapter 3) and the further silencing of children.

Conclusion

Children's experience of childhood will depend on social constructions of childhood, and the attitudes and behaviour of the adults on whom children depend for their care, protection and development. This chapter drew attention to adults' perceptions of children and their rights, and the history of parent–child relations, with an emphasis on parental discipline of children. At first sight, the professional 'discovery' of child abuse appeared to change perceptions of those parent–child relations. It is clear, however, that the silencing of children continues. Further discussion of the UNCRC (1989), as it relates to lawful physical punishment, is discussed with other legal issues in the next chapter.

3

Legal responses to physical punishment

Introduction

In the 19th century, in response to a request to support proposed UK legislation preventing parental cruelty to children, Lord Shaftesbury replied: 'The evils you state are enormous and indisputable, but they are of so private, internal and domestic a character as to be beyond the reach of legislation' (cited in Cobley, 1995, p. 15). This chapter explores some legal perspectives on physical discipline of children, and gives an overview of differing common law and legislative responses to physical punishment.

A child is defined in Article 1 of the UN Convention on the Rights of the Child (UNCRC) (1989) as 'every human being below the age of eighteen years unless under the law applicable to the child, majority is attained earlier'. In countries such as Australia, Canada, New Zealand, the UK and the US the age of majority is 18 or 19, at which time the person legally assumes control over his or her body, decisions and actions. With some exceptions, for example Gillick v. West Norfolk & Wisbech Area Health Authority and Department of Health & Social Security (1985), until the age of majority parents have legal control over and legal responsibilities to children. 'Gillick competence' refers to the ability of a particular child under the age of 17 to fully understand a proposed medical treatment, at

Physical Punishment in Childhood: The Rights of the Child, by Bernadette J. Saunders and Chris Goddard
Copyright © 2010 John Wiley & Sons, Ltd.

which time the parent's right to determine whether or not that child will have that treatment ends.

In many English-speaking countries children continue to be the only people who may be lawfully physically punished, and the 'social and legal endorsement of hitting children is one of the most symbolic indications of their low status' (Lansdown, 1994, p. 43). Childhood, for children forced to live in homes characterized by violence or aggression, might be described as 'an age-defined category of oppressed people' (Hill and Tisdall, 1997, p. 204). Children's voices may be silenced and abusive responses to children can be hidden (Lee, 2001). Young children's limited autonomy and dependence renders them particularly vulnerable to adults' abuse of power. Violence that might otherwise be deemed criminal may be termed 'physical punishment', and thus considered legally and morally acceptable child discipline (Straus, 1994).

The United Nations Convention on the Rights of the Child (1989)

Every country in the world, except the United States and Somalia, has ratified the United Nations Convention on the Rights of the Child (1989) (UNCRC). It comprises 54 articles which derive from three main themes: the 'best interest of the child, evolving capacity of the child, and respect for the human dignity of the child', and children's rights in the convention may be grouped into four categories: 'rights to survival, protection, development and participation' (Limber and Flekkoy, 1995, pp. 4, 5). Participation suggests 'dialogue', 'negotiation' and 'peaceful resolution of conflict' in contrast to forceful conflict resolution (Freeman, 1999, p. 136). Indeed, Article 12(1) stipulates children's right to comment on issues that affect them:

> States Parties shall assure to the child who is capable of forming his or her own views the right to express those views freely in all matters affecting the child, the views of the child being given due weight in accordance with the age and maturity of the child. (UNCRC, 1989)

Article 42 of the convention necessitates the dissemination of the UNCRC's principles 'to adults and children alike', yet many countries fail to conform either to this or to full implementation. Signatories are expected to ensure that children are accorded their rights, including taking every measure to protect children 'from all forms of physical or mental violence, injury or abuse, neglect or negligent treatment, maltreatment or exploitation' (Article

19(1), UNCRC, 1989). Further, Article 37 of the convention states that 'States Parties shall ensure that [n]o child shall be subjected to torture or other cruel, inhuman or degrading treatment or punishment'.

Limited physical punishment, some argue, is not an infringement of children's human rights. If 'reasonable correction' is defined and limited, legal arguments 'that the criminal law authorised or excused inhuman or degrading treatment or punishment contrary to international human rights law' are complicated (Bronitt and McSherry, 2001, p. 557). Freeman maintains, however, that the 'concept of privacy encompasses the concept of bodily integrity' and even mild physical punishment would breach international law that non-discriminately guarantees a person's privacy (1999, p. 137). He refers specifically to Article 17 of the Covenant on Civil and Political Rights, which 'in effect rules out corporal punishment of children on privacy grounds' (Freeman, 1999, p. 138).

The UN Committee's latest comment on physical punishment refutes State parties' allowance of '"reasonable" or "moderate" corporal punishment' at any 'level'. The principle of children's 'best interests' gives 'due weight' to children's views, and cannot defend practices that are inconsistent with children's 'human dignity and right to physical integrity': 'The committee emphasizes that eliminating violent and humiliating punishment of children, through law reform and other necessary measures, is an immediate and unqualified obligation of States Parties' (Committee on the Rights of the Child, 2006, pp. 6–8).

Physical punishment or the assault of children

Clarity is particularly important in child protection because child abuse definitions guide prevention and intervention measures. In societies that tolerate violence in any form, thresholds of acceptable violence may be blurred and definitions of actions that might constitute child abuse imprecise (Gough, 1996). Broadly, child abuse may be defined as 'a significant harm done or anticipated to a child as a result of human action. The action may be intentional or reckless and inflicted by individuals, groups, agencies or by the state' (Cooper, 1993, p. 1).

Physical punishment might fall within such a broad definition. However, child abuse is a socially constructed phenomenon. Its parameters adjust continually as cultural values and opinions change over time. In countries such as Australia, the UK, the US and Canada, the physical assault of children by parents, even using implements, may be excused particularly if it occurs in the home as discipline or control. Children's relative size, stage of human development and powerlessness appear to moderate judgements about the seriousness of punitive violence directed at them.

The common law defence to criminal assault

Definitions of criminal assault may vary in different jurisdictions around the world. Australia, for example, has a federal system with six independent states, two territories and a federal government, each with their own jurisdictions.

Common law or 'judge-made law' stems from 'the commonsense of the community, crystallised and formulated' over time (Cashmore and de Haas, 1995, p. 14). In Victoria, where this research was undertaken, minor criminal assault is defined as 'actual intended use of unlawful force to another person without their consent' (Fagan v. Metropolitan Police Commissioner [1969] 1 Q.B. 439). More serious criminal assault is defined in the Crimes Act ((Vic) 1958, s.16) as 'causing serious injury … without lawful excuse, intentionally'; s.17 as 'causing serious injury … without lawful excuse, recklessly'; and s.18 as 'causing injury … without lawful excuse, intentionally or recklessly'. Nicholson makes it clear that police only intervene in 'more serious assaults' as the principle *de minimus non curat lex* serves to ensure that law 'does not concern itself with trivialities' (2008, p. 12). In view of this, he contends that 'gentle correction of a toddler', for example, does not constitute assault and would not face prosecution.

Judgements in criminal assault trials rest on subjective and objective tests (Waller and Williams, 2001). With regard to the use of physical force to discipline a child, a parent or person acting *in loco parentis* (identified below as 'D') will have criminally assaulted a child if the punishment is subjectively and objectively unreasonable. Gillies explains that:

> Corporal punishment is subjectively reasonable when D acts in the belief that it is reasonable to resort to physical chastisement, and that the quantum of such chastisement is reasonable. Further, D must act out of a desire to correct the child, and not for 'the gratification of passion or of rage'.
>
> The chastisement is objectively reasonable when a reasonable person would not regard the decision to resort to force, or the quantum of force employed, as unreasonable. In considering whether punishment is reasonable, regard must be had to all the relevant circumstances. (Gillies, 1997, p. 332)

The use of 'reasonable' force to correct a child is not a parental right; it is only a defence (Ambikapathy, 2003). The defence of 'reasonable chastisement' or 'lawful correction' of a child became common law in 1860 when Lord Chief Justice Cockburn, in the case R v. Hopley in the UK, stated that:

> By the law a parent ... may for the purpose of correcting what is evil in the child, inflict moderate and reasonable corporal punishment. ... If it be administered for the gratification of passion or of rage, or if it be immoderate and excessive in its nature or degree or if it be protracted beyond the child's powers of endurance, or with an instrument unfitted for the purpose ... the violence is unlawful. (R v. Hopley, 1860, 2 F and F 202)

Justice Scholl made a similar statement in a 1955 judgement in Victoria, Australia in which he found the 'reasonable chastisement' defence did not apply in the case R v. Terry. Hugh Terry was living with the mother of 19-month-old Brenda Duncan, whom he struck and killed. Terry claimed his intent was lawful correction, with her mother's permission. A jury found him guilty of the lesser charge of manslaughter rather than murder. The judge advised the jury:

> There are strict limits to the right of a parent to inflict reasonable and moderate corporal punishment on his or her child for the purpose of correcting the child in wrong behaviour ... the punishment must be moderate and reasonable ... have a proper relation to the age, physique and mentality of the child, and ... it must be carried out with a reasonable means or instrument. (R v. Terry [1955] VLR 114)

In some jurisdictions, including some Australian states (Victoria, South Australia and the Australian Capital Territory), parents and other adults charged with criminal assault of children in their care retain recourse to common law to excuse their actions. Indeed, Wells (2008) notes that common law remains a defence to a charge of assault, ranging from common assault to grievous bodily harm and potentially even to manslaughter or murder. Some Australian states have, in part, codified this defence. New South Wales, for example, was the first Australian state to attempt to define the words 'moderate' and 'reasonable' (see below).

The imprecision of laws concerned with physical punishment allows considerable discretion as to whether the assault of a child is even prosecuted (Tasmanian Law Reform Institute, 2003). Indeed, in Australia, 'few parents are investigated, let alone convicted of child assault' (Bagaric, 2009). When cases come to court, further discretion and variations in sentencing are found in judicial responses. Moreover, most cases are heard in lower courts which are not courts of record. Case law emanating from higher courts is scant and often controversial (some case examples are cited below). Child advocates frequently point out that assaults against children are minimized when sentences given for assaults against adults are compared with those afforded to adults who assault, and even kill, children in their care (see, for example, Goddard and Tucci, 2007; Milfull and Schetzer, 2000).

In law, the concept of 'reasonableness' serves to determine standards of acceptable conduct of people whose behaviour could harm others: 'the imagined reasonable person exhibits morals, intelligence and knowledge reflecting community standards and perceptions' (Minow and Rakoff, 1998, p. 42). Given an apparent lack of community consensus on what, if any, actions constitute reasonable assault of children, this 'reasonableness' test is problematic. Further, as the 'lawful correction' defence affords parents or guardians the option of physically punishing their children as discipline, including with an 'instrument' but 'not for the gratification of passion or rage', it requires that the parent calmly chooses a 'reasonable' form of physical punishment with the intent to instruct. Forethought and the infliction of physical punishment in a controlled and benevolent manner appear integral to the validity of the defence. Research suggests, however, that a parent or guardian will often physically punish a child as a reflexive action (Simons *et al.*, 1991) or as a result of pent-up frustrations, fears or anger (Gough and Reavey, 1997; Rodriguez and Richardson, 2007). Many parents, it appears, do not consider the 'reasonableness' of the physical punishment they use before they strike a child.

In this context, Freeman cautions that abuse is a label retrospectively applied, and 'those who skate on thin ice cannot expect a sign to alert them to the exact point where the ice will cave in' (Freeman, 1994, p. 23). Legal and social endorsement of physical punishment gives parents permission to respond to children in a manner which places children at risk. Harm suffered by children may be unintended, accidental or well motivated (see Chapter 9).

In light of this, the common law defence 'lawful correction of children' can be criticized because it amounts to authorized harm to children, and may endanger them. Johnson suggests that the 'mere existence of the privilege is an acknowledgement that, as a society, we condone the harm of children for the purposes of teaching them acceptable behavior' (1998, p. 418). English law, Foster and Gingell observe, creates 'a category of lawful assault on children' (1999, p. 191). The explicit use of the word 'smack', they contend, 'reflects a determination to distinguish blows struck against children from blows struck against adults. The same blows against an adult would be an assault' (Foster and Gingell, 1999, p. 191). The defence of lawful correction 'infringes the security interests of victims of corrective force', and unlike any other legal defences, it discriminates against children because of their age and position in the family (Carter, 2004, p. 58). Hammarberg and Newell similarly expose this paradox and the 'affront to humanity' that smaller and more vulnerable people should be less protected from assault than adults (2000, p. 3). Keating, moreover, describes 'the defence of "discipline"' as 'outdated, vague and potentially dangerous to children' (2006, p. 394).

Some arguments against the common law defence of 'reasonable chastisement'

As Mount observes, law is not only 'a direct regulator of behaviour'; it 'may be introduced as a symbolic gesture or affirmation of a principle. This is particularly so in relation to "moral" issues' (1995, p. 1004).

Lawful correction and 'reasonable' force

Opposing the view that parents are entitled to a defence of lawful correction if charged with the assault of a child in their care is the view that children are entitled to physical integrity and protection from harm (Naylor and Saunders, 2009). Indeed, as Ludbrook (1995, p. 123) notes, Blackstone (1723–80) in his *Commentaries on the Laws of England* contended that the 'law cannot draw the line between different degrees of violence … every man's person being sacred, and no other having the right to meddle with it, in any the slightest manner'. Blackstone, however, made the physical punishment of children an exception to this decree and, as Ludbrook (1995, p. 124) suggests, common law has held firm to Halsbury's comment that 'an act is not an assault if it is done in the course of lawful correction of a child by its [sic] parents'. Bodily integrity thus appears to be a human right which may legally be denied to children (Ludbrook, 1995).

Vieth (1994) contends that the concept of 'reasonable' force is a fallacy stemming from history rather than logic. It is illogical to denounce assaults between marriage partners and assaults between siblings but to approve the assault of a child by his or her parent. He argues that because of the physical and emotional vulnerability of a child relative to an adult, 'the parental assault of a child warrants prohibition to a greater extent than assaults between other family members' (Vieth, 1994, p. 46).

Kearney (1995) asserts that parents should be afforded an excuse for the disciplinary assault of children only if they have no other alternatives, and she places responsibility on the state to ensure that parents are provided with knowledge of alternatives. If the state will not assist, she contends, it cannot limit parents' use of physical punishment: 'The test thus balances the interests of parents and children in a way that is sensitive to the needs of both groups' (Kearney, 1995, p. 51).

Parent–child relations and the privacy of the home

Several arguments have been proposed in relation to state regulation of practices that may occur in the privacy of the home or within the 'family's jurisdiction', such as child-rearing (Durrant, 1994). Some have argued that parents' self-governance ensures child-rearing diversity and, as parents generally consider children's best interests, state intervention may be more damaging than helpful to children (Thompson, 1993). Further, as parents' perceived right to discipline children rests on their 'primacy' in the relationship, directives about better ways to discipline may greatly annoy them (Garner, 1998, p. 15). On the other hand, a decision by the state to allow potentially harmful child-rearing behaviours reinforces parents' use of such practices (Gelles and Straus, 1988), and may be perceived as intruding upon parenting by condoning parents' adoption of such practices (Durrant, 1994, p. 130).

Conversely, Mount espouses the effectiveness of laws that are 'symbolic or educative' rather than associated with criminal sanctions because they may subtly affect people's ideas about family and family relationships (1995, p. 1005). Leach (1992) extends this argument when she stresses the ineffectiveness of punitive approaches in changing adults' or children's behaviours. Rather than being punished, she contends that people need to be encouraged to learn about and adopt alternative 'desirable' behaviours which make them 'feel good' (Leach, 1992, quoted in Mount, 1995, p. 1003). Countries that have banned physical punishment perceive legislative reform to be educative rather than punitive. Education campaigns and social supports for parents are thus integral to the process.

Retributive and utilitarian justifications

Traditionally, legal punishment may be justified in terms of either 'retributivist' theory, typified by the maxims 'an eye for an eye' and 'the punishment should fit the crime', or 'consequentialist' theory, which perceives punishment to have a deterrent effect, producing 'the greatest happiness to the greatest number' (Turner, 2002, p. 199). Turner contends that deterrence theories can provide justification for punishing children but any theory that includes elements of retribution cannot. She argues, however, that neither of these theories can justify the corporal punishment of children. Retribution as justification, she contends, requires 'moral guilt' and presumes that the person being punished is 'rational and autonomous', neither of which characterize children in law (Turner, 2003, p. 225). Moreover, retribution implies 'just deserts' yet precedents demonstrate that corporal punishment may need to seriously harm the child for it to be considered unreasonable by the judiciary (Turner, 2003, p. 225).

On the other hand, utilitarian theories value punishment as a precursor to behavioural change and as a deterrent. Thus, an appeal to utilitarian theory to justify corporal punishment of children would hinge on the practice actually correcting or improving children's behaviour. Turner (2003) contends that this is also an ill-founded assumption given that social science research (see Gershoff, 2002b for an overview) indicates that at best physical punishment will immediately and temporarily give pause to aberrant behaviour but may cause harm to the child. It therefore follows that laws which provide a defence to assault on the grounds of lawful correction of children are 'anomalous' because they attempt to justify corporal punishment of children (Turner, 2003, p. 226).

Similarities between tolerance of parental physical punishment and tolerance of men's violence towards their wives

In the past, husbands, masters and employers could physically punish wives, servants, slaves and apprentices, knowing that should their actions come to the attention of the courts they could justify and defend them through recourse to social norms and special defences stemming from common law or legislation (Bronitt and McSherry, 2001). Blackstone in his *Commentaries on the Laws of England* recorded: 'The husband also (by the old law) might give his wife moderate correction ... in the same moderation that a man is allowed to correct his servants or children' (1979, pp. 432–3).

Centuries later, in Western industrialized countries, legal and social tolerance of violent responses to women in their homes lessened only by degrees (Turner, 2002). The 'rule of thumb' story, suggesting that it was legally permissible for a man to beat his wife with a rod not thicker than his thumb, is often cited as an example (Conway-Turner and Cherrin, 1998; Hoff Sommers, 1994). The idea that spousal violence directed at a woman infringes her human rights and is morally wrong slowly gained societal acceptance.

Historically, the community and the judiciary have been inclined to limit violence before questioning its legitimacy. In England, prior to the reign of Charles II in 1660, a husband was permitted to severely beat his wife for some behaviours for her benefit, while being restricted to 'moderate correction' for other misdemeanours (Dobash and Dobash, 1979, p. 61). Women, like children, were considered to be naturally inferior to men, and husbands were accorded the right to control their wives through 'domestic chastisement' in the privacy of their home (Dobash and Dobash, 1979, p. 74). Freeman (2007) observes that, like children, women were considered non-persons. In Bradwell v. Illinois 83 US (16 Wall.) 130 (1872), for example, Justice Bradley stated: 'The natural and proper timidity and delicacy which belongs to the female sex evidently unfits it for many of the occupations of civil life … a woman [has] no legal existence separate from her husband'.

Historically, members of the judiciary and general community have perceived women and children to provoke violence by unreasonably challenging their subjugation to their 'superiors'. Women, like children, may be perceived to 'need' or to 'have deserved' physical punishment (Dobash and Dobash, 1979, p. 12), and violent means of control in the home have been a private matter where 'it is better to draw the curtain' and 'shut out the public gaze and leave the parties to forget and forgive' (State v. Oliver 70 NC 60, 1874, cited in Dobash and Dobash, 1979).

Dobash and Dobash (1979) note that in the 17th, 18th and 19th centuries a man was not censured for physically beating his wife, as long as it was limited. Wife beating was excusable if the woman challenged her husband's power, 'nagged', or failed to meet his standards (Dobash and Dobash, 1979). In 18th-century France, physical punishment of women by their husbands was limited to 'blows, thumps, kicks or punches on the back if they leave no lasting traces' (Dobash and Dobash, 1979, p. 56, quoting Castan, 1976, p. 5). Husbands were not permitted to use 'sharp edged or crushing instruments' and were not allowed 'to direct blows to the head or sensitive or vital organs'. Indeed, 'it was the moderate use of physical punishment that separated the "reasonable husband from the brute"' (Dobash and Dobash, 1979, p. 57, quoting Castan, 1976, p. 5). These restrictions on violence against women bear close resemblance to restrictions in the New South Wales Crimes Amendment (Child Protection – Physical Mistreatment) Act 2001 and the Children Act 2004 in the UK, which limit rather than condemn parental violence against children (discussed in more detail below).

In Australia, the Royal Commission on Human Relationships *Final Report* stated: 'We are now appalled by acts to which our ancestors would have been indifferent. It is part of a growing awareness that the human rights, dignity and integrity of every man, woman and child should be protected' (1977, p. 159). However, despite today's intolerance of violence against women, and documented evidence of the process by which this change has occurred, reluctance to condemn violence against children remains strong. McGillivray highlights the numerous limitations in 'secular law' on the use of physical force to correct children: 'instruments' and 'sites of punishment', 'reasons for punishment', 'who can administer punishment', 'degree of force', risk of harm' and 'susceptibility to punishment' (1997a, p. 211). Law, McGillivray observes, is 'a shifting geojurisprudence of licit and illicit body contacts' (1997a, p. 211). Indeed, violent responses to children that may now result in a conviction, because the perpetrator is unable to use the defence of lawful correction, were once 'simply a fact of childhood' (McGillivray, 1997a, p. 211). Moral arguments against lawful violence against children appear to be less powerful than arguments upholding adults' rights and children's subordinate status. It is significant that when the defence of lawful correction is allowed in an assault trial it is more likely to be successful when the child is portrayed as '"difficult", "wilful" "undisciplined", "disobedient", "provoking", "obstinate", "hard to manage", "resistant" or "having behavioural problems"' (McGillivray, 1997a, p. 220).

Countries that have banned physical punishment

At the time of writing, corporal punishment of children is legally prohibited in schools in 107 countries, and as a penal sentence in 149 countries (End All Corporal Punishment of Children, 2009). Physical punishment has only been banned outright in 24 countries, however. Sweden, in 1979, was the first country to legislate against all physical punishment and, in 2007, New Zealand was the first English-speaking country to enforce a ban (see Wood *et al.*, 2008). In Italy and Nepal, the prohibition of physical punishment is embodied only in Supreme Court judgements. Legislative prohibition occurred in eight countries – Sweden, Finland, Norway, Austria, Cyprus, Denmark, Latvia and Croatia – between 1979 and 1999, and in 16 countries – Germany, Israel, Bulgaria, Iceland, Ukraine, Romania, Hungary, Greece, Portugal, Netherlands, Venezuela, Uruguay, Spain, New Zealand, Costa Rica, Republic of Moldova – between 2000 and 2008 (End All Corporal Punishment of Children, 2009). The Council of Europe (2008), with 47 member states, has launched a campaign for universal prohibition.

Sweden

In Sweden, after 1920, a man could not legally beat his wife and his servants but physical punishment of children was allowed (Boyson, 2002, drawing on Hauser, 1988). In 1959 Sweden removed its criminal defence of lawful correction in cases of assault against children and in 1979 the country definitively banned all physical punishment with the following addition to its civil code (Durrant, 2006):

> Children are entitled to care, security and a good upbringing. Children are to be treated with respect for their person and individuality and may not be subjected to physical punishment or other injurious or humiliating treatment. (Parenthood and Guardianship Code, Section I, Chapter 6)

The acceptability of physical punishment in Sweden decreased from 53% in 1965 to 10% in 1999, at which time only 6% of Swedes under the age of 35 condoned it (Durrant, 1999). Attitudinal change occurred through various means. Boyson (2002) observes that the social democratic welfare systems of Scandinavia rest on principles of universalism and equality; high expenditure, standards of service and public benefits are aligned with maximum employment, and the state actively responds to the needs of families. Children are seen as social capital, hence hitting them would be inconsistent. Along with legislative change, the difficulties of parenting were recognized by providing social welfare supports for families. Supports included home visitation by nurses to provide parenting advice and to give parents devices that contribute to safety in the home, such as locks and electric outlet plugs. Such support decreases the likelihood of parental stress, frustration and anger that may result in violent responses to children. Parenting education also occurred through the provision of brochures, written in various languages, which provided information about alternative means of discipline, and detailing sources of further information and assistance. Parenting advice on the sides of milk cartons and responsible media reporting about the new law were particularly effective (Palmerus, 1999).

A recent Innocenti report on children's well-being in 21 industrialized countries (UNICEF, 2007) found that all countries have flaws that need attention. However, countries were ranked on six dimensions of child well-being: 'material well-being; health and safety; educational well-being; family and peer relationships; behaviours and risks; and subjective well-being'. On each dimension Sweden ranked close to or in the top third of countries who promote, and cater for children's well-being (UNICEF, 2007). Northern European countries the Netherlands, Sweden, Denmark and Finland, all of which have banned the physical punishment of children, were the best achievers.

Durrant (2004) notes that children's right to be protected, as enshrined in the UNCRC, was the primary principle underlying law reform in Sweden.

This right to protection also underpinned Sweden's social policy reforms, and Durrant notes that this influences the time it takes for societies to achieve non-violent child-rearing. Remarkably, by 1981, 99% of Swedish people were aware of physical punishment prohibition (Ziegert, 1983). While the 1979 law was designed to be educative rather than punitive (Flynn, 1996), injured children can sue for damages, parents' use of physical punishment may influence custody cases, and the penal code provides for prosecution of parents (Freeman, 1999).

The impact of Sweden's 1979 legislation is the subject of much discussion and contention in the literature (see, for example, Beckett, 2005; Roberts, 2000). Some research suggests that a small number of Swedes continue to use physical punishment because the adults are stressed, their children continuously misbehave, or for religious reasons (Durrant *et al.*, 2003). Other research proposes that children do not expect to be physically punished by their parents as 'verbal control/firm command' is the normal approach to discipline (Sorbring *et al.*, 2003, p. 64). Surprisingly however, some children, especially boys, may still expect to be hit for transgressions such as hitting a sibling or pursuing a dangerous activity such as touching a stove (Sorbring *et al.*, 2003). It appears that some parents' motivations for using physical punishment may remain strong despite the ban. Moreover, ongoing education about child development and alternatives will always be needed.

Notably, reports of child abuse by family members quadrupled in Sweden from early 1980 to the late 1990s (Annerback *et al.*, 2007). However, this was expected given heightened sensitivity to adults' responses to children, and knowledge that abusive parents may have significant family or other problems that preclude them from being influenced by the law. The analysis by Annerback *et al.* (2007) of all suspected child abuse reports to police in one district of Sweden between 1986 and 1996 revealed that reports mainly related to suspected abuse by socially disadvantaged biological parents. The researchers suggest that this may be because these parents were more closely monitored. Severe abuse cases, Annerback *et al.* (2007) observe, are often known to social services in relation to minor abuse reports. As Newell proposed, 'increased sensitivity' to child abuse resulting from the ban probably results in earlier reports of abuse (1989, p. 85). However, Annerback *et al.* (2007) express concern that minor abuse reports might escalate in severity if not taken seriously and acted upon.

Sweden's child fatality statistics are also the subject of considerable interest and debate in the literature. A 2001 Innocenti report, 'Child death by injury in rich nations', found that 'at least 12,000 child deaths a year could be prevented if all OECD countries had the same child injury death rate as Sweden' (UNICEF, 2001, p. 2). This report cautioned that distinguishing between intentional and unintentional injuries suffered by children is often difficult. However, in relation to the annual number of deaths from injuries (unintentional and intentional) per 100,000 children in the age group one to 14 years old, occurring between 1991 and 1995, Sweden registered the lowest number of deaths at 5.2 compared to, for example, Korea at 25.6.

Countries that continue to permit physical punishment

At the time of writing, in 29 countries, including Malaysia, Singapore, and Saudi Arabia, children continue to be caned, whipped or flogged as lawful punishment in the penal system. Ninety-one countries permit physical punishment in schools, including 21 states in the US (Human Rights Watch, 2008). In 173 countries, including the US, the UK, Canada and Australia, physical punishment continues to be sanctioned in the home. Twenty-three countries have committed to prohibition in all settings or are actively debating law reform (End All Corporal Punishment of Children, 2009).

Promisingly, in recent cases in India, Fiji, Kenya, Namibia, Nepal, South Africa and Zambia, high courts have ruled in favour of children's right not to be physically punished (e.g. Parents' Forum for Meaningful Education v. Union of India, 2000 and, in Fiji, Naushad Ali v. State, 2002) (Durrant, 2008).

The historical development of child protection and physical punishment legislation in the US, UK and Australia

In the US, animal cruelty laws preceded child protection legislation. Indeed, animal cruelty laws were said to be relied upon when intervention was required to protect a child named Mary Ellen Wilson from parental assault in 1874 (Swain, 1998). In 1877, the New York Society for the Prevention of Cruelty to Children, founded in 1874, and several Societies for the Prevention of Cruelty to Animals from throughout the country, joined together to form the American Humane Association (AHA). The AHA (2008) has had a formal policy against corporal punishment of children in any setting since 1995.

In 1889 in the UK, the Prevention of Cruelty to, and Protection of, Children Act 1889 (UK) determined penalties for wilful ill-treatment, neglect and abandonment by custodians of children (boys under 14 and girls under 16) which caused unnecessary pain or damage to health (Swain, 1998). In 2008 the National Society for the Prevention of Cruelty to Children (NSPCC) in the UK proposed that 'the law on the physical punishment of children should be changed to give children the same protection under the laws on assault as adults' (NSPCC, 2008). Consequent to the Children Act (2004), parents retain the right to physically punish their children and use the defence of 'reasonable chastisement' if charged with common assault but they do not retain the defence if punishment results in 'grazes, scratches, abrasions, minor bruising, swelling, superficial cuts or a black eye' (Crown Prosecution Service, 2007). This new legislation, the NSPCC (2008) maintains, is confusing and leaves children vulnerable to abuse.

Among the first Australian statute laws concerned with children's welfare and protection were the Neglected and Criminal Children's Act 1864 (Victoria) and the Infant Life Protection Act 1890 (Victoria). Neglect, rather than physical or sexual assault of children, was the major concern of statutory authorities and voluntary child protection organizations in the first half of the 20th century (Hill and Tisdall, 1997; Swain, 1998). Attention refocused on physical assault when Kempe *et al.* (1962) produced convincing evidence of 'battered-child syndrome', as noted above. Consequently, the idea 'of parents as the natural protectors of children' had to be questioned because 'significant numbers of children are seriously hurt or even killed by their parents' (Hill and Tisdale, 1997, p. 198).

Limiting rather than banning physical punishment

In some countries, calls for physical punishment law reform have received little or no response. Rayner observes:

> No Australian government has yet been prepared to address one of the prime causes of child abuse, the excesses of 'discipline' to children in the form of 'corporal punishment', 'smacking' or 'spanking' – all euphemisms for what would certainly be assaults if they were inflicted on anyone other than children. (1994a, p. 65)

In recent years, the Common Law legal systems of the UK, Canada and New South Wales in Australia have limited rather than removed parents' right to use physical punishment as a response to their children. The following questions, Freeman suggests, should thus be posed: 'What is a "loving smack"? Or a "safe smack"?' (1999, p. 138). Does the law allow infants or children with a disability to be 'smacked'? Can children be 'smacked' on the head, the face or have their ears boxed? And what about a child's bottom, Freeman (1999) asks, given possible sexual undertones. Does age, 'Gillick competence', clothing or implement use impact on permissibility? Freeman also points out the incongruity that some would tolerate 'a punch with a fist or a powerful blow with the hand but rule out a strap on the palm of the hand or back of the leg' (Freeman, 1999, p. 138).

United Kingdom

The Criminal Justice (Scotland) Act (2003) defines blows to the head, shaking, and the use of implements as unjustifiable assault of children, restricting the common law defence of lawful correction of children. The England and Wales (Children Act (2004)) and Northern Ireland (Law Reform (Miscellaneous Provisions) Order (2006)) disallow a defence of 'reasonable punishment' in cases of serious assault ('bodily harm'), allowing a 'reasonable punishment' defence in common assault cases (End All Corporal Punishment of Children, 2009).

Canada

In Canada, a 2004 Supreme Court judgement (Canadian Foundation for Children, Youth and the Law v. Canada (Attorney General)) upheld parents' rights to physically punish children aged between two and 12; implement use, blows to the head, and physical punishment of children with a disability and by teachers were prohibited (Watkinson, 2006). Recent court cases suggest 'confusion and contradiction' as the judiciary is faced with the challenge of deciding 'which limitation on reasonable force "trumps" the others' (Durrant *et al.*, 2008, p. 246). In 2007, the Standing Senate Committee on Human Rights recommended repeal by 2009 of section 43 of the Criminal Code which allows for the use of force as a means of correction (End All Corporal Punishment of Children, 2009).

Australia, the UNCRC and physical punishment law

At the time of writing, legislation prohibits physical punishment in all schools in Victoria, Tasmania and the Australian Capital Territory, and law reform is proposed in South Australia. Ministerial guidelines prohibit physical punishment in schools in New South Wales, and policy discourages it in Queensland and Western Australia but the defence of 'reasonable chastisement' is available (End All Corporal Punishment of Children, 2009). Notably, around the world, physical punishment is usually banned in schools before parental physical punishment is limited in the home or in public.

Australia's commitment to the UNCRC came into effect in September 1991 but 18 years later the Convention is not fully reflected in Australian law. Ratification of the UNCRC proceeded despite protests from segments of the Australian community who felt parents' rights would be threatened (Goddard and Carew, 1993). Jones (1999) argues, however, that the UNCRC is 'pro-family' and 'pro-parent' and fears about the impact of the Convention stem from a lack of knowledge and understanding of its principles; prompting the need for a major education campaign.

A 1997 inquiry into Australian legal and child protection systems, *'Seen and Heard': Priority for Children in the Legal Process* (Australian Law Reform Commission, 1997), established that Australia was not fulfilling its commitments under the UNCRC (1989). The inquiry report proposed that children should have the same protection from assault as adults but recommended the banning of physical punishment only in schools (Recommendation 50, p. 217). Parents' or guardians' perceived right to physically punish their children was not challenged (Model Criminal Code Officers Committee, 1998). In the same year, Australia received a strong rebuke from the UN Committee on the Rights of the Child regarding its treatment of children. Mrs Karp, a member of the UN Committee, 'deplored the apparent differences in interpretation of the question of corporal punishment' and stated that this 'implied ... a double standard' where children and adults were concerned (Summary of the 404th Meeting: Australia, 22/12/97). She advised the Australian Government to revise its stance. Further, the committee recommended education campaigns to bring about attitudinal change (Hodgkin, 1997). In the UN Committee's view 'even mild corporal punishment represents a profound invasion of rights and a fundamental discrimination against children' (Save the Children, 2001, p. 17), regardless of adults' disciplinary motivations and cultural or religious beliefs or traditions (Leach, 1994).

In 1998, in spite of the UN Committee's position, the Model Criminal Code Officers Committee (MCCOC) confirmed that the Australian Government upheld the view that Article 19(1) of the UNCRC did not require the banning of parental physical punishment. In light of this, the MCCOC proposed that the following parental behaviours should constitute *unrea-*

sonable physical punishment of a child: '(a) causing or threatening to cause harm to a child that lasts for more than a short period; or (b) causing harm to a child by use of a stick, belt or other object (other than an open hand)' (1998, p. 130). As discussed below, legislative reform in the state of New South Wales ignored proposal (b). In this context, the UN Committee responded to Australia's 2005 periodic report with concern about any lawful corporal punishment of children 'under the label "reasonable chastisement" and other similar provisions in states' legislation' (Concluding Observations CRC – Australia , p. 7).

Physical punishment, common law and statute in Australia

Lawful correction legislation in New South Wales, Australia

An amendment to the Crimes Act 1900 (NSW) – The New South Wales Crimes Amendment (Child Protection – Physical Mistreatment) Act 2001 (formerly known as the (*Child Protection – Excessive Punishment*) Bill 2000) – came into effect in NSW in December 2002, following a 12-month community education campaign. This legislation determined that parents' use of 'physical force' would not be considered 'reasonable if the force is applied: to any part of the head or neck of the child or to any other part of the body of the child in such a way as to be likely to cause harm to the child that lasts for more than a short period' (Crimes Act 1900 (NSW) S.61AA (2) (b)). A 'short period' was not defined in the act. Moreover, in the original bill, the use of implements, such as a belt or stick, to hit a child, and the use of a closed fist were also to have been considered unlawful but these explicit limitations were excluded from the final act. These amendments weakened the bill and retained 'as before, an element of uncertainty and confusion' (Corbett, 2001, p. 14063).

The act states that a parent's use of 'force' against a child 'could reasonably be considered trivial or negligible' (Crimes Act 1900 (NSW) S.61AA (2) (b)) and, if so, would not be deemed unreasonable. The Legal Aid Commission suggested it is therefore conceivable that, given past approval of wooden spoons and belts as suitable instruments with which to hit children, their use may 'continue to be seen by the adults sitting as today's judiciary as "trivial or negligible", despite the fact that these implements can often cause serious physical injuries to children' (Standing Committee on Law and Justice, 2000, p. 36). What is meant by 'trivial or negligible' is 'subjective', as Calvert contends: 'What some people consider reasonable chastisement, other people consider excessive punishment' (Standing Committee on Law and Justice, 2000, p. 37). Similarly, law enforcement officers', the judiciary's and society's estimations of 'trivial' are culturally and histori-cally determined (Turner, 2002).

Turner highlights the gradual changes in degrees of violence tolerated against women (noted above) and asks whether the law should follow the same path with respect to violence against children. She argues that if the law adopted a zero tolerance stance against hitting or 'spanking' children its trivialization would diminish and gradually disappear, simultaneously influencing both the police and others who observe disciplinary violence (Turner, 2002). Davis's (1991) research reveals that in a society that sanc-tions parental violence towards children, adult observation of a child being hit repeatedly in public is more likely to be ignored than to be commented upon, and even less likely to be reported to protective authorities.

In essence, the 2001 NSW legislation codifies parents' right to physically punish their children and the use of an implement may still be considered reasonable. While making a statement about the unacceptability of some forms of violence towards children, the act formally confirms a commit-ment to denying children the same rights to physical integrity as adults.

The law in Victoria, Australia

Law reflects a society's 'values and ideologies' (Durrant and Olsen, 1997, p. 445). As mentioned above, a parent in Victoria, Australia charged with the assault of a child in their care may still use the common law defence of reasonable chastisement to lawfully excuse their actions. Since 2007, however, teachers in Victoria have been prohibited from administering corporal punishment as a means of discipline or control in any state or private school.

Corporal punishment in schools

In Victoria, the corporal punishment of students was banned in state schools in 1983. A working party of school teachers, principals, welfare professionals and parents also strongly urged the Minister of Education to abolish physical punishment in private schools. They presented several arguments to support abolition: it was morally wrong, not compatible with an enjoyable, effective learning environment, prohibited in other areas of the law, and banned in many other countries (Working Party on the Aboli-tion of Corporal Punishment, 1983). Corporal punishment was seen as an infringement of children's rights and paramount in dividing teachers and students: 'middle class boys may accept such punishment as part of the ethics of the school, working class boys may regard it as evidence of the moral bankruptcy of the school which preaches against violence but also practises it' (Ware, 1983, p. 7). Until 2007, however, private schools retained the discretion to use physical punishment with parents' permission, and within the bounds of the applicable common law.

Historically, corporal punishment in schools reinforced children's inferior status. Corporal punishment was administered by ostensibly caring adults for the child's own good yet there were numerous instances of abuse to which the Victorian Education Department responded too timidly (Simpson, 1996). Indeed, Simpson raises the possibility that children's questioning of the reasonableness of corporal punishment may have resulted in their defiance of teachers' authority.

Some significant court cases in Australia, the US and UK

Many cases of parental assault of children that are prosecuted in lower courts receive public attention only through the media. Court transcripts may only be available for cases heard in courts which hear serious indictable offences. Newspaper articles, however, report legal professionals' comments, and record penalties enforced by magistrates in lower courts as well as judges in higher courts, sometimes assisted by juries. Often court reporters' accounts of legal opinion about the 'reasonableness' of physical punishment highlight children's vulnerability and inadequate protection from harm. Media reporting of child assault by caregivers can also stimulate intense public debate about the legitimacy of physical punishment.

Australian courts have deemed 'cricket bats, cricket stumps and fists' as 'reasonable instruments' with which to punish (Horin, 1995a, p. 4) and, even when found guilty of assault, many parents have escaped penalties and the recording of convictions (Horin, 1995b). Some Australian cases serve to illustrate the vulnerability of children and sentencing which appears to minimize child assault.

A four-year-old girl who refused to 'put her legs inside the family car' was reportedly struck and kicked on her legs and buttocks up to 40 times by her father, a man who had been similarly 'disciplined' as a child. Bruises and red marks resulted. The magistrate is reported to have said, 'If you lose your temper once you can lose it again'. The man was placed on a 12-month good behaviour bond, and was required to donate to a charity and attend an anger management course. No conviction was recorded (Gilchrist, 2002, p. 13).

A man on a suspended sentence for splitting his son's head open with a metal walking stick was re-arrested six months later for beating and kicking his son for eating too slowly. For the combined offences, the man received a six-month jail sentence (Turner, 2004).

A father tied his eight-year-old son's hands and feet before thrashing his bare buttocks with a belt, causing 'big black bruises'. He was sentenced 'to a one-year community-based order including 100 hours of unpaid community work'. The judge reportedly acknowledged that the father was at the 'end of his tether' before, as argued by the prosecution, he 'had lost his temper and gone beyond the reasonable use of force'. The child's wrongdoing: spending 'a lot of his pocket money' (Darragh, 2005, p. 5).

A man who had breached 13 suspended sentences and community-based orders received an 18-month jail term for beating his five-year-old son. As in case 2, the child's transgression was eating too slowly. The child was extensively bruised 'over his face … legs … behind his ears … all over his stomach' and he had 'contusions inside his mouth … scratching on his back described as red raw … a fractured left cheekbone and … rib' (The Queen v. Damien Paul Ripper, 2006).

Other Australian cases which have recently sparked controversy include a case in which a judge reportedly 'sent a "dangerous message" condoning child abuse' when he sentenced a mother to six months probation with no conviction recorded. It was reported that the mother, in a rage, used a belt to beat her nine-year-old daughter 'up to seven times on the stomach, back and chest … the plaited pattern of the belt could be seen on the girl's skin'. The judge reportedly said, 'Pressures in child rearing frequently lead to the raising of the temper' (*News Nation*, 2007).

In another case a mother with two previous convictions for violence was sentenced to two years probation for reportedly whipping her children. Her nine-year-old daughter suffered 14 lashes for failing to clean her room. Her seven-year-old son received 'five lashes on his buttocks and back of his neck for not cleaning his room to [his mother's] approved standard [and] five whacks on his shins with a fly squatter for fidgeting because he was cold, while helping to wash up' (Keim and Wenham, 2008).

In the US, a recent editorial (*News Sentinel*, 2008) commented upon social workers' distress given the outcome of a case in which a mother 'whipped' her 11-year-old son, with an electrical cord or belt, causing bruising on his thighs, arms and buttocks. The child reportedly stole some of her clothes to give to a friend. In a lower court, the mother was convicted of battery at which time the judge reportedly said, 'This is a tough area of law ... because you know that a person's intent was not to do the wrong thing. ... I don't have a good answer as to where to draw the line'. On appeal to the Indiana Supreme Court, however, four of the five justices reportedly decided the mother's 'discipline did not cross the line into criminal conduct', but they unanimously agreed on the limited amount of 'case law providing guidance as to what constitutes proper and reasonable parental discipline of children' (Boen, 2008).

The following 1994 case, and the media attention that surrounded it, highlighted law in relation to physical punishment in the UK.

A v. The United Kingdom

In Britain in 1993 authorities became aware that a stepfather had beaten his nine-year-old son, known as 'A', with a garden cane. Reportedly, the boy had tried to stab one of his brothers (Muir *et al.*, 1996). A paediatric examination revealed bruising suggestive of previous severe beatings and, in 1990, child protection authorities had registered the boy and his brother as physically abused (Bainham, 1999). In 1994, the stepfather was tried before a jury for assault occasioning actual bodily harm. The jury acquitted him after consideration of the common law defence of reasonable chastisement. Dissatisfied, 'A' and his natural father 'B' pursued a further hearing in the European Court of Human Rights on the grounds that the UK court decision breached Article 3 (Prohibition of torture and inhumane or degrading treatment or punishment) of the European Convention on Human Rights (ECHR). They argued that the defence of reasonable chastisement only applies to the assault of children, giving children less protection from assault than adults. They also drew attention to international condemnation of parental physical punishment, which contravenes Article 19(1) of the UNCRC (1989). The ECHR judgement in the case, known as A v. the United Kingdom, was delivered in September 1998. Detrick summarized its content, noting that the stepfather's 'treatment of the applicant' was harsh enough to attain 'the level prohibited by Article 3 of the ECHR' and, indeed, 'English law', which required the prosecution to 'prove that an assault on a child went beyond the limits of reasonable punishment, had not provided [the applicant] adequate protection' (1998, p. 336).

The 1998 ECHR ruling placed obligations on the UK Government to change existing law to 'protect children from "inhuman and degrading treatment"' (Department of Health, 2000, p. 12). As Turner (2002) observes, parents sometimes fail with regard to their children's welfare so unquestioned parental discretion is inherently risky for children. A v. the United Kingdom and other similar cases attest to this.

Conclusion

Historically, changing the status of oppressed people has been slow and incremental as it usually involves a diminution in the perceived rights of a more powerful group of people, such as men in the case of women and adults in the case of children. Throughout time 'smaller, weaker and less powerful people have been protected or liberated only when their rights as equal human beings have been asserted and recognized by society in both law and practice' (Saunders and Goddard, 1999, p. 16). While the passing of legislation may not guarantee changes in people's attitudes or behaviour, laws 'may be introduced as a symbolic gesture or affirmation of a principle' (Mount, 1995, p. 1004). With the exception of lawful correction of children by parents, the once-lawful degrading treatment of other groups of people may now be considered a part of history in some English-speaking countries.

Women, like many children today, were regarded as possessions; inferior beings who could be subjected by their husbands to disrespectful and humiliating treatment. Societal and legal tolerance of male violence against women, particularly in the privacy of the home, has been slow to change. Recent law reform that limits rather than bans physical punishment of children appears remarkably similar.

4

Conducting sensitive and ethical research with children and adults

Introduction

Parental physical punishment is a controversial issue, as noted in the previous chapter. The distinction between lawful physical punishment and child abuse is complex, and the literature and newspaper articles related to physical punishment highlight challenging themes and issues.

The qualitative research upon which this book is based was conducted in Victoria, Australia. It sought to capture the insights of some Australian children, parents and grandparents, and professionals whose work brought them into contact with children in clinical and legal settings, schools, preschools and hospitals. This chapter briefly outlines the practical and ethical process undertaken to gather, analyse and report participants' contributions (for further details see Saunders, 2005).

The impetus for this study

Countries around the world are increasingly considering the legitimacy of physical punishment of children. An understanding of factors that may

Physical Punishment in Childhood: The Rights of the Child, by Bernadette J. Saunders
and Chris Goddard
Copyright © 2010 John Wiley & Sons, Ltd.

either motivate or inhibit changes in attitudes and behaviours is vital. Knowledge about both adults' and children's experiences of, and views about, physical punishment is important. Awareness of its incidence, nature, effectiveness and effects, as well as the motives and rationales that perpetuate its use is essential.

Research design

This research sought to document children's and adults' accounts of, and perspectives on, family life, parenting and disciplinary practices, particularly physical punishment, and to ascertain participants' views in relation to the status and rights of children and parents. It proposed to give children a voice in current debates on physical punishment.

Method

The establishment of a sample

An Advisory Group comprising managers, practitioners and professionals whose work focused, at least in part, on children and families provided specialist knowledge, facilitated access to research participants, provided a forum to raise and discuss ethical issues, and enabled the distribution of information about the research. Both purposeful and snowball sampling were used (Kuzel, 1999).

As the subject of this research was controversial and sensitive, and because the research involved interviews with children, initially the sample of children, particularly for focus groups, was difficult to establish. Organizations and children's guardians acted as gatekeepers who restricted children from participating. At one school six children were permitted to take part in focus groups after 75 notices had been sent to families. At another school, eight children participated. Several schools did not participate, despite the principals' endorsement, because parents were not willing for their children to take part.

Purposive sampling

The primary selection criteria for this research sample were children over the age of eight, including children who had received counselling in response to abuse or neglect; parents; grandparents; and professionals who worked with children. As one of the foci of this research was the intergenerational transmission of family violence, family members from different generations within a family were also sought.

People who were interested in participating were contacted by phone or email, given information about the project, and their verbal and written agreement to participate was sought. Written consent from parents/carers was sought before children were interviewed. Child participants also signed the consent form, and verbally agreed to be involved in interviews before they began. Participants were made aware that they could withdraw from the research at any time or they could choose only to answer some questions. All participants were assured of anonymity.

Information packages were sent to the schools and notices about the research were sent to all parents with children over eight. A copy of the questionnaire booklet was available for parents to peruse at the school office. Parents who allowed their children to participate sent completed consent forms back to the school, co-signed by their children.

To recruit children who had received counselling for abuse and neglect, children's counsellors provided information to parents of children whom they considered might be interested in, and unlikely to be harmed by, participation. The counsellors were provided with explanatory letters and consent forms to either send by mail or make available to families who could then, without any pressure, initiate an inquiry about the research. Alternatively, parents gave the counsellor permission to provide their contact details so they could be contacted to discuss participation.

Snowball sampling

Both members of the advisory group and research participants selectively distributed information which resulted in an increase in the numbers of participants who were willing to contribute their views, experiences and insights.

Semi-structured interviews

Qualitative research techniques provide the researcher with an opportunity to explore issues deeply and comprehensively. Participants spend time thinking issues through, reflecting upon them, and sometimes arriving at different conclusions at the end of the interview to those that they had at the beginning. Each participant was assured at the beginning of an interview that the research aimed to document the anonymous life stories and differing viewpoints of individuals at different ages and from various backgrounds. Moreover, there were no right or wrong answers to questions, with the exception of factual personal details such as age and occupation.

When participants' comments appear inconsistent, qualitative data collection methods provide scope to draw the participant's attention to these apparent inconsistencies, and explore their views further. This enables enhanced insight into participants' world views and the motivations/rationales for their behaviour. In-depth interviews also capture evolving views, and enable clarification of words and thoughts in order to clearly document participants' life stories, feelings and attitudes.

Qualitative research methods accommodate a social work perspective. Through in-depth interviewing the researcher seeks to perceive and understand the world from the participants' viewpoint, in their own words, and at their own pace. The qualitative research interview may be empowering for participants because they have an opportunity to be listened to (without critical or confirming comment from the researcher), to mull over past experiences and to clarify their thoughts. The research interview is distinct from therapy but has some complementary characteristics. The researcher must be aware of and acknowledge personal biases and experiences related to the research question or issue so that the researcher's views are not imposed on the participant, and the researcher can uncritically hear what the participants are communicating. Moreover, the professional orientation of the social work researcher may assist in determining if an interview should cease on ethical grounds, such as causing the participant stress or discomfort.

All the adults participated in individual semi-structured interviews in their homes or workplaces. Children participated either in individual semi-structured interviews mainly in their homes or in focus groups at school. In individual semi-structured interviews, children and adults talked about their childhood experiences, particularly experiences of physical punishment as a recipient and/or as a person knowledgeable about the physical punishment of siblings, friends or other children. Children and adults also contributed their views and ideas about childhood, physical punishment, discipline and children's/parents' rights.

Adult interviews took about 90 minutes, and 20- to 60-minute interviews were conducted with children. Children were provided with pencils, paper and a picture to colour in if they wished but only a few children engaged in this activity. Set, mainly open, questions were asked, and participants were encouraged to raise any related issues that came to mind. Participants' comments were explored with questions not on the questionnaire.

Children's focus groups

Focus groups '*clarify, extend, qualify or contest findings on the same topic produced by other methods*: multi methods cannot validate, but they can deepen ... understanding' (Bloor *et al.*, 2001, p. 91, emphases in original). Schools allocated rooms for focus groups and meeting times. Children verbally expressed their willingness to participate before the group commenced. Children were asked not to disclose other participants' comments outside the group.

To begin, a similar approach to Willow and Hyder's (1998) consultation with four- to eight-year-old children was adopted. 'Curious Quizzey', a character created for this research's colour-in questionnaire booklet, expressed curiosity about children's thoughts and feelings regarding physical punishment and emphasized the importance of documenting children's views. Though entertained by this approach, eight- to 13-year-old participants appeared not to engage with the fictitious inquisitor. Rather, initial responses to the research questions led to the children entering into lively, frank, in-depth discussions. Children shared their views about physical punishment and were encouraged to talk generally rather than personally about physical punishment. Each child was asked to say their name before they contributed to discussion, and each child in turn was given an opportunity to make a comment if they wished. Children were provided with marker pens with which they could scribble on the booklets or colour in the Curious Quizzey character. Many children of all ages scribbled and coloured in the pictures whilst they participated in group discussion.

Reflexivity or 'representation of voice'

Qualitative researchers need to be self-reflective and self-critical (Miller and Crabtree, 1999) as 'the researcher, the method and the data are ... reflexively interconnected' (Mauthner and Doucet, 2003, p. 414). The researcher interprets participants' contributions and decides which extracts from transcripts illustrate the messages gained from the research process. The analysis is 'subjective' and 'interpretive' (Mauthner and Doucet, 2003, p. 415). Personal, academic and pragmatic influences and constraints must be acknowledged to avoid bias and misinterpretations of participants' contributions. Alternative explanations and discrepant examples are always highlighted. Articulation of the researcher's background and perspectives enables contextualization of the findings (Mauthner and Doucet, 2003).

The Australian Research Council funded this research in partnership with the Australian Childhood Foundation. In Australia, physical punishment appeared to be perceived as a defensible and an indispensable means of discipline. As parents, we recognized the challenges and difficulties of parenting. We were keen to explore not only people's experiences and views about physical punishment, but also how receptive people were to

changes in policy and parenting practice and what supports and/or education might encourage more respectful discipline of children. In our view,
children deserve at least the same rights to physical integrity and protection
from harm as adults.

Ethical conduct

Ethical issues and questions pervade all research (Waldrop, 2004). Monash
University's Standing Committee on Ethics in Research Involving Humans
granted ethics approval. Six participating organizations also granted ethics
approval.

Alderson proposes that researchers, particularly those who involve children as participants, should ask themselves the following questions: 'What
are the hidden values and interests? Who benefits? How is power used,
abused, shared? Are children seen as problems, villains or contributors? Do
the researchers aim to rescue, or criticise or respect children?' (2004, p. 110).
The answers to these questions will determine the methods used and the
manner in which the research is carried out.

Beauchamp and Walters highlight three basic ethical principles to which
all research involving human persons must adhere: autonomy, which refers
to self-regulation through 'adequate understanding' and freedom from
others' control and 'personal limitations' that disallow choice (1989, p. 28);
beneficence, which guards against harming research participants, and
endeavours to achieve some good; and justice, which ensures that participants are treated in a manner that is 'fair, due and owed' (1989, p. 32).
Moreover, the principle of justice is enforced when minority and disadvantaged groups are heard and vulnerable individuals are protected (Orb
et al., 2001, p. 96).

In light of these ethical principles, prior to conducting research, researchers must obtain participants' informed consent. They must choose and
want to participate. This choice should be based on plain language information which is provided about the research. Participants must be informed
that they can withdraw from the research at any time without undesirable
repercussions, and they must be well informed about the nature and
requirements of participation. Further, they need to be informed about
how the information that they share in the research is to be handled, and
that their contributions to the research may be published (Greig and Taylor,
1999).

In this research, all of this information was provided in the documentation given to participants, and in telephone or email communication, prior

to their participation. Further clarification and responses to questions, and opportunities to withdraw from the research, were given on the day of the interviews.

Ethical issues in research with children

Alderson contends that researchers who 'take ethics very seriously' will adopt 'methods' which ensure that children are respected (2004, p. 110). In research involving children at least two considerations are paramount: the child's right to be consulted and heard, and the need for protection from possible trauma (Mudaly and Goddard, 2006). Qualitative research with children is based on the premise that children 'are knowledgeable about their worlds, that these worlds are special and noteworthy, and that we as adults can benefit by viewing the world through their hearts and minds' (Fine and Sandstrom, 1988, p. 12).

Qualitative research may thus be a means of empowering children and motivating positive changes in their status and treatment. Mayall observes that children's contributions to research 'serve as thought-provokers and indicators for changes in social policies affecting children: as regards their rights, their relationships with adults … the services offered and available to them, the social institutions and environments which structure their lives' (Mayall, 1994, p. 7). At the same time, children's powerlessness and vulnerability may expose them to harm and exploitation. Research involving children thus demands heightened attention to sensitive and ethical conduct.

Children's distress emanating from participation in the research

In the explanatory information given to children's carers, it was explained that if children found discussion about physical punishment distressing they would be offered debriefing and, if necessary, counselling support. As physical punishment is common and may be legitimate, many children who had experienced being physically punished talked about it as a normal behaviour to which children were accustomed. Given this perception of normality, discussion about it did not appear to cause children distress in a way that raised concern for their well-being. Children expressed a range of emotions during interviews. When children disclosed unpleasant memories the researcher was always ready to either redirect the discussion or determine whether they wanted to continue the interview, or stop and debrief. Physical punishment that may be described as mild or acceptable is not an experience that children enjoy. However, children were able to talk about their experiences and express their views in a thought-provoking and insightful manner. When interviews and focus groups ended, none of the children appeared to be upset or unsettled by either the research interview or focus group experience. Children were not offered incentives to partici-pate in this research. However, they were sent a bookmark with letters thanking them for their time and contribution.

Guarding against risks to children

Mudaly and Goddard (2009) propose several strategies that help minimize the risks to which children who have been abused would be exposed by participating in research. These strategies guided the conduct of this research, particularly when interviewing the five children who had received counselling for abuse. These children had all completed or almost com-pleted their counselling. They had talked about their abuse, and they had been listened to and believed. Involvement in this research was therefore less likely to create anxieties or to resurrect unresolved issues. Through therapy, these children had established strong relationships with their counsellors and would therefore have been comfortable about deciding not to participate. These children knew that they had ongoing support from a counsellor.

Children who took part in this research all verbally expressed their will-ingness to participate prior to the start of the interview. They were also aware that they could discontinue the interview at any time by saying 'let's finish now' or 'I don't want to talk any more'. As children may have been in the habit of agreeing with adult agendas it was not possible to be com-pletely certain that children were truly giving their assent to participate (Willow and Hyder, 1998). However, the children participated enthusiasti-cally and had much to say about their experiences of, and views about, physical punishment. Children were not pressured to discuss abusive expe-riences. Moreover, all children were informed that they could say 'pass' if they did not wish to answer a question. Finally, the child's main carers were not placed under any pressure to encourage their child's participation.

Strategies in place if a child disclosed legally defined abuse

Even when confidentiality has been assured and the researcher is not man-dated to report abuse to child protection authorities (as is the case in the state of Victoria) it is important to report suspected child abuse to child protection authorities (Mudaly and Goddard, 2009). Otherwise that child may remain in a harmful environment. At the beginning of children's interviews they were informed that their contributions would remain anonymous as long as they were not in any danger of being seriously hurt by an adult. This reflected information about the research given to parents.

In focus groups conducted in schools children were not encouraged to talk specifically about their home situations. However, if a child wanted to talk with someone about their personal experiences, school personnel (who, in the state of Victoria, are mandated to report abuse) were to be asked to respond to the child as in normal school procedures. Child participants did not disclose recently occurring, legally defined abuse in either interviews or focus groups so none of the above procedures occurred.

Parents' informed consent and children's assent to participate

Permission for children to participate is obtained through the consent of the children's parents or guardians, who are expected to act in the child's best interests. This may present problems when the interests of the child and the interests of the parent conflict, such as in situations where parents may not wish children to disclose information about parental behaviours towards children that may be perceived as inappropriate or abusive. Many children will not be allowed to participate (Thomas and O'Kane, 1998; Willow and Hyder, 1998). Masson observes that 'gatekeepers have a positive, protective function, sheltering children and young people from potential harm and testing the motives of those who want access to them … However, gatekeepers can also use their position to censor children and young people' (2000, p. 36). Legally children cannot consent to participate but they can be well prepared to make a decision about whether to give their assent (see, for example, Ford *et al.*, 2007).

Confidentiality

Children were informed, in a manner that ensured their understanding, that their views and statements would be highly valued and anonymously presented in any publications. On one occasion, after completing the children's interviews, a parent asked about her children's responses to the research questions. She was assured that the children had not disclosed any information about which she was probably not already aware, and that she could perhaps discuss the research with the children with a view to sharing each other's thoughts about the issue. She appeared to consider this approach to be a reasonable one.

Organization, coding and analysis

Qualitative research involves 'a nonmathematical process of interpretation, carried out for the purpose of discovering concepts and relationships in raw data and then organizing these into a theoretical explanatory scheme'

(Strauss and Corbin, 1998, p. 11). However, all research involves analytic movement 'from ideas to data as well as from data to ideas' (Hammersley, 1992, p. 48). Although qualitative research does not generally quantify data, 'simple counts are sometimes used and may provide a useful summary of some aspects of the analysis' (Pope *et al.*, 2000, p. 114). For questions where there was a limited choice of answers, such as yes/no/don't know, all participants' responses were grouped according to the question number so that the number of participants answering the question in the same way was apparent. Each closed question was followed in the interview by an open-ended explanatory question, the responses to which were explored to arrive at an understanding of the participant's choice of response.

Data analysis

The data were analysed and coded using both pen and paper and a QSR data analysis program. The process was inductive, in that themes emerged directly from the participants' contributions, and deductive in that themes emanating from the literature review and other knowledge sources were discovered in the participants' contributions. This research was guided by a three-stage coding and analysis process that begins with the organization of the raw data by using a template that may have emanated from the literature review or categories readily apparent in the data. The second stage involves identifying themes and patterns in the data, making connections between them, and developing insights and possible explanations. The third stage involves the researcher in the task of 'corroborating' or 'legitimating' the insights and explanations by searching for deviant cases and ensuring the integrity of the tentative conclusions (Miller and Crabtree, 1999, pp. 135–7). Strauss (1987) proposed a similar analysis process which he termed 'open coding', 'axial coding', and 'selective coding'.

Interviews, followed by transcription, began the process of immersion in the data. 'In vivo' coding (Strauss, 1987), where key words or phrases were identified in the transcripts, occurred often, as did exploration of the data to make free nodes using computer software (QSR), some of which were later incorporated into themes. The initial thorough coding of this research data identified multiple themes which were then condensed by finding commonalities in the themes, identifying sub-categories, making connections, identifying patterns and making decisions as to which were the key themes in the data. Berg proposes, as a guide, that at least three 'occurrences of something' constitutes a pattern (Berg, 2004, p. 287). Themes were organized to 'represent the account' (Miller and Crabtree, 1999, p. 137) under the original themes derived from the literature that were rediscovered in the data, questions asked in the interviews that stimulated insightful participant contributions, and additional, unanticipated themes that emerged from the data. The final analysis sought to ensure that all views expressed were acknowledged and incorporated, especially cases/comments that deviated from common themes and possible explanations. Berg suggests that in the final stage of analysis the researcher seeks to explain 'thematic (categorical) patterns' by answering whether they reinforce or question previous similar research and then the researcher attempts to explain these differences or similarities (2004, p. 287).

Integrity, replicability and generalizability

Arminio and Hultgren suggest that evidence that research is 'credible', 'representative', and 'trustworthy' includes 'triangulation, peer debriefing and respondent debriefing or confirmability' (2002, p. 457). Barbour maintains that 'triangulation addresses the issue of internal validity by using more than one method of data collection' (2001, p. 1117). She further contends that qualitative research findings are not threatened by 'contradictions (or exceptions)' as these simply challenge the researcher to refine any emerging theories (Barbour, 2001, p. 1117).

This research used a multi-method approach to increase the numbers of children who could contribute their views on an issue that affects them. Common themes emerged from both types of data, and focus groups were particularly effective in giving children the opportunity to explore and develop ideas raised within the group. However, this research sought to acknowledge 'the existence of multiple views of equal validity' (Barbour, 2001, p. 1117). A multi-method approach did not therefore validate findings but rather added depth and richness (Mays and Pope, 2000).

Peer debriefing involves meeting with a peer or peers 'for the purpose of exploring aspects of the inquiry that might otherwise remain only implicit within the inquirer's mind' (Lincoln and Guba, 1985, p. 308). Ezzy (2002) maintains that peer debriefing is beneficial because it increases the researcher's awareness of his or her personal values and theoretical perspectives and the influence of these on the research process and on the ethical conduct of the research; stimulates discussion about evolving thoughts and theories emanating from data collection and analysis; and provides a forum for discussion about methodological issues. The authors reviewed and discussed each stage of the research and participated in both formal and informal discussion with colleagues.

The research results reflect, as closely as possible, participants' contributions as they were expressed at the time they were interviewed. Conceivably, their views on this issue may have changed since the interview. Indeed, the experience of involvement in the research may have prompted further thought and thus attitudinal and behavioural change but this would need to be the focus of further research as it was not a part of this research plan. Documentation of the 'stories' that are produced by research 'carries great responsibility and the need for integrity, honesty, and rigorous analytic procedures' (Jones, 2002, pp. 467–8). The researcher is required to determine 'the main issues and problems with which the informants were grappling' and then to document 'enough conceptual detail and descriptive quotations' to facilitate the reader's comprehension (Strauss and Corbin, 1998, p. 252). Throughout the interviews the researcher's understanding of what participants had said was checked frequently using 'summary techniques' and 'controlled non-directive probing' (Alston and Bowles, 2003, pp. 118–19).

Silverman (2000) suggests that validity in qualitative research is established when discordant data have been incorporated and raw data are well differentiated from the researcher's analysis and interpretation. Reliability, Silverman suggests, is established through clear documentation of the research process and the way in which the raw data were analysed. The audit trail for this research took a number of forms: ethics applications, the questionnaires, the interview tapes, the typed transcripts of interviews, the QSR database, research journal entries during data collection, memos and notes, Advisory Group minutes, conference papers and presentations, and publications. Typed transcripts were checked against taped interviews and any apparent discrepancies were corrected. Huberman and Miles refer to this process as 'descriptive validity' (2002, p. 45).

A small, purposive sample is not representative of any particular group of people so the results of this research cannot be generalized.

Description of the research sample

Forty adults and 31 children participated in this research. The 31 children included 17 children who were interviewed individually, and 14 children who participated in one of four focus groups..

The 31 children (16 girls and 15 boys) were predominantly Anglo-Australian, of various socio-economic backgrounds, and aged between eight and 17 years. Seven children had not been physically disciplined, and five children had received counselling for abuse.

The children's voices in this study do not differentiate between the contributions of children known to have been abused and those of children

Table 1 Summary of the research method used, numbers and ages of children

Participants	Numbers	Age range (yrs.)
Children N = 31		
Individual interviews	9	8–10
Focus Groups × 2	6	8–10
Individual interviews	5	11–13
Focus Groups × 2	8	11–13
Individual interviews	3	14–17
Total	31	

who had been physically punished as the themes that emerged from analysis of the transcripts represented both groups. There is some differentiation in the results between children who had and who had not been physically punished, but there appeared to be none in terms of gender. Throughout the text children are referred to by their ages.

Forty adults were interviewed. Twenty-one of the adults were interviewed as professionals. Of these 21, 15 were also interviewed as parents. The remaining 19 (out of the 40) were interviewed solely as parents. In total, therefore, 34 parents were interviewed. They came from various socio-economic backgrounds, and included 26 mothers (two were single mothers), and eight fathers (one was a single father). Of these, seven were also grandparents. While all of the grandparents, except one teacher, were retired, the parents' occupations included home duties, unskilled work and professional work. The 21 professionals had a variety of roles in social work, psychology, health, education and law enforcement, and their work brought them into contact with children and families.

Conclusion

This research sought to give children, parents, grandparents and professionals an opportunity to reflect upon physical punishment, and to contribute to discussion about the issue. Despite being recipients of physical punishment, children have rarely been consulted when physical punishment is debated and legislative reform considered. We contend that physical punishment has played a significant role in silencing children's voices. This research builds on an emerging field of research that encourages and supports children who wish to speak about their views and experiences. In the following chapters, we present children's voices alongside those of adults.

5

Experiences of physical punishment at home, at school and in public places

Introduction

Childhood may be 'defined by corporal punishment' (McGillivray, 1997b, p. 241). Children may be physically punished for normal childhood behaviours that adults perceive as challenging or disobedient, and this and other types of family violence mostly occur in homes where children are assumed to be safe (Gelles and Cornell, 1990; May-Chahal and Cawson, 2005). Determining the nature and incidence of aggression between family members is challenging. Parents may underestimate, or publicly conceal, violent responses to children for fear of being labelled abusive or reported to child protection services and, when parents publicly hit children, observers rarely intervene on children's behalf (Davis, 1991).

In this context, the meaning of the words that parents and others choose to describe children's physical punishment may be ambiguous. This chapter explores language inconsistencies with a view to enhancing understanding of adults' and children's descriptions of physical punishment at school, at home and in public. To begin, however, we highlight some research that gives an indication of the current nature and incidence of physical punishment in the US, the UK, Canada and Australia.

Physical Punishment in Childhood: The Rights of the Child, by Bernadette J. Saunders and Chris Goddard
Copyright © 2010 John Wiley & Sons, Ltd.

Reported use of parental physical punishment

Physical punishment research rarely involves both parents, yet Nobes and Smith (2000) found that while 90.9% of fathers admitted hitting their children, mothers reported that only 55% of fathers had done so. Similarly, mothers' reports may underestimate mother-to-child violence when compared to children's accounts (Kolko *et al.*, 1996), and children are rarely consulted in physical punishment research. Further, both parents and children may minimize the severity and frequency of violence (Sariola and Utela, 1992). For some parents and children physical punishment may be so normal that estimates of its occurrence will not reflect reality (Giles-Sims *et al.*, 1995).

We know, however, that many babies are physically punished even before they reach their first birthday (see, for example, Combs-Orme and Cain, 2008; Socolar and Stein, 1995; Straus and Stewart, 1999), and between the age of 18 months and three years the numbers increase (Socolar *et al.*, 2007; Virtrup *et al.*, 2006). Preschool children tend to be physically punished more than older children (Holden *et al.*, 1995; Wauchope and Straus, 1990) but adolescents are also physically punished (see, for example, Agathonos-Georgopoulou, 1997; Straus and Stewart, 1999; Sunday *et al.*, 2008). Despite under-reporting and increasing ambivalence about its acceptability, the reported use of physical punishment remains high (Benjet and Kazdin, 2003; Department of Health, 2000; Leach, 1994; Straus and Mathur, 1996).

In the US, Straus and Stewart (1999) claimed that the prevalence of physical punishment was around 90%: 35% of parents hit infants under 12 months old, over half of the parents hit their 12-year-old children, approximately one in five parents continued to hit their 16- to 17-year-old children, and 28% admitted using belts and paddles to hit their 5- to 12-year-old children. More recent research involving 191 US adolescents, half of whom were known to child protection services, suggests that mothers' 'physical abuse/punishment' of adolescents may be underestimated, especially 'physical abuse/punishment' of daughters (Sunday *et al.*, 2008, pp. 15–16). Deitz (2000) found that 26% of parents reported at least one incident of hitting a child's face, head or ears, pinching the child, or using a hard object, and Graziano *et al.* (1996) found that 30% of parents used physical punishment that resulted in intense pain, bruises or raised welts. Moreover, 35% of the children reported that they had been punished with sticks, paddles, whips and cords.

In the UK almost three-quarters of a randomly selected sample of 2,869 young adults aged 18 to 24 reported having been mildly and infrequently slapped on the leg, arm, hand or bottom (May-Chahal and Cawson, 2005). A 2008 National Society for the Prevention of Cruelty to Children (NSPCC) survey of 1,900 parents found that one in eight children, and 7% of young people aged 15–17 had been hit in the previous 12 months (Carvel, 2008). A 2007 NSPCC survey of 1,000 adults revealed that 77% believed smacking is becoming less acceptable. However, it also revealed that 41% of respondents had seen a child hit in public in the previous six months (End All Corporal Punishment of Children, 2009), prompting an NSPCC (2007) campaign to 'create smack-free shopping'. In a nationally representative UK study (Ghate *et al.*, 2003), 71% of parents reported physically punishing their children, and in the past year 58% had resorting to 'smacking' or slapping whereas 9% had resorted to more severe physical punishment.

In Canada, prevalence of physical punishment appeared to be around 51% (Oldershaw, 2002). Representative surveys of mothers in Quebec (Clement and Cumberland, 2007) revealed decreased levels of physical punishment, such as slapping a child's hand, arm, leg or bottom, between 1999 (47.7%) and 2004 (42.9%), with more severe violence, such as hitting with implements or above the shoulders, remaining around 6.4%. Attitudes favouring physical punishment also declined. The 1999 survey revealed that while children over three and under six were most frequently slapped, almost 50% of children under two had been physically punished (Clement *et al.*, 2000, cited in Gagne *et al.*, 2007). A telephone survey of 1,000 adults in Quebec (Gagne *et al.*, 2007) found that 66.4% had been physically punished and more than 10% said they were often hit.

In Australia many children are physically punished by their parents. Recent representative polling research suggests that a belief in the need to 'smack' children remains high but appears to be declining (Tucci *et al.*, 2002; 2006a). Seventy-five percent of Australians in 2002 compared to 69% in 2006 agreed that 'it is sometimes necessary to smack a naughty child'. Tolerance of smacking increased as children approached the age of five years. Three percent of Australians surveyed in 2002 and 1% in 2006 felt that reasonable physical punishment could leave a red mark on the child for a few days. Hitting children around the head, shaking children, and hitting children under five appeared to be the least tolerated.

Current meanings attributed to physical punishment

This research did not attempt to define physical punishment. Rather it explored its manifestations from the participants' perspectives. Their perspectives were wide ranging, and reinforced concerns about the 'fuzzy' distinction between 'legitimate' physical punishment and child abuse (Freeman, 1994, p. 21), discussed in Chapter 1. In some families children are occasionally hit with the hand on the bottom and extremities, causing minimal pain. Other children are physically punished by various painful means, sometimes to the extent that they sustain marks or injuries, and sometimes with implements such as belts or wooden spoons. Inevitably children experience some degree of physical pain but may not be injured, as Straus's commonly used definition (1994) suggests. Participants' perceptions suggest that children are most often hit with an open hand, but hitting children with implements, pinching, biting, shaking, and throwing objects at children were also considered common. Professionals more frequently saw severe forms of punishment, such as burns and cuts.

To ascertain the meaning that adult participants ascribed to terms commonly used to refer to physical actions directed at children as a means of discipline or control, they were asked to describe the actions they associated with 'physical discipline', 'physical punishment', 'a good smack', and 'assault'. They were also asked if, and in what ways, they differentiated these terms from one another. Further, adults were asked to consider the aptness of the words 'violent' and 'abusive' to describe actions falling under the aforementioned terms (see Chapter 6).

Is physical 'discipline' different from physical 'punishment'?

The terms 'physical punishment' and 'physical discipline' appeared to be used interchangeably:

> It's semantics, they're the same. (mother)

However, when given the opportunity to differentiate between these two expressions, just over half of the participants perceived a difference, typically related to adults' motives and intentions. Physical responses to children were perceived to differ in intensity, though opinions differed about whether physical 'punishment' or physical 'discipline' was likely to be more painful. Some suggested that physical discipline has good intent, is instructive and is therefore nobler than physical punishment, which may be considered retributive and may be harsher. Discipline was seen as 'proactive' and 'more measured' while punishment is 'reactive' and 'cold-hearted':

> You try disciplining them before you start abusing them. (mother)

Others focused on the mental state of the parent, suggesting that physical punishment is harsher than physical discipline – which is more of a last resort or spontaneous response to inappropriate or annoying behaviours:

Punishment is … premeditated. (father)

A grandparent, however, expressed the opposite view, seeing physical discipline as 'more regimented and … severe'.

Words currently used to describe physical punishment

Adult participants used the following, frequently euphemistic, words and expressions to describe familiar physical means of discipline or punishment:

> smack, hit, slap, flogging, whack, belting, swat, strap, cuts, thrashing, hiding, tap, six of the best, bum warmers, beating, assault, blow, putting over the knee, wailing, paddling, punching, shaking, kicking, biting, pinching, pushing, shoving, striking, hitting with objects, throwing, pulling hair, scratching, cuff around the ear, hit with a spoon, clip over the ear, wallop, poking, clip over the lughole, backhander [and] bashing.

The current meaning of 'a good smack'

Parents commonly threaten a non-compliant child with 'a good smack'. When asked what this might imply, participants suggested 'a good smack' might describe hitting which either punishes or disciplines a child. Parents' intent may be retributive, educative or without forethought:

> A good smack … is bordering on beating … there's some pleasure gained. (social worker)

> Hard enough for [the child] to realize … 'I've done something wrong'. (mother)

> Enough for them to understand that they have gone outside the realms of acceptability. You might get a few tears. (father)

> A single strike … reactionary or instinctive. (grandfather)

Alternatively, a 'good smack' may refer to the intensity of the hit and how much it hurts:

> A real strong whack. (psychologist)

> It would raise concern around the extent of force … and degree of control used by the parent. (social worker)

> A really hard slap in the face. (social worker)

> Smacked intensively … painfully. (father)

Inflicting pain. (father)

It would sting ... leave a couple of finger marks. (grandmother)

A 'good smack' may also refer to how it is delivered:

With a wooden spoon. (grandmother)

A good open-handed slap ... around the legs, the bottom or ... face. (social worker)

On the backside. (teacher)

On the leg or ... arm ... with a hand. Not a huge amount of force. (mother)

Actions currently associated with the assault of a child

Given the 'reasonableness' requirement inherent in legally sanctioned physical punishment (see Chapter 3), responses to the question, 'When I use the word "assault" what actions directed at children by parents, guardians or teachers do you think of?' were thought-provoking. A 'reasonable' person's understanding of 'assault' in the context of physical punishment seems likely to be inconsistent. 'Assault' may mean:

Extremely direct, purposeful, beating (social worker)

Being hit once ... with an open hand, across the upper body or face. (teacher)

A much more aggressive action ... with the use of an implement ... or ... punching ... shaking or kicking. (social worker)

From a slap or a smack right through ... (mother)

'Assault' may be associated with injury:

A real risk of physical injury ... premeditated and without restraint. (father)

On the other hand, arousing fear in a child may be enough to be considered 'assault':

Where the adult is imposing their physical force or their size ... in a way that is quite intimidating to ... and causes fear in a child. (teacher)

'Assault' may only refer to

hitting ... around the head. (father)

[hitting] with an implement. (father)

Finally, it may be an 'assault' only if the parent intended to harm the child:

> Outside the boundary of discipline. (health worker)

> Meted out in some uncontrolled way, or deliberately with the level of force that has been excessive, left injuries. (social worker)

People's perceptions of the meaning of the terms 'physical discipline', 'physical punishment', 'a good smack' and 'assault' are inconsistent, and the boundaries that differentiate acceptable from unacceptable disciplinary responses to children are imprecise. Contributing to this lack of clarity is the large number of words, many of which are euphemistic, from which people may choose to describe violence directed at children. Choosing one word over another to describe a particular physical response to a child may both reflect and influence judgements about acceptability and whether particular actions are reasonable to adopt as a means of discipline or control (discussed further in Chapter 6).

Adults' memories of physical punishment in childhood

Many adults remembered that as children they had accepted legally and socially sanctioned physical punishment at home and at school, and believed it was necessary. The threat of physical punishment, coupled with its even occasional use, instilled fear in children which was intensified when they witnessed other children's physical punishment. Indeed, some children appeared to be affected in ways similar to children who have experienced intimate partner violence (see, for example, Bedi and Goddard, 2007; Mullender *et al.*, 2002).

Adults recalled that, as children, they learnt that adults responsible for their care and protection were 'the boss' and their 'owners' so they could legitimately hurt them. Physical punishment taught children that 'adults had ultimate power':

> If you made them angry enough or ... did the wrong thing ... a child is at their mercy.

> Physical punishment was just normal. It hurt and I was scared ... you are so powerless.

Seeing other children hit made the child witness a 'victim', 'silenced'. As children, adults remembered they needed to 'be really good' to avoid getting hurt and this curbed their 'freedom'. Several participants recalled how much, as children, they wanted to please their parents. Some spoke of how they had 'disappointed' their parents, even 'fallen from grace', when their father physically punished them. Physical punishment reinforced children's inferior position in society:

> My parents saw us as children ... I certainly felt ... lesser than them, like not as important.

> Physical discipline taught me that you really don't get much of a say. Adults don't listen ... don't respect you.

Physical punishment at home and at school was:

> Rejecting ... being put down. Children have no rights and ... children were like nobody. You're a child ... you don't really count.

In many if not most childhoods, pain and tears were common, and tears were often shed in private to avoid giving adults too much in return for their demeaning punishment. In school, one participant

> used to feel sick. My teacher's aim was to make me cry, and nothing would make me cry, no way ... just the shame of it. There was no way I would cry in front of everybody.

Another participant said:

> I didn't want to cry ... I wasn't going to show that it hurt.

Another's refusal to cry gave the impression:

> 'You're not hurting me' ... that was pride kicking in.

Experiences at home

Participants recalled being physically punished at home for:

> not eating; theft, household damage and outrageous behaviour; being very bad or naughty; challenging rules and limits; being disrespectful; answering back; not doing chores; shoplifting; wagging school; arguing in the car; doing dangerous things; swearing; fighting with siblings; picking apples; mud over good clothes; being very cheeky; not doing things; rudeness; and, as a teenager, sneaking out of the house.

Physical punishment was 'an acceptable norm' which 'everybody did', and many parents believed children 'needed' it to encourage obedience:

It was commonplace ... the way to raise children.

A 'good smack' was meant to teach children 'a lesson' about appropriate behaviour, and some participants' parents, many of whom had also experienced physical punishment as children, believed that if you 'spare the rod you would spoil the child'. Physical punishment may have been 'the only way' that parents knew how to discipline. Moreover, parents were perceived to be often tired, stressed or angry:

> My mother felt under an enormous amount of stress, had experienced physical punishment in her own childhood ... and that was what she chose to use at the time.

Another participant 'was the eldest of seven children ... Mum had had a couple of nervous breakdowns, dad was struggling with his work', and another observed that physical punishment resulted from 'loss of temper, just ... feeling pushed to the limit'. Implements, such as 'belts', 'spoons', 'straps', 'jug cords', 'slippers' and 'sticks' were often used. 'Red marks', 'bruises' and 'welts' were not uncommon outcomes, resulting in feelings of embarrassment, anger, fear, resentment, sadness, even hatred. Children felt wronged, indignant and belittled. Several participants recalled having to wait for punishment 'until your father comes home'. This, one adult observed, was 'horrible', like 'sitting on death row'. In this context, participants' accounts of physical punishment at home, including witnessing their siblings' punishment, present a glimpse of childhoods lived under the threat of pain and humiliation.

At the same time, many adults remembered physical punishment occurring in homes that were also caring and supportive:

> We were pretty spoilt ... but ... we were pretty disciplined as well.

> For unacceptable behaviour ... you'd either get a smack or be sent to your room but acceptable behaviour ... mum and dad would praise and encourage.

One participant knew that if he was 'disobedient', he'd get hit but:

> Friday nights ... there'd always be lollies in dad's pocket ... for being good.

Another recalled:

> We got praised if we did things right but if we didn't we were hit with a strap and jug cord on the backside ... I hated them for it.

Adults vividly remembered the trauma associated with being physically punished by very angry parents. Yet similar angry responses were perpetuated from one generation to the next (see Chapter 9):

> My dad's rule of thumb was never hit a child unless in anger. It sounds strange but when you think about it there's some logic to it. … His thing was you shouldn't think I'm going to hit you now because you've been bad. It would have to be heat of the moment, passionate.

In some families, fear enhanced the power of threats. One participant's father would say:

> 'Right, lay across the bed'. … Nine times out of 10 dad used a slipper. The threat of it kept you on your toes. You didn't want it to happen.

Some participants described adults' complicity:

> Dad slapped me across the ear … just one belt. Mum … goes, 'Are you alright?' and I said, 'No, my ears hurt', and she goes, 'Good'.

> I remember not eating and mum picking up a big spoon and … whack on my finger … purely sort of rage. … My finger was damaged. In those days … doctor would have said, 'Well do it next time too'. I remember feeling really scared. Living with a single parent you have only got one source of love and care … I just became a completely compliant child.

Many adults remembered the fear of 'getting caught again':

> Coming home late … I must have been 12 … I was hit across the back, backside … half a dozen times. Dad was waiting for me … I hadn't told them where I was going. Mum had a favourite piece of cord. … It made me afraid of my parents … always on my toes … a bit wary and worried.

At the age of 15, this participant left the house without asking permission. On her return:

> Dad grabbed me by the hair … dragged me up the stairs, and … made me kneel over the bed. … He belted me with the belt across the buttocks maybe … eight times. … It made me more wary of being caught, perhaps a bit sneaky … I was very angry but [never] dared to show that.

Another remembered being 'frightened' after her dad had kicked her:

> I was caught smoking … I must have been about 12. … My dad had a terrible temper … I had the strap a few times … welts on my leg and … the wooden spoon on my bottom. … It made me more on guard.

Witnessing siblings' physical punishment

While children witnessing violence between adults in the home has been recognized as child abuse (McGee, 1997; Mullender *et al.*, 2002), there appears to have been little comment on the impact on children of witnessing other children's physical punishment (Lansdown, 2000; Turner, 2002). Defined broadly, 'witnessing' includes the 'multiple ways' children may be exposed to other children's physical punishment, including directly observing the violence, hearing it, knowing about it, and experiencing its aftereffects (Edelson, 1999, p. 844).

Children with siblings who lived in a family where physical punishment was used inevitably either saw or heard the physical punishment of their siblings. Adult participants reflected upon times when, as children, they felt fearful and distressed and wanted to intervene to stop parents from hurting siblings or friends. Children sometimes felt responsibility for other children's punishment, and were unable to comfort the physically punished child. Children who have witnessed violence between adults in the home express similar reactions to the violence (McGee, 1997; Mullender *et al.*, 2002). One adult recalled:

> Dad was giving my younger brother the strap, and … I got really distraught … saying … 'Stop it, stop it'.

Another adult remembered the instruments used to hit her siblings:

> Hand, stick, hairbrush. … Sometimes I would cry if I would see them being hit … I'd be distressed. It often made me really angry at my parents … very upset. I felt very powerless.

One vividly described her mother 'chasing' her brother with a 'plastic racquet'. Her mother 'whacked him' and 'left imprints':

> I just felt devastated for him … I didn't like watching him being hit with an implement and … cower.

Adults remembered as children fearing that they would also be hit. One participant recalled her brother

> getting the strap … you feel more upset in some ways when it's happening with someone else. … I was frightened at home because you are thinking, 'Oh my God it might be me next'.

Another recalled her brother

getting a slap to the back of the legs ... the clip around the ear, and I can picture Dad fighting him to the ground and hitting him uncontrollably. It was frightening. I feared that that could happen to me.

One adult's only means of escape from her father's violent response to her sister was to close her eyes:

She was really insolent and would stand up to my father and I remember ... I shut my eyes ... I remember the noise and her crying and ... the whack noises ... I remember his anger.

Feeling unsafe, another described how she would escape to her bedroom:

I would physically remove myself while it was happening ... go to my room and shut the door.

Another remembered:

A girlfriend ... used to get belted. If I was at her house playing, I would always run home scared. I was a real wuss because I had never seen anything like it. ... I just couldn't handle it. I used to hide her under my bed and mum would find out ... and ring up her mum, and then she would get a belting, and my mum would say to me it's my fault.

Some adults recalled that they reacted to other children's pain with uncomfortable relief that 'it wasn't me' this time, and they sometimes felt responsible:

I often remember Dad ... hitting my brothers when they wouldn't go to sleep ... maybe 10 or 15 times each. It was actually my fault ... I felt ... sick in the stomach thinking, 'Thank God it was them and not me this time'.

I was glad it wasn't me ... I remember my youngest sister getting a thrashing ... the noise she made, 'Dad, Dad, don't, don't!' ... more noise than the boys did ... we didn't bellow [but] he would keep on going until he made you cry.

Another recalled feeling that all children 'really are vulnerable':

I thought, 'They're getting a smack and I'm not' ... I remember being scared ... This only happens to kids. I'm a kid.

One participant recalled trying to intervene. Her brother

did naughty things and I used to lie to protect him. I hated it when he was hurt … I'd get in the middle [and] be pulled out of the way and he'd get the smack anyway.

Others remembered disempowerment and distress when a sibling was in pain:

I remember hearing my brother screaming. The rest of us would be in absolute fear … that we were going to get it. Our fear was also in sympathy for him and our helplessness. We couldn't help him … he was made to sit alone … sobbing. He had all these marks and his face would be tear-stained. We were wanting to … tell him how sad and sorry we were but … we were scared.

I can remember the distress … and the helplessness … I didn't feel like I could do anything but also … the guilt that I didn't intervene. I can remember … my dad taking his belt off and strapping my brother several times across his back.

Experiences at school

For some, physical punishment at school was remembered as 'a bit of theatre'. Adults in authority 'made a spectacle of it'. Black humour crept into some participants' reflections on this 'theatre' and 'spectacle', yet today most adults would be outraged at physical punishment of children at school:

If a teacher did any of those things today they would be before the disciplinary board. (teacher)

Historically, 'the old adage of "spare the rod, spoil the child" typified many teachers' approach to children' (psychologist). While some have changed their views, there remains 'a generation of school teachers that rue [not] being able to physically hit a child with a ruler' (social worker), and parents may still say:

In the old days … they belted kids. If we had the old days back we could certainly keep … kids in line.

Physical punishment 'was just the way things were done' and was commonly justified as 'social control':

You whip it out of them when they're 12 or 13, and you won't have trouble later. (health worker)

Physical punishment at school could be harsh and frequent. Implements hung on classroom walls, or were placed in children's view to threaten pain for misbehaviour:

> The cane ... was more to frighten us to do the right thing.

Welts and cuts were, however, regularly inflicted, and a 'normal' part of many childhoods. If not victimized, children were exposed to other children's physical punishment:

> The ruler across the hand ... hurt, and it was humiliating. There was a whole process to it ... sitting outside the principal's office so you were clearly visible. You had a sense of powerlessness ... a level of fear.

The consequence for 'those who didn't learn the times table' was:

> Stand in front of the class and ... whack, whack, whack, whack, whack, whack, whack.

Adults recalled the pain they experienced, the 'awkwardness' and tears, and how they learnt to be 'cunning' or 'cautious':

> The queue for the black strap ... the stinging ... being told if you didn't hold still ... you'd get worse. I don't think I ever cried at school ... 'cause ... that gave them far too much.

> Being dragged up to the board to do a sum, and not being able to do it and ... getting my hair pulled, getting shoved, pulled around by the hair. I was in shock emotionally. It made me more cautious ... probably restricted my learning ... I was so anxious.

Another recounted an ink spill:

> The teacher went ballistic, 'Outside!' and ... with a cane whacked me three or four times across the backs of the legs. I couldn't sit down afterwards. I can remember getting whacks on the knuckles. ... In the playground, 'Come here, bend over', and whack. I felt ... extreme discomfort ... very, very pained. It was often embarrassing or humiliating ... in front of a group, often with little explanation. Crying ... was always awkward. It would make you more cunning. ... You lived in fear.

Witnessing other children being hit

As in the home environment, children who witnessed violence directed at a sibling, friend or fellow student were affected:

You are frightened.

They'd use a yardstick ... you could see marks on children's hands ... I was scared stiff. ... You knew there was a cane waiting for you if you did the wrong thing.

The boys getting the cuts. ... He gave them six of the best. It was a lesson to everybody. Six whacks of the strap. Three on each hand. ... They held their hands afterward, one or two might have cried. ... I was frightened. It made my blood run cold.

A 'big ruler' came to mind for one participant:

Being told to come out the front ... bend over and the teacher whacks ... saying, 'This is what happens'. Kids would cry, would really get upset.

In school some children also felt uncomfortable relief in the presence of another child's suffering because at least 'it's not me' this time.

I was regularly struck at school, horribly with various implements but never around the head with a hand. ... others ... got injuries from it ... I was standing next to a kid who turned to me and spoke [and the teacher] just thumped this kid to the side of the head so hard he crashed into me ... I thought I was next. ... This kid was just crying, the whole side of his face was all red. Your overwhelming sense is, 'Thank God it's not me'.

In summary, adult participants' recollections of their childhood revealed that physical punishment occurred regularly at home and was once common in schools:

It used to be quite abusive. (social worker)

As noted above, physical punishment was prohibited in Victorian state schools more than 25 years ago.

The current prevalence and nature of physical punishment: professionals' perceptions

Increasingly people are questioning the acceptability of parental physical punishment, but many adults still resort to it, despite their childhood experiences. Many also continue to believe that parenting practices are no one else's business. Changes in parental physical punishment have been described as 'qualitative rather than quantitative' (Leach, 1999, p. 6). It still commonly occurs, though its nature and severity may have changed.

Privacy of the home

Strengthening societal intolerance of physical punishment raised professionals' concerns about the privacy of the home:

> They do it in their house and no one sees it. (psychologist)

> It worries me what happens at home. (social worker)

> Usually people stop if it is out in public but what happens to the child afterwards is one of my concerns. (social worker)

> If you are at home you can snap. (health worker)

> Physical punishment is probably happening less ... but then I don't really know what goes on in people's homes. (teacher)

As an integral component of some parents' disciplinary repertoire, professionals remarked:

> Some parents feel guilty if they use physical discipline with their children. ... If they ever do open up very much ... it's really often out of sheer frustration of not knowing what else to do. (teacher)

> Parents might consciously ... not raise it because of fear. (social worker)

Moreover, 'children are aware of the taboos' and this makes it 'difficult' for children to talk:

> Physical discipline at home still occurs [but] there is kind of a lid on it. (teacher)

In this context, the likelihood of professional intervention is greater in poorer families (Mount, 1995) because they may be less resourceful than wealthier, more articulate people in concealing or accounting for bruises and injuries to children resulting from physical punishment:

> The middle and upper class are better at hiding it. (social worker)

> Nearly all discipline occurs behind closed doors. ... The mum who has got a mild intellectual disability ... strikes her child repeatedly ... sends him out on the street to play, and all the bruises and marks are evident. She is going to be getting a knock on the door. ... At the other end of the social spectrum ... the child stays home from school and the bruises and marks go away, or there is much more of the coercion of the child, 'I am sorry ... please don't tell anyone'. We get one group saying, 'It's the great unwashed out there that are the problem'. [But] there might be a whole group of ... middle class, wealthy, socially supported people ... who are doing horrible things to their kids each day but I don't see them. (health worker)

Physical punishment in common use

Professionals were asked to draw on their personal and professional experiences to suggest how common they thought it was for parents to physically punish their children in the following ways: with an open hand; with an implement; by pulling hair, throwing objects at children, shaking or pinching children. They were asked to identify the types of implements that they are aware of parents using, and to disclose other means of discipline that they were aware of parents using to change, modify or eliminate a child's behaviour.

Twenty of the 21 professionals perceived that hitting children with an open hand is common or very common:

It's what I've observed, it's what I hear, it's what I've done. (social worker)

I smack my children … and most of my friends … have smacked their children. … Every day in the supermarket you'll see somebody smack their child … on the street, all the time. (health worker)

A social worker observed that in her agency

a lot of families have experienced many generations of family violence. … It has become a part of their lifestyle and belief system.

In contrast, a teacher thought that hitting children, even with an open hand, was not common because there is 'a social stigma attached to hitting children'. Other professionals suggested that physical punishment with an implement is less socially acceptable:

I just don't hear people talking about it. (teacher)

I've not heard as many accounts of physical abuse with an implement as with an open hand. (social worker)

Another social worker suggested that 'there is a growing understanding' that it is an assault. However, 16 professionals thought that physically punishing children even with an implement was common. These professionals had reason to believe:

Using something to hit a child is reasonable in a lot of people's minds. (social worker)

It's common enough for it to be a problem for children. (psychologist).

There's widespread use of the wooden spoon … as a fairly acceptable way of disciplining a child. … People still believe if you spare the rod you'll be spoiling the child. (social worker)

A health worker observed that there appear to be 'two broad groups' of parents who use implements. One group 'will go to the drawer and get the implement out', and they will threaten to use 'the wooden spoon or whatever', and the other group in a 'rage' pick up and use 'anything'. Implements that professional participants had direct knowledge of parents using to punish children included

> wooden spoons; a bit of wood; rubber hoses; kitchen implements; sticks; belts; garden hoses; electrical cords; a plastic, rubber plant; straps; canes; rods; footwear; spoons; a back-scratcher; a remote control; cups; spoons; the ruler; cords; fly swat; leather strapping; rubber seals off car windows; pipes; tree branches; wood with the sharp pointy end of nails sticking out; hairbrush; cigarette; fishing rods; bricks; whips; [and] irons.

Sixteen professionals thought that pulling children's hair, shaking and pinching children and throwing objects at children were common or very common disciplinary practices. Further, they described various methods of physically hurting children that they perceived to be common. Social workers observed:

> I have … seen children being shaken and … pulled around.

> You get people saying, 'I picked up something and I threw it at him because I was just so frustrated'.

A teacher had 'seen children get their hair pulled … ears pulled'. Other social workers recalled that 'pushing and shoving is very common', and

> parents sometimes use pinching. … Often it's on the arm, a real hard pinch that often left marks. … Pulling hair usually occurs when the parent was doing the hair and the child was fussing.

A health worker said, 'I have pinched my kids a couple of times', and a social worker expressed 'alarm' that her 'two-year-old is a biter' and many 'times people have said to me, "Why don't you just bite him back?" '.
When toilet training resulted in an accident, a health worker recalled a child being put 'in the bath' resulting in 'third degree burns all over the buttocks and genitalia'. Social workers talked about parents

> picking a child up and putting them down with force [resulting in bruising].

> Using lighters to burn them, cigarette burns, using sharp things to prick them or cut them.

Tying children up or to a chair or something and putting their hand on a hot stove or hot object.

A psychologist knew of parents forcing children 'to remain really still', and a social worker described

holding children up against the wall ... if the child's urinating in the wrong place ... hitting the child on the penis ... putting pegs on the penis or ... hitting right on the mouth, making kids stand in corners ... in particular positions or hold heavy things.

On the other hand, professionals had also had contact with children who had not been physically punished:

People ... say ... that they talk to and reason with their child or ... use time-out and that is what their parents did with them.

Speaking as a parent, another professional commented:

Physical punishment isn't what we do.

The exact incidence of physical punishment is impossible to ascertain as it occurs mostly in the home. The privacy of the home was a concern to many participants and some suggested that disapproval of physical punishment may be making the practice more clandestine. Forrester and Harwin (2000) and Gershoff (2002b) also raise this concern. While hitting children with an open hand was the most commonly used and observed physical disciplinary response to children, many professional participants believed that hitting children with implements, pinching, biting, shaking, and throwing objects at children was not uncommon. Moreover, more severe forms of physical punishment, such as burns and cuts, were too frequently evidenced.

Physical punishment: parents' accounts

Participants' willingness to participate in this research suggested that they held a conviction about the appropriateness or inappropriateness of physical punishment as a means of discipline, and they talked about their parenting practices. Fifteen parents (just under half) said that, prior to becoming a parent, discipline of children was not a subject on which they had strong views, nor one that they discussed with their partner.

Twenty-two parents felt that one partner in the relationship was dominant in decisions about discipline. With the support of their partners, only four considered physical punishment to be unacceptable. Three of these were professionals and one a foster carer. Six couples were committed to the use of physical punishment. Eighteen parents had not received any education related to parenting, though 25 parents had read books, magazines or other materials about parenting. Twenty-nine parents had had support from family or community services. None felt that their disciplinary practices went beyond societal norms or legal sanction. Participating families all disclosed information about their lives and family values that suggested that in their own way they were loving and supportive of each family member.

Two examples follow of parental physical punishment in apparently nurturing family environments. The first illustrates a parent who resorts to limited physical punishment and is knowledgeable about normal child behaviours. This health worker believed that 'a little touch of violence is a part of every child's security', and described

> trying to paint in the laundry one day and [pre-school child] knocked the paint over and I smacked him and I started again. And then he did it again and I smacked him again. And then, when he did it again I thought, 'Right, time to pack up the paint' ... I knew that if I smacked him again, it would definitely be a hard smack and ... he was just being inquisitive and wanting to learn.

The second example illustrates that parents who espouse that it is wrong to hit can lose control and hit children, sometimes severely. A grandmother commented:

> I've seen my daughters and daughters-in-law ... get really aggravated to the point where they've ... given my grandchildren several slaps ... because they've let things go too far. ... They're thinking to themselves, 'Oh no, I shouldn't hit them' and when they do let fire it almost amounts to child abuse because they've let the situation get out of control.

Seven parents claimed that they had never used physical punishment as a means of discipline, or had done so only once. Two parents acknowledged physically punishing their children often. The remainder used physical punishment occasionally or rarely. Thirteen parents acknowledged that one of their children was punished physically more often than their other children. The types of physical punishment that participants used are outlined below and parents' motives and reasons for using it are the focus of Chapter 9. All of the parents also used one or more of the following or similar other means of discipline:

> Withdrawal of privileges; time-out; extra chores; involve them in other things; be firm, say no, and then distract; get them to apologize; raised voice; stars; reward systems; catch kids being good, encourage positive behaviours; into bed for a rest; negotiation; compromise; threats of holding back privileges or rewards; reasoning; they get pocket money and if they misbehave they get a fine; sitting at the table for five minutes; yelling; clean your room; and confined to the house.

The nature of parental physical punishment

Parents described hitting their children at least once with an open hand:

> On child's backside … one whack or five …; with my hand … just a slap … bang … to their rear end; Once nearer to a beating; I smacked their bottoms … six of the best. … My daughter bruised; minor to severe … repeated hitting; I've occasionally hit … grabbed them by the arms … smacking. You … do hurt the child; a slap … I've kicked them; I certainly haven't smacked them as high school kids but … their father has.

Some described using wooden spoons, and one used 'all sorts of implements' to hit children. A parent told how a friend

> tried to bite her child to say, 'This is what happens when you bite', but she didn't realize her strength. … She was… really distressed. The teeth marks on that little child were awful. She was trying to teach the child. … My son bit someone once and I … said, 'Hey look!' [and bit him] but I … didn't hurt. You are trying to teach them … give them an idea.

Another parent disclosed:

> Until recently I hadn't hurt my child … My [two-year-old] daughter was pinching me very hard and I said, 'stop…that really hurts!' … I pinched her back. I made her cry … I was just trying to show her the effect of what she's doing to me. … She thinks about it now.

Mothers' and fathers' comments suggested that the numbers of children who are physically punished by parents remains high (Lansdown, 2000), and the nature of physical punishment still ranges from mild to severe

(Gough and Reavey, 1997). However, hitting children with the hand is reportedly used most frequently and may continue into adolescence (see also Agathonos-Georgopoulou, 1997; Straus and Stewart, 1999). Parents also use alternative means of discipline.

Physical punishment in public

When participants were asked about their reactions to seeing a child being physically punished in public, responses were mixed:

> When I see people in the supermarket sometimes I think that child deserved it. ... Other times, I think that poor little child. So, I have conflicting thoughts. (health worker)

> Each to their own, I don't interfere. (parent)

> Good on you for not being intimidated by the fact that you're out. (parent)

Some participants empathized with parents' 'frustration' and sympathized with the parent hitting children 'in public when they probably wouldn't want to do that'. A parent observed:

> Sometimes these mothers are just tired.

It was generally acknowledged that, when in public at least, parents often feel bereft of alternatives:

> If they had any other choice or alternative then they would probably try that. (psychologist)

> I wish people could realize that there are other ways. (mother)

> Poor parents. ...They haven't got any other strategies. Their child is causing them difficulty ... I feel sorry for them. (grandmother)

Some adults remarked that 'placed in the same situation', they 'would probably resort to some very similar actions'. Grandparents recalled thinking:

> 'It's about time'... It doesn't trouble me. I've been there done that too many times. I don't criticize other people unless they're hitting children about the head or doing something unacceptable.

> The child may have deserved it ... I'd give them one sharp smack.

Many participants, some of whom had physically punished their own children, were nevertheless affected when they saw a child hit:

I cringe, I wish they wouldn't do it. (social worker)

It's awful, unpleasant, an ugliness in the world. (parent)

I feel quite ill inside, it churns me up. (parent)

Some described feeling 'angry' and 'really mad':

You see children's little faces crumple … they cry and it is just horrible to watch. (parent)

For some, memories of childhood physical punishment and concern for the child aroused empathy:

Whenever I see a child being hit, I don't feel well, I don't feel happy about it because I know that that child is sustaining a degree of pain. (health worker)

I feel uncomfortable … anger and … empathy for what that child is experiencing. I feel like I need to do something about it … this is not right. (social worker)

I can see that the child is being hurt, on both levels, emotional and physical, and it just seems like the parent's out of control. (social worker)

Given public displays of parental violence, one parent was concerned about her 4- and 10-year-old children who had never been physically punished:

If you're in a shopping centre … and my children see a child being whacked, I think they fear it. … My daughter's teacher made my daughter pull the hair of another child because he'd just pulled my daughter's hair. My daughter was quite upset by it.

Adults' fear of big people

As a child faced with being hit by an adult, a health worker recalled:

I was little and he looked so big, and it was … scary. … Dad would have terrible tempers when he lost his cool.

Despite children's small stature and subsequent vulnerability, only 14 of the 40 adult participants said that they would comment or intervene if they saw a child being physically punished in a public place. Eighteen participants said that they would not, and the remainder possibly would, depending on the situation. Confusion in the community about what is and what is not acceptable physical punishment contributed to observers' inaction:

> If there was a clear position … I would feel empowered to intervene but … parents have absolute autonomy over their kids. (social worker)

Most interveners were professionals. However, almost half of them acknowledged, with some dismay, that the size or gender of the parent would affect their decision:

> I would fear that I'd get hit, especially seeing blokes in public who are out of control. … I've seen a guy who was really horrible and his size and his level of violence. … I didn't intervene with him … he was a pretty scary guy. (social worker)

> If I thought they were going to turn around and belt me I might be less likely to intervene, which is a bit sad really. (psychologist)

> It would make me a little more cautious if it was a very big aggressive man. (social worker)

> If it's a big man with tattoos and rough-looking I would be more scared to intervene … but … if I'm scared, what is it like for the child? (social worker)

Some participants observed that physically disciplining a child in public may be a parent's 'cry for help', and an opportunity not only to immediately protect a child but to enable further protective intervention:

> I have been told by friends to bugger off and mind my own business. But I have also had people almost relieved that someone had stopped them. (psychologist)

Physical punishment in public affects not only the child but others who witness it. Adults' concerns about intervening in observed incidents of parental physical punishment because of fear of being hurt themselves, and because it is legally and socially sanctioned, highlighted children's vulnerability.

Physical punishment at home and in public: children's perspectives

Hitting children is 'normal'

Seven of the 17 children individually interviewed thought that all parents physically punish their children. Two children didn't know whether this was the case. Physical punishment seemed predictable:

From my experience ... adults would at some stage get frustrated enough to shake ... or slap children. (13 yrs)

It just gets too much for the parents and then they can't just sit down and talk to children about it. (14 yrs)

Children are a handful and ... parents can't keep their cool. It would have to get to the time when enough was enough. (16 yrs)

For many children, being hit is

just something that the parent does, everyday life. ... it's just sort of natural. (12 yrs)

I get physical punishment a lot ... so many times it doesn't really bother me any more. (10 yrs)

When children have 'done something bad', a smack is 'going to happen' (12 yrs). A 10-year-old observed that adults smacking adults is not 'the normal way of living ... parents normally smack children', and a 12-year-old maintained that children think

smacking is normal. ... They love their parents, and they don't wanna think that their parents are doing something sort of illegal almost.

What actually happens when children are hit

Children remembered scenes of bigger, stronger adults hitting them or hitting another child, usually a sibling. An eight-year-old recalled

the adult's face. They get really mad and ... angry ... they start yelling out, an' you can hear like, like they come up and their face is going red, like 'eeeeeee' like that ... they're feeling really mad ... can't control their temper so they just hit.

Another child suggested that hitting is

not a very nice thing to do to people. Adults just mainly swing their arm and hit you ... the little child is standing down, and they slap them ... instead of grabbing 'em. It could be hard ...or anythink. ... It's the same thing as being told off but different sort of. The smack is a bit worser because you get something on your body but telling off you don't get anythink ... it hurts and you feel the pain inside. (8 yrs)

A 12-year-old talked about 'someone else's hand' making 'a loud bang' which 'children hear' and 'a big person tells 'em off; punishing you'. Other children recalled:

Hurting, lots of pain … crying … sometimes you like … get a red mark …
a smack, a big kaboom … like when the hand hits, like going really fast, and
then it hits you really hard, and 'cause you're only a child and parents are a
lot stronger, so that's why it hurts. (9 yrs)

A smack is when someone gets their hand and smacks them with the front
… it hurts a lot … You pull your arm back, get the person, and smack them
on the bum. … Throw your arm at them, and you hit them. (10 yrs)

Children's bodies and minds may feel pain when adults responsible for
their care and protection

get really mad so they started hitting you with their hands on your bottom
and it really, really hurts … children may understand or they may not …
sometimes it leaves red marks, it's that hard. (9 yrs)

Many children's comments suggested acceptance of physical punishment
at home and in public, especially when they are small. Some children even
justified physical punishment (see Chapter 9). An 11-year-old said children
'usually' get hit 'at home':

When you're young sometimes your bottom and as you get older sometimes
my parents slapped me on my legs and … arms.

And an 8-year-old said:

Usually big kids don't get smacked in public very much but … little kids get
smacked a lot while they're in public. Older kids … might get smacked at
home. …When you're talking about the body, well anywhere really … I
usually get smacked … from the waist down.

When asked where it was acceptable for parents to smack them, children
volunteered various body parts but they generally disapproved of parents
hitting them on the face. Children said that they could be hit

on their bottoms or on the side, on their face sometimes … on your bottom
you have protect. (8 yrs)

sometimes [on] their hand … their cheeks … their bottom and … their back
… I know that happens lots of times. (9 yrs)

basically on the bottom, leg … arm … or back would be okay. (13 yrs)

anywhere if you're really naughty but it should be on your hand if you're a
baby, or your bottom or … thigh if you're a little kid. (8 yrs)

Seeking children's opinions about acceptable places to hit them highlighted the incongruous nature of sanctioned physical punishment. To any other group of people in Australia this question would be ludicrous:

> Smacking is bad but the bottom is just as good a place as any. … if children are trying to grab something, a hand is good. It's not okay, but it's good, it's not as bad as other places. (10 yrs)

> It sort of depends on how hard the adult hits you and … where they hit you, 'cause if they hit you over the head … that's bad, maybe on the bottom that's a bit better. I think most adults do more than one. (12 yrs)

When asked 'Why is it okay to smack on those places?', another 12-year-old replied:

> The bottom and the thigh have a bit more strength and, for the babies, the hand … would be okay to slap them … but not that hard.

The nature of children's physical punishment

An eight-year-old described how yelling often accompanies physical punishment:

> My mum usually yells at me and smacks me at the same time … sometimes you get the play smack, sometimes you get really smacked … you can get really big bruises … 'cause even if I get touched a little bit I still get bruised.

After hitting a sibling, a 12-year-old said: 'I got smacked … and … sent to my room'. A 13-year-old recalled having nightmares when younger and keeping her parents 'awake all night':

> They would want me to tell them what the dream was and I … couldn't … so that would really, really frustrate them … make them angry … I was definitely smacked and very, very upset.

Two 10-year-olds said:

> Dad hit me … I shouldn't have got the smack and I was very annoyed with dad so I didn't talk to him for the rest of the day … and he felt bad, I think.

> Dad smacked me a few times, dragged me and shook me and put me on the floor. I felt quite scared you know … very bad. He didn't really hurt me … but I was very scared an' you don't like your dad doing things like that. But

he hardly ever does that ... it's not nice like having your father ... who's mean ... not a nice thought that you can't rely on him. Mum hasn't really done anything serious but she does it more times – smacking me.

Some children talked about the use of implements for punishment. A 9-year-old mentioned a boy at school who 'gets spanked with the wooden spoon by his mum' and an 11-year-old said 'we get a ... belt. My dad uses it'. Other children commented:

[Implements] will hurt a lot ... Dad used to threaten me with a wooden spoon and I used to go, 'Ugh okay, okay I won't do it'. (10 yrs)

Parents don't always use their hand – they could use a wooden spoon or a cricket bat to smack you too, and it's not always on the backside, it could be anywhere really. ... One of my old friends she says that whenever she is really naughty she gets the wooden spoon, and all her sisters. (8 yrs)

Three children referred to physical punishment on the head or mouth; two of these children had received counselling for abuse. A 12-year-old described how her sister got 'smacked across her head', and an 8-year-old thought that children 'could have to go to hospital'. His brother 'got banged on the head and now he can't talk as well'. Another 8-year-old talked about how 'you would get your mouth washed out with soap' or hit 'for swearing if you had no soap'. When asked whether she thought that children sometimes should be smacked or physically punished, she said:

Yes ... they've done something wrong or prob'ly hurt their brother or sister, so they should deserve one.

A 12-year-old hated having her arms squeezed:

I don't mean to swear ... but something might slip out and then mum will get all angry at me and she might squeeze my arms really tight, really near the muscles and that hurts.

Witnessing physical punishment of siblings and friends

When asked about times when they, their siblings or other children had been in 'big trouble' with mum or dad, some children talked less freely about their own and other children's physical punishment at home instead opting to talk about 'grounding', removal of privileges and time-out. However, some expressed their discomfort and powerlessness when confronted with other children's distress when they were being physically punished or threatened. A 12-year-old was confused when he observed a small child:

> Just playing around in the chemist and then she just walked out the doors and the mother ... hit her hard. ... Then she just picked her up and was hugging her.

A 9-year-old talked about when his 'brother drew on a wall ... we got into a lot of trouble and got smacked'. When asked about his brother's response to the smack, he said he 'cried and was angry at my mother and my dad'. A 12-year-old felt 'sad' when she saw her sibling hit 'across her head' for 'arguing'.

Physical punishment 'intimidates' children (10 yrs). Feeling 'scared' when she observed her father hurting her brother, a 12-year-old said she thought 'he might go off and do something to me':

> [My brother] accidentally scratched my dad's car and dad picked him up off his bike and dragged him along with one arm. ... Dad was just over-angry ... his new car being precious.

In focus groups, children suggested that children who were physically punished thought about ways to escape:

> If it doesn't hurt too much they sort of walk off ... sad and want to like run away from home ... but if it hurts they usually go in their room ... and think 'What am I gonna do to stop this from happening?' (9 yrs)

> Sometimes kids just like run away ... they don't face their fears and stuff and I don't think that [parents] should just smack because nothing is as precious as your children's feelings. (11 yrs)

Another child described feeling sad and disempowered:

> My best friend and her little brother started having a fight and their mum smacked them and sent my friend to her room. She started crying ... I couldn't go in ... I felt sorry for her. (8 yrs)

A 10-year-old 'felt a bit worried' when she observed her 4-year-old cousin being hit:

> I was gonna you know ... kind of ... I dunno ... I felt sorry for her.

Another 10-year-old was anxious but tried to offer her friend reassurance:

> My friend … stayed over my house too late and her parents threatened her by phone. They said, 'Come home now, your dad is going to hit you'. She was crying in the car when we were going to drop her off. She said, 'My dad is going to hit me'.

Children also described being hit in public where 'everybody's looking at you' (9 yrs); 'where everyone can see me?' (10 yrs). Other children may be witnesses:

> It's embarrassing … everyone stares at you, especially around your friends, and they go, 'Your dad … and your mum's so mean because they smacked you'. (12 yrs)

Children talked about themselves or other children being smacked, squeezed, dragged along the ground, shaken, belted, banged on the head, having mouths washed out with soap, or threatened with physical punishment both at home and in public. Some children referred to being hit with implements. Children also expressed discomfort and powerlessness when they were confronted with other children's distress at being physically punished or threatened. Alternatives or accompaniments to physical punishment such as being yelled at, having to give away favourite pieces of clothing, the removal of privileges, being 'grounded' (i.e. restrictions on activities outside the home), time-out, and discussing their behaviour, were also mentioned.

Conclusion

Children and adults have described physical punishment in the privacy of the home, in schools and in public places. Their accounts suggest that the nature and extent of physical punishment considered 'normal' may have changed and there is now a greater tendency to question its appropriateness. However, for many children it appears that physical punishment at home continues to be normalized.

6

Public and professional perceptions of the effectiveness of physical punishment

Introduction

Both broad and narrow definitions of child abuse tend to focus on parents' actions or the resultant harm to the child. These determine the point at which society legitimizes intervention in the privacy of the home, imposing standards of parental behaviour, and monitoring family life (Futterman, 2003). Research (Whitney et al., 2006) that compared child welfare professionals' ratings of child disciplinary practices in 1977 and 2001 revealed increased severity ratings for spanking, shaking, verbally abusing, and publicly embarrassing children. Research of this nature, including Giovannoni and Becerra's (1979) seminal study, demonstrates that perceptions of child maltreatment change as knowledge is enhanced. Indeed, Gracia and Herrero's (2008) research suggests that people who believe that physical punishment is an indispensable parenting technique underestimate the extent of child abuse in society.

Australian research suggests that the community generally does not realize the seriousness, extent and cost of child abuse (Tucci et al., 2006b). A recent study (Taylor et al., 2008) cast light on the enormity of the problem, estimating the staggering economic cost of child abuse to Australian society. Education to enhance public awareness of the problem may

Physical Punishment in Childhood: The Rights of the Child, by Bernadette J. Saunders and Chris Goddard
Copyright © 2010 John Wiley & Sons, Ltd.

motivate positive changes in parenting behaviour (Gracia and Herrero, 2008).

In this chapter we extend our exploration of the meaning given to words associated with physical punishment. In particular we focus on the descriptors 'violent', 'violence' and 'child abuse'. When used in reference to the physical punishment of children, these language choices spark strong reactions. We explore participants' understanding of these descriptors and whether they associate them with parents' disciplinary responses to children. We then present some professionals' concerns about physical punishment, and contextualize these among differing personal and professional perceptions of the effectiveness of physical punishment.

The association of physical punishment with violence and child abuse

Is physical punishment violent?

Some children's comments suggested that reference to 'smacking' and physical punishment as 'violent' and 'violence' aptly emphasized its nature and impact. A 12-year-old observed that physical punishment probably makes children 'angrier':

> They'll grow up thinking that ... violence is a way to sort things out.

And, in focus groups, children maintained:

> Smacking ... is really violent. (9 yrs)

> It's wrong to smack because it's sort of like having violence. (11 yrs)

A 10-year-old associated violence with being hit frequently:

> Dad's not really violent. He doesn't go for smacking as much as mum.

Most adult participants considered all the actions that they described in Chapter 5 as 'physical punishment', 'physical discipline', 'a good smack' and 'assault' to be violent. However, when asked for a reaction to the use of the word 'violence' to describe physical punishment, inconsistencies appeared. For some, 'violence' accurately described all physical punishment. The word 'violence' is 'accurate ... that's what it is' (teacher), 'it is a violent act ... quite out of context' (health worker), and to describe physical punishment 'the word violence is similar to the word assault. ... We need to be using it more' (social worker).

> I think [violence] should be used because it makes you realize that it is a violent act. Like starting this interview I started thinking, 'I suppose it is not that bad really ... a little whack, so long as it doesn't leave a mark'. But when you think about it really, what is to stop you going over that line? What do you do the next time, if the child keeps doing it? Do you smack harder? Harder and harder? (parent)

Eight of the 40 adults considered that some physically punishing actions were not violent. The nature of the action and the impact on the child were significant considerations. A parent and a health worker did not consider a 'smack' or a 'slap' to be violent. Another parent specified as not violent:

> A blow to the rear or hands ... that doesn't hurt or cause undue pain.

The parent's mental state was a consideration:

> If a child is smacked as a last resort I don't see that as being violent or assault ... whether it means tears or not ... any form of malice or premeditation and repeated ... that's ...violent. (parent)

Parental intent was also an influential factor. A grandmother maintained that 'a corrective smack' that 'won't hurt' is not violent, and a teacher suggested 'an intention to hurt the child' is integral to violence. Other adults perceived a continuum of physical actions directed at children, with the less severe end not being violent. A health worker did not 'view a smack necessarily as violence' but said 'beating up children ... pinching ... that's violent'. Similarly, a teacher 'would not define all physical punishment as being violence'. Some adults considered milder physical punishment to be relatively inconsequential, though possibly at the beginning of a continuum of violence.

> I see ... real violence ... there's varying forms of violent. (social worker)

However, when asked how they reacted to the use of the word 'violence' to describe the act of a husband or partner hitting his or her partner, adult participants appeared not to question that this was violence. Interestingly, when prompted to differentiate between violence between adults and the act of a parent hitting a child, many participants who did not wish to consider hitting a child to be 'violence' found the comparison challenging. Some participants, on reflection, concluded that both acts amounted to violence:

> I think for someone to hit another adult, there is obviously a fight happening … I would say that if a person was to hit another adult they're obviously having a fight and lost control.

When asked if smacking a child when a parent is out of control is violence, the same participant replied, 'semi-violence'. A psychologist observed that physical punishment may be normalized and 'depersonalized' as 'an act of shaping a child's behaviour'. Rather than focusing upon the violent nature of 'hitting', parents focus on a behavioural 'outcome' and this mindset disregards the child's right not to be hit, 'just like no adult has a right to hit another adult'.

Is physical punishment child abuse?

Twelve of the 40 adults, ten of whom were professionals, considered that they had been abused as children. Eleven adults, nine of whom were professionals, categorized all physical punishment as either abusive or child abuse. It 'is a mild form of child abuse' (parent) and can't be 'anything but abusive' (psychologist). The distinction was important, as some professionals observed that sanctioned physical punishment does not meet the criteria to be considered child abuse or, specifically, to indicate a child in need of protection, according to legislation in Victoria.

> [Physical punishment] is pretty much socially sanctioned … unless kids have got … good photographable marks. … A lot of kids have lots … of bruises and marks before anything is done to protect them. (social worker)

> [Physical punishment] is abusive. But … in society smacking children is condoned and accepted and doesn't constitute child abuse. (social worker)

Participants reflected on their own childhoods, their work experience and their parenting experience, and 28 adults perceived differences between physical punishment and child abuse. These related to the severity and nature of the action, chronicity, parent–child relationship, family context, parent's motivation, child's age, and effect on the child.

Physical punishment is not abuse; it sits at one end of a continuum

The 'extent to which society is willing to risk danger to the child before intervening' remains 'very unclear' (Stanley and Goddard, 2002, p. 24). Many professionals who work with children and families, some of whom are mandated to report child abuse, continue to tolerate or condone physical punishment (Goddard *et al.*, 2002; Straus, 2000). Mount observes that the policies of police and social welfare departments define what they consider to be 'reasonable', and police policy may often result in ignoring 'domestic discipline' (1995, p. 987).

This research added support to previous research (Chan *et al.*, 2002) that personal experiences and attitudes appear to influence professional tolerance of physical punishment. Consequently, children may remain in violent families without recourse to protective services or counselling. The following professionals' observations are illustrative. A social worker considered that hitting a child with a 'block of wood' exceeded what is 'reasonable'. However, despite the incident being reported to child protection authorities, the child went home and 'nothing was done'. Another social worker recalled a 15-year-old girl

> seen in the emergency department ... with bruising to her head and face as a result of a physical assault by her father. ... She'd been seen ... last year after a similar assault by her father ... assaulted with an electrical cord and child protection were involved. ... She'd been left in a situation where it occurred again.

'The definitions of abuse', according to one social worker, are 'narrowed' and only 'severe abuse is being dealt with'. Police officers, however, commented:

> Some organizations think that children shouldn't be hit no matter what whereas other people think that there are times when children need to be physically disciplined. ... Child protection are of the opinion that children should not be hit at all. My opinion is that ... it can be appropriate for a child to be physically disciplined.

> Child protection workers are different to us. A lot of them would tell parents that they are not allowed to smack ever. And parents get like different messages ... from us that well you can but it has to be reasonable. Personal experience comes into it a lot. You just kind of decide job by job and take in all the circumstances and a lot of it is your gut feeling. ...We are a little paranoid about people going over the top but probably a little bit more tolerant than say maybe the child protection people.

Some participants did not consider physical punishment to be abusive:

> [Physical punishment] is not abuse ... there is a sliding scale. (social worker)

> [Physical punishment and abuse] are within the same continuum. ... It's to do with force and intention. Intending to hurt ... using more force than is necessary ... that's abuse. If it's a smack with an open hand and not a huge amount of force it's discipline. (teacher)

> There's a normal sort of range of human interaction ... physical punishment
> doesn't have to be abuse. (parent)

Illegality and severity are components of abuse

Child abuse is not defined in legislation in the state of Victoria, Australia. However, as noted in Chapter 3, common law suggests that physical punishment should be reasonable, taking into consideration the reason for the punishment and the age, physical build and the mental state of the child, as well as any implement used. The Children, Youth and Families Act 2005 (Victoria) determines that a child requires protection if the actions or inactions of a parent cause, or are likely to cause, the child harm. However, adults may differ in their perception of the meaning of the words 'reasonable' and 'harm'. The following participants' comments suggest factors that individuals may consider.

A social worker considered a smack 'on the bottom' as 'unnecessary and inappropriate' but not 'abusive'. However, the extent of the punishment and the long-term effects may make a difference. A parent remembered rarely being hit but never in excess so 'it didn't cause me any lasting stress'. Similarly, a police officer said:

> I don't believe that my parents did anything that was against the law. ...
> Abuse ... has long-term implications.

Perceptions of deservedness and the part played by the child were mitigating factors:

> Physical punishment was always deserved and ... never really went beyond
> the boundary. ... I don't believe it's done me any harm. (police officer)

> If a child knows that it's done something that's outside the boundaries that's
> been set and they get a slap, I don't consider that to be child abuse.
> (grandparent)

To be considered abusive, physical punishment may have to be severe. A grandparent maintained:

> Child abuse is ... a smack ... above the waist or ... a child sent sprawling on
> the floor.

A social worker noted 'severity [and] the use of objects', and emphasised that to qualify as abuse, 'the motivation was abusive'.

Age is significant:

Anything that is done against a real junior ... more than a gentle discipline or a smack. (parent)

Others felt that child abuse is:

Physical punishment that ... left marks. (social worker)

Hit so badly the child is not able to walk ... lost a tooth ... bloody nose. (parent)

An injury caused or hitting in inappropriate parts of the body, the head, using instruments ... I do condone smacking and that depends on ages. (police officer)

The child's environment may mitigate abuse

In this context, a psychologist observed that:

Children can and do believe that they deserve to be hit [but] if physical discipline is used and there is ... positive and nurturing kind of feedback as well then the child is less likely to be emotionally harmed. ... Where there's no injury ... in a context where a whole range of emotions are expressed to children physical punishment is not abuse.

Some participants did not consider their physical punishment in childhood as abusive because they felt loved, safe and appropriately disciplined. They recalled:

Happy times with ... a caring and loving ... family. Physical discipline ... wasn't a regular occurrence. (parent)

I was brought up in a safe environment ... not physically, emotionally or sexually distressed in an inappropriate way. (parent)

I was never badly treated ... got plenty of love. (grandparent)

Some participants drew attention to the self-interested and destructive nature of child abuse in contrast to ostensibly child-focused physical punishment as discipline:

My mother just constantly slapped us around ... stamped out whatever spontaneity I had as a child. ... She was angry ... it was not about me. (social worker)

Abuse ... is about hate ... about power. (parent)

Physical discipline ... is ... relating to that child's well-being whereas ... abuse is not. (parent)

I wasn't hurt physically in an unkind way. (social worker)

'Remorse' and 'unresolved social issues' may mitigate responses to children's injuries resulting from physical punishment:

> A child with three red stripes across the bottom or the face ... talk to the parent ... there is almost inevitably enormous remorse ... often a lot of pathology happening within the house ... social issues ... unresolved, and I just couldn't sit in judgement of that. ... I would term that ... physical discipline that's resulted in some injuries. Child abuse ... slightly wider issue of the delivery of punishment or injuries that were really outside that fine line ... repeated episodes ... where the age of the child is out of all context with the type of discipline. (health worker)

Child abuse is undeserved, frequent or unjust

Physical punishment that bears little relationship to the child's misdemeanour may be seen as abusive:

> Punishment that was totally undeserved and out of all proportion to the alleged offence ... was abuse. (health worker)

Another health worker maintained that to be abusive physical punishment would have to occur often:

> Abuse [is] when you are ... hurting your child ... regularly, constantly.

Some participants perceived abuse to have occurred when the child could not identify a precipitating action or event, and the violence was intense and frightening. One parent mentioned occasions when a child is 'belted, whether the parents think there is a reason or not'. A social worker felt that key points indicating possible abuse were 'frequency ... intent too ... and even the way they were hit. It was in the eyes ... and the force.'

Other participants drew attention to lack of forethought as a characteristic of abuse; lashing out without consideration of alternatives:

> Punished physically without having any understanding or explanation about what's happening, and ... as a first avenue of discipline. (teacher)

> Abuse ... occurs when the adult reacts automatically ... emotionally and unfairly. (grandparent)

Abuse has a more intense emotional impact on the child

Many participants perceived abuse to be emotionally or psychologically damaging, creating fear and diminishing the child's self-esteem and sense of self. A social worker talked about feelings of 'rejection' and 'lack of security' when 'physical attacks' were 'inconsistent':

They left me frightened ... led me to not feel safe ... not good about myself.

Parents proposed:

Hurting the child to such an extent ... a child is unable to be itself.

Abused children have black eyes and blood lips ... repeatedly told that they're useless or hopeless.

A teacher perceived abuse as:

A feeling of being demeaned ... of fear ... of having no control.

Abuse denies children their right to be nurtured and to enjoy life:

Being injured ... hurt ... treated poorly ... unfairly, being unhappy as a kid. (police officer)

Abuse places children on guard:

Living in a constant state of fear ... that your parent is going to hurt you [thinking] you could get hurt. (teacher)

Professionals' concerns about physical punishment

Physical punishment presents a risk of spiralling into 'full blown' child abuse (Elliman and Lynch, 2000, p. 198). When asked about their use of physical punishment, parents may be inclined to normalize their own physical disciplinary practices, perceiving only more severe punishment as abusive. Reluctant to admit any natural tendency for physical punishment practices to escalate in severity at a future point in time, they may normalize their own more severe disciplinary practices (Leach, 1999).

By its nature physical punishment may be viewed as existing at the lower end of a continuum which can lead to severe abuse (Gershoff, 2002a; Graziano, 1994; Pollard, 2003; Straus, 2000). Indeed, the link between parental disciplinary force in response to perceived misconduct or disobedience and resultant child abuse has been documented for decades (Gil, 1970; Kadushin and Martin, 1981). Turner (2002) in reference to Robertshaw's (1994) research reveals that 22 children between the ages of three months and five years died in Canada in 1977 from injuries inflicted during parental physical punishment. Similarly, an unpublished US study (Hyman, 1994 cited in Pollard 2003), reveals that 41% of parents who had murdered their children used discipline as a defence. Intent to discipline, silence and/or to punish an infant or child is a common precursor in child homicide cases (Cavanagh *et al.*, 2007; Crittendon and Craig, 1990; Nielssen *et al.*, 2009; Stroud and Pritchard, 2001; Wilczynski, 1997a). Cavanagh *et al.* quote from the case files of convicted child murderers. One 'perpetrator' said that while removing the child's clothes at bath time 'he started messing about and I ended up slapping and hitting him on the head', and another 'perpetrator' stated that 'in sheer frustration ... he hit the crying child' twice but 'something flipped', and he did not appreciate that he had used enough 'force' to murder the infant (2007, p. 742–3).

The links between physical punishment and severe abuse are noted frequently in the literature. Indeed, Garbarino provocatively questions whether 'physical abuse is simply too much of a good thing?' (1996, p. 159). Freeman (2008, p. 6) observes that the 'majority' of physical abuse cases begin as 'moderate correction'. Most physical abuse stems from severe punishment rather than intentional maltreatment (Fergusson and Lynskey, 1997; Whipple and Richey, 1997). Parents who have hurt their children badly very often explain that it occurred because of 'their right to punish their child and, okay, it got a bit out of hand' (Peter Newell, quoted in Murdoch, 1992, p. 12). Browne (1995) observes an escalation in parents' responses to children who ignore an initial request. Stress mounts to the point where abusive parents resort to violence to regain control. Recent research in the US (Zolotar *et al.*, 2008) cautions that heightened concern about 'spanking' escalating into abuse is warranted when parents hit children often and with objects.

In contexts where physical punishment is sanctioned in law and culture, both the idea of causing a child pain and the motivations and rationales fuelling its use may be normalized and considered appropriate. Arguably, the more a society condones physical punishment the more often it will be used – thus increasing the risk of severe and fatal injury to small children who are particularly vulnerable (Straus, 1994). Violence that in other circumstances would be considered unacceptable or criminal may not be questioned. Nine case studies of mothers who were convicted of fatal child abuse (Korbin, 1989; 1991) revealed that prior to the fatal event they received reassurance from neighbours, family and friends. They were told that they were 'good mothers' and the children's bruises and welts confirmed the difficulties of child-rearing. This allowed the mothers, as Thompson (1995) observes, to rationalize and at times defend their behaviours as not serious and not abusive despite eventually resulting in children's deaths. Moreover, in one of Korbin's case studies, threats of assault to a sister who witnessed her niece's beating halted her intervention. Korbin (1989; 1991) found that in all of the case studies hitting was acceptable family and extended family behaviour. Hence, a report to child protection authorities might risk exposing commonly practised abusive family behaviours. Thompson remarked:

> There seemed to be little consensus ... as to how to define the parameters of appropriate parental conduct (and instead, undue deference to parental authority) or how to respond when clearly abusive behaviour was witnessed (and instead undue deference to family privacy). (1995, p. 70)

In communities where parental physical punishment is legally and socially acceptable, limitations on parents' perceived rights may be considered an unwarranted invasion of family privacy. Yet in some families the habitual use of violence to resolve conflict and to relieve stress may result in injury:

> '[T]riggers' that occur just before many fatal assaults on infants and young children ... include a baby's inconsolable crying, feeding difficulties, a toddler's failed toilet training, and highly exaggerated parental perceptions of acts of 'disobedience' ... most physical abuse fatalities are caused by enraged or extremely stressed fathers or other male caretakers ... beating [babies' and children's] heads and bodies, shaking them violently, intentionally suffocating them, immersing them in scalding water, and performing other brutal acts. (US Advisory Board on Child Abuse and Neglect, 1995, pp. 12–13)

Inquiries into, and media reports of, child deaths frequently highlight children's experiences of chronic and abusive physical punishment known about, but not acted upon, by community professionals and child protection workers. Three child deaths in Victoria, Australia are pertinent. Daniel Valerio, only two years old at the time of his death in 1992, had experienced multiple and severe bruising. His stepfather and murderer perceived Daniel to be naughty (Rayner, 1994b). Daniel's four-year-old brother told police that bruising on his own face, arm and legs had been caused by being hit with a stick by his stepfather and by being slapped by his mother (Goddard and Liddell, 1995). Daniel's brother produced the weapon, but the police did not press charges in response to his report. Indeed, both Daniel and his brother remained in the 'care' of their mother and stepfather until the tragedy of Daniel's death.

> Confusion about, or reluctance to condemn, corporal punishment of a child ... appeared to play a part in Daniel Valerio's case. (Goddard, 1996, p. 182)

In another example, Ferguson and Webber (1996) reported that, weeks before her death, five-year-old Amanda Clark begged a child protection worker not to send her home. Her case was closed by child protection services one week before she died, despite unresolved concerns about previous physical punishment (Boreham, 1996, p. 1). A child protection report noted that Amanda had been

> subjected to cruel and extreme forms of punishment and discipline, including being tied up or locked in her room for more than 24 hours ... Amanda died of massive brain injuries. ... Her mother and stepfather admitted to shaking her after she had wet her bed. (Ferguson and Webber, 1996, p. 4)

Similarly, 20-month-old Dillion Palfrey died in 1996 two days after his mother's partner slapped him across the face causing him to fall back and sustain severe head injuries. His mother then picked him up and shook him. Although the family was well known to protective services and other community professionals, effective protective action had not been taken (Davies, 1996).

More recent examples include the deaths of Victoria Climbié in the UK in 2000, and Ciara Jobes in the US in 2002, both of whom were known to child protection services and were subjected to harsh physical punishment at the hands of their 'carers'. Lord Laming, Chairman of the Climbié Inquiry, commented that 'a major context' for the child's abuse was 'discipline and punishment. ...Victoria's abuse began with little smacks' and her 'great aunt told the inquiry that there was nothing wrong with smacking'. Lord Laming recalled acting in cases of child abuse and 'losing cases on a defence of reasonable chastisement'. 'I would have thought', he reflected, 'that violence towards children should be taken as seriously – or more seriously – than violence towards adults' (House of Commons, 2003).

Some very recent cases highlight children's continued vulnerability. In 2007 Stuart McMaster was tried in Victoria for the death in 2005 of five-year-old Cody Hutchings. Cody suffered from Williams syndrome, a genetic condition the judge said caused developmental delay, associated behavioural problems, poor sleeping and irritable behaviour. McMaster, Cody's mother's partner, had adopted the role of disciplinarian. He modified a belt to become a heavy strap to more severely beat Cody who, the court heard, pleaded in vain for mercy: 'Don't call the strap man, dad.' McMaster had beaten Cody many times. The post-mortem examination found more than 160 bruises on his head, neck, chest, abdomen, arms, legs, penis and buttocks. He had also suffered a gash to the forehead, a tear in the mouth, two skull fractures, a torn liver, and a tear to the mesentery, the structure that holds the internal organs in place (see Goddard, 2007).

In December 2008 in Queensland, a mother (who remains anonymous to protect the child's identity) was jailed for six years for three counts of cruelty and one count of grievous bodily harm. In the *Courier Mail* newspaper (Keim, 2008), her two-year-old son is described as having 'horrific injuries and close to death' having suffered 'beatings in the guise of discipline. His legs [were] bound so tightly they turned purple.' The child was reportedly admitted to Mater Children's Hospital with severe bruising and injuries to the brain, body, head and limbs. The mother, expecting her fourth child, was reported to have also watched her partner physically punish the boy and his sisters for behaviours like glancing at him the 'wrong way'. The prosecutor in this case reportedly said, 'it was only a matter of fortune this is not a murder'. In the same week, another *Courier Mail* article (Wenham, 2008) draws attention to a Department of Justice and Attorney-General Review of Queensland Police Service data. Wenham reports that between 2006 and 2007 there were 134 cases of 'excessive discipline' and in 80 cases 'sticks, belts, brooms, kitchen utensils, pieces of hose' and 'cattle prods' were used. In 85 cases, children were 'hit about the head' and in 13 they were 'punched and kicked'.

In the US in February 2009, Kimberley Trenor was convicted for the murder of her two-year-old daughter Riley Ann Sawyer, frequently identified in the media as 'Baby Grace'. The mother and the child's stepfather, Royce Ziegler, reportedly subjected the child to 'an all day disciplinary session' in which she was whipped with a belt, her head held under bath water, her face pushed into a pillow, and her body repeatedly thrown onto a tiled floor (Rice, 2009b). Members of the jury were reported to have cried as the mother told how Riley 'looked at her during the beating and said "I love you"'. Ziegler reportedly suggested that this was manipulative behaviour, saying 'We need to break her' (Rice, 2009a).

Stanley and Goddard (2002) suggest that the threshold of tolerance of physical punishment may be higher for children living in dysfunctional/violent families known to child protection services. Stepchildren, some argue, are disproportionately abused because step-parents are more likely to be indifferent, hostile and less loving than natural parents (Daly and Wilson, 1991). Presumably this might apply to all non-genetically related cohabitees in a family. Deep affection, Daly and Wilson (1991) contend, stimulates enhanced parental protection and alertness to extrinsic danger and this disinclines parents to injure children irresponsibly or angrily. Gelles (1991) argues, however, that whereas fatal abuse might result from parental divestment, sublethal abuse may stem from parents investing more rather than less in the abused but alive child.

Together these arguments explain why most parents, even those who regularly resort to mild physical punishment, may be inhibited from progressing to severe abuse. More serious forms of abuse may be more likely to occur in hostile family environments where parents (biological, step or de facto) have minimal emotional investment in children and use violence indiscriminately. Abuse may be 'the most extreme expression of a parent's incapacity to form an attachment to a child' (Argles, 1980, p. 35, quoted in Stanley and Goddard, 1995, p. 27) and some parents do plan to cause severe and even fatal injury to their children (Gelles, 1996). But while a violent continuum or progression might characterize some families, most parents' disciplinary behaviour is probably unlikely to progress through a continuum because it is 'guided by limits' (Gelles, 1996, p. 85). One unforeseen act of violence may, however, unintentionally overstep boundaries. Children are often injured when they are struggling to resist an angry parent. The location of the blows and the resultant injury is frequently not under a parent's control and younger, smaller children's body parts are particularly vulnerable to injury (Claussen and Crittendon, 1991).

In societies that sanction disciplinary violence, children are without doubt susceptible to harm. In a recent *World Report on Violence*, Pinheiro comments:

> Violence against children persists as a permanent threat where authoritarian relationships between adults and children remain. The belief that adults have unlimited rights in the upbringing of a child compromises any approach to stop and prevent violence committed within the home, school or state institution. (2006, p. xviii)

Simultaneously sanctioning and failing to clearly define acceptable physical punishment suggest adult indifference and irresponsibility in relation to children's well-being:

> It should be clear legally ... what's acceptable and what's not acceptable. ... We can't all have the same definition of what physical punishment or physical discipline is. ... Without a clear definition there can't be adequate protection. (social worker)

Children are vulnerable

For some children living in violent families, physical punishment and unintended assault may be difficult to distinguish:

> Kids ... get caught up in family violence situations ... they might be pushed aside ... or hit in the face in the generally kind of chaotic and abusive family situation. I don't think we have had many cases that have been purely around physical abuse, physical discipline. (social worker)

Physical punishment is sanctioned despite the risks it poses to children's safety. A hospital social worker talked about 'a little girl' who had 'just died'. She had a fractured skull which is ... more severe than what she would have gotten in a major, massive car accident. ... I have real troubles understanding how an adult can inflict that on a child and kill her, you know, from just smacking her kid ... most of us don't continue down that road, most of us stop, thank God, but the few that don't, I don't think we understand why that is. ... All of us at times have had enough and want to chuck [children] out the window. (social worker)

A parent who was physically punished as a child but is now committed to not using it, recalled similar emotions:

There have been times where I've thought, 'I could give you a whack across the backside' or even to the point where I've thought, you know, when you've got a baby crying constantly and you've had no sleep and you think, 'I could just throw you out that window'.

Permitting physical punishment establishes a climate in which parents may more easily use harsh physical punishment in response to children's transgressions. A health worker talked about 'physical discipline that's resulted in some injuries'.

People assume they can stop at a smack ... but that's not always the case. (social worker)

Often the physically disciplined ones come from normal loving families ... but they have lost their mind a little bit and gone over the top. (police officer)

A social worker observed that most child abusers 'haven't intended to severely hurt their children or cause such serious injury'. Children's attempts to avoid parental assaults may result in children suffering indiscriminate or accidental physical pain or injury:

Sometimes ... a parent has meant to hit a child in one particular place and the child's moved and then they hit them somewhere else. (police officer)

Other related comments included:

There's a difference between a parent that is ... out of control ... versus the parent who [says], 'don't put your finger in that fire', and takes the swipe to get the hand out of the way. ... The more anger ... intensity, the more likely it's gonna have a negative impact. (psychologist)

Where children are injured it's often as a result of an angry or frustrated response ... a reaction ... and many of the parents are really remorseful. ... Often parents don't set out to hurt their children. So initially ... to teach

> them right from wrong and it's about who's defining what's right and wrong. …When children end up being injured … the parents are out of control and usually they're … unsupported or carrying a lot of problems. (social worker)

While children's vulnerability is increased when parents are permitted to punish them physically, legal and social sanction also increase people's exposure to children's physical punishment – which in turn enhances its acceptability. Exposure as a child, parent or professional to the difficulties of parenting may further impact upon one's tolerance of physical punishment and whether it is judged to be appropriate and necessary or abusive and unnecessary.

Some professionals maintained that to gain attention and achieve compliance, shock, pain or both may stop children 'in their tracks':

> Other strategies are abandoned because they haven't got that instant response from the child. (social worker)

> As they get bigger they tend to do like more out of control things that need to be crunched. (police officer)

A police officer further suggested that physical coercion may be required to instil civilized values in young children:

> People who have no control over their kids … end up ringing when the kid is 12, and is throwing a knife at them and/or having a go at them, 'Come and fix my kid, come and speak to it'. We can't fix it. Like you lost control when it was about two. … You have just been inconsistent and … really soft and wishy washy. The kid doesn't know where it stands, runs rings around you and you can't magically fix it at 12.

Consequently, when this police officer knows a parent has hit a child, she thinks:

> Good, at least there is someone there who has got control of them and if they do something out of control they get a smack.

Social workers observed:

> Physical discipline is a tolerance issue.

> So many children experience being slapped or hit or disciplined in a physical way because generally society condones it.

A psychologist could thus readily 'accept and engage with parents … if the physical discipline doesn't cause any injury and isn't within an environment of fear, criticism or negativity'.

Social issues also have an impact upon professionals' assessments and responses. A health worker conceded:

> I would be prepared to tolerate ... the smack around the legs or the hand in a young child, in children. I can't see a situation where I would be prepared to tolerate it in an adult ... if a parent uses an implement on an infant ... that's not on. ... The recalcitrant 9-year-old ... who got half a dozen stripes across his bum from the strap. ... I would be wanting to know all about the social background and circumstances rather than saying that parents are guilty. A smack that leaves a red mark on a child – I think we look behind it rather than at it.

Social workers cautioned, however, that:

> Less education ... greater social problems, like financial worries, drug and alcohol use, poverty, overcrowding ... physical discipline is much more accepted and ... expected [yet] the combination of those factors increases the risk of explosive behaviour.

> [Parents] often [have] a sense of frustration, powerlessness themselves, a difficult relationship with that child, difficult family context, financial, a whole range of problems ... and then the extra demands of a child that is annoying them is enough to prompt them to take [physical] action.

Another social worker observed:

> Physical punishment is more readily condoned in the more socially and financially disadvantaged.

However, she suggested that 'wealthier' families may use physical discipline because they 'have had a history of having had physical discipline used against them' but they may also be more likely to evaluate 'other options'.

Some professionals observed that physically punishing an animal is unacceptable: 'If people saw that on the street they'd be unhappy about it but it seems like it's okay to do that to a child'. Others posed some challenging questions:

> If you hit another adult, then it is assault. ... Why should it make a difference with a child? There is a strong power relationship between adults and children ... parents believe they can get away with it.

> When I do...community education work I say 'you don't allow your child's crèche ... kindergarten or school to physically discipline your child ... but it is okay for you to. What makes it okay for you?' Parents find that really difficult to answer.

The effectiveness of physical punishment

As we have noted, parents have long insisted on children's unquestioning obedience. Yet unrealistic restrictions on children's behaviour conflict with their natural spontaneity and inquisitiveness. Instinctively, children will do whatever interests, excites or appeals to them and, if they disobey or displease adults, punishment frequently results (Walvin, 1982). Physical punishment may be effective in getting young children to respond immediately to parental commands (Baumrind, 1996; Gershoff, 2002a; Larzelere, 2000). However, the effectiveness of physical punishment decreases as children grow bigger and may retaliate.

Frequent and harsh physical punishment may encourage rather than curb antisocial behaviour (Gershoff, 2002a; Straus and Mouradian, 1998), and it may teach violent conflict resolution (Gershoff, 2002a; Straus, 1994). Physical punishment is unlikely to enhance children's moral and social perspective as it causes physical pain rather than developing the child's understanding of the impact of their behaviour and why they are expected to behave differently. When hurt and upset, children may have difficulty understanding parents' reasons for punishing them, rendering disciplinary goals unachievable. Turner argues that, rather than learning 'internal rational control', children may only learn not to get caught (2002, p. 197). The anger which 'pain and indignity' incites may also override both children's 'repentance' and their 'cooperation' (Leach, 1979, p. 440). Physical punishment may also confuse children who perceive it as a parental right and unquestionably accept it as such (Graziano *et al.*, 1996), simultaneously associating love and care with the infliction of pain (Graziano, 1994). This may, however, break down trusting and warm parent–child relationships.

From a practical perspective, Larzelere's research suggests that:

> A combination of [corporal or non-corporal] punishment and reasoning delays the next misbehaviour recurrence in toddlers significantly longer than does punishment alone, reasoning alone, or other discipline responses. (1994, p. 205)

When combined with reasoning, other punishment such as 'time-out' was found to be slightly more effective than physical punishment in reducing the recurrence of a toddler's disobedience (Larzelere, 1994). Non-compliant preschool children who are given explanations in addition to punishment will, Larzelere *et al.* (1998) maintain, be better behaved and listen to parents' explanations – rendering future punishment unnecessary. They recommend using physical punishment as a last resort when both verbal reasoning and non-corporal punishment have failed to achieve compliance.

This, they conclude, appears likely to be an effective disciplinary sequence because the child's distasteful experience of physical punishment will subsequently make him or her more compliant in response both to non-corporal punishment and verbal reasoning. However, for physical punishment to effectively deter children's unacceptable behaviour and reduce the likelihood of a negative impact, Baumrind maintains that it ought to be administered

> without guilt, under controlled circumstances in a measured fashion, where both parent and child are aware of the reason for its use, in private [and] for wilful defiance rather than childish irresponsibility. (1996, p. 831)

Further, it should only be used with children older than 18 months and prior to puberty (Baumrind, 1996). Holden similarly contends that to be effective physical punishment must be consistent, 'immediate', initially 'intense' and not 'signalled by a discriminative stimulus' (2002, p. 591). He adds that, on each of these requirements, parents are destined to failure. Drawing on a number of studies, Parke maintains that to be effective, punishment depends on 'interparental consistency', and parental conflict may intensify punishment because of 'displaced anger' or lowered tolerance of children's behaviours (2002, p. 598). It seems that explanations alone may be more effective in deterring unacceptable behaviour (Cashmore and de Haas, 1995).

Parents' perceptions of the effectiveness of physical punishment

Sixteen parent participants thought that physically punishing children could effectively inhibit repetition of the punished behaviour:

> It gives a very strong message to the child that that was unacceptable. ... I am not saying I am condoning it ... but it is effective.

In one family, the parents appeared to have few doubts about the necessity, effectiveness and appropriateness of physical punishment:

> Definitely the demons seem to leave [child] for a good five or six months afterwards. He seems to not need threatening or any realignment. ... I know people who have got children ... who have never been physically disciplined because the parents don't believe in it. You can almost see through their body language and looking into their eyes ... they're not endearing. ... One little person is almost evil.

The other parent stated:

> I'm not a violent person by nature. Being violent is the last resort ... a case
> of saying, in a very strong way, that you [child] have pushed the bounds ...
> you have challenged this house to that point and this is the reaction we're
> gonna have. ... I've run out of doing the nice word bit ... the subtle soft
> threats and ... withdraw the minor privileges. ... In this household, where
> there has been continuity for 20 years and the meeting of minds, they know
> full damn well that if I was to smack them there is no point ... running off
> to [my wife]. She'd say straight away, 'You probably deserved it and you're
> lucky I didn't get to you first'.

For this parent, 'consistent' physical punishment:

> Had the intended reaction and it's been very rare that ... I've smacked them
> for the same reason. I normally don't have to go through the same rubbish
> twice.

Other parents also seemed convinced that 'it gets the message across ...
they don't do it again':

> If a child's going to run on the road, or touch a hot stove, or stick an imple-
> ment into a power socket, I think a short sharp smack is effective in imme-
> diately teaching them [but] it's probably not the only thing that's effective.

Effectiveness appears to rest on children's avoidance of pain: 'it inflicts pain
... fear of pain'.

> After one or two times she had the wooden spoon or smack on her bottom,
> she never did those things. The physical effect would be 'Ouch, it hurt'. So if
> mummy will give me another ouch ... forget it.

Some parents use physical punishment in a limited, controlled manner to
achieve immediate compliance:

> Slapping or smacking... is controlled. 'I can slap my child' means 'I know
> how much force I am using ... how often I can do it. I know the science I
> am doing.'... Physical punishment gives a very strong message to the child
> that that was unacceptable ... it is effective ... short term.

Describing physical punishment as 'instantaneous', this parent said:

> They understand succinctly that they've stepped over the line. Other punish-
> ment ... drags out.

Another parent felt physical punishment was effective only if children understand 'why' it is being used; 'just physical violence on its own is not effective'.

Some parents' perceptions of effectiveness related not only to behaviour modification but to arousing remorse:

> My children come to me and admit they've done the wrong thing. ... I gave [10-year-old] a smack a couple of weeks ago and he said, 'Sorry dad, I shouldn't have hit [sibling]'. [His sister] is the same. She comes up and wants to kiss me to death ... 'I'm sorry dad' and sit on my knee ... whereas if I tell her she's not watching television she goes off and sulks.

Physical punishment may be counter-productive

Twelve parents drew attention to the ineffectiveness and counter-productiveness of physical punishment:

> The children ... haven't modified their behaviour ... other things are more effective.

> I don't think it has any long-term effects around stopping the child engaging in that behaviour.

A grandparent recalled the futility of physically punishing her daughter:

> I figured out how to deal with her on a different basis. She was defiant. ... If you smacked her she'd fire right up back at you.

Some parents acknowledged that physical punishment may be more of an uncontrolled rather than effective response to children:

> When I use physical punishment it's just out of sheer frustration ... not really working through solving the problem. It's just a reaction, it's not a solution.

Another parent asserted that children's powerlessness and vulnerability are undesirably enforced:

> Physical violence, physical force towards children ... might have the impact of stopping what you want them to stop doing ... but it also gives other messages about who has got the total power and where they sit in the relationship. So ... any form of physical punishment ... has a detrimental impact on them.

Several parents suggested that recognition of wrongdoing is dispelled by children's anger and distress:

> It doesn't achieve anything, it just makes everybody upset.

> If you're so scared and you're being hurt, there's no way anybody learns. ... All your energy is directed ... to physical and emotional pain.

One parent said that physical punishment doesn't teach 'the child to do things in better ways'. He continued:

> It actually takes the focus off the issue at hand. ... Once the child's belted ... they just get angry at the parent. They stop thinking about what they've done wrong. It's not dealing with the issue. It's diffusing it ... bringing in another issue to cloud it all away.

Another parent observed that 'particularly pre-verbal children' do not 'make a connection between physical punishment and what they've actually done'. 'For older children', she maintained:

> It raises a whole lot of other emotional feelings. They are less likely to do what you are wanting them to do. You make them feel angry, resentful.

One parent thought that physical punishment had the potential to break a 'deadlock'. However, she conceded that this may not produce a constructive change in the parent–child relationship:

> The physical violence changes it; not necessarily for the better but at least the situation moves.

Other ways parents felt physical punishment was not effective included:

> It's basically telling a child that it's okay to hit.

> Violence just becomes an acceptable method of solving problems, an acceptable end point of an argument.

> It sets up all sorts of inappropriate role modelling for conflict resolution. It suggests that violence is an appropriate and legitimate way of resolving difficulties.

> Any smacking or hitting ... has the potential to cause emotional harm, give children wrong messages about resolution of things. Hitting anyone is a violent fact ... and gives a message that violence and assaulting one another is okay, and it's not.

> Physical punishment often can exacerbate an issue. It doesn't seem to be dealing with ... the thing that you are trying to address. The child learns nothing about what they need to be doing, and basically gets a lesson in how to be violent.

Physical punishment may also effectively devalue children, foster poor self-esteem and contribute to a fearful and coercive environment:

Children can and do believe that they deserve to be hit. Physical discipline can instil fear. It's got to do with … frequency and … other messages being communicated to that child. Harm is mitigated by the environment. When children are smacked … a whole range of messages about their value are being reinforced.

In contrast to Gershoff's (2002a) findings, some parents in this research were convinced that painful physical punishment is effective in modifying children's behaviour not only immediately but for a longer period or permanently. Other parents were convinced that physical punishment did not achieve desirable behaviour change. Indeed it could be counterproductive, subjugating children and breaking bonds of love and trust presumed to characterize a parent–child relationship (see Gershoff, 2002b; Graziano, 1994). Physical punishment may arouse anger, fear and resentment that detracts from the issue requiring discipline (see Chapter 8), and children may learn to resort to violence as a means of resolving conflict (McCord, 1996; Turner, 2002). Significantly, none of the parents in this research who used physical punishment had stopped using it because it had resulted in children no longer needing it. The use of physical punishment was, however, perceived to occur less often as children grew older; confirming previous research findings (Holden *et al.*, 1995; Wauchope and Straus, 1990).

Children's perceptions of the effectiveness of physical punishment

An 8-year-old seemed convinced of physical punishment's effectiveness:

Children … 5 to 10 … could like get really bad if the mothers don't teach them a lesson. [If] children … get teached a lesson then you will be better. The lesson that they learn is like not to get smacked, not to smack anyone else … and why it's not okay to be naughty. When you grow up it will teach you not to do anything bad.

While physical punishment undoubtedly hurts and arouses fear in children (see Chapter 8), many children observed that physical punishment was often ineffective or effective in undesirable ways. A 10-year-old asserted that 'instead of adults using their mind and their head they use action instead'. Other children wanted parents to know:

You get smacked and … you can nearly 99% guarantee that they'll go do it again anyway. (14 yrs)

It's wrong to smack because it doesn't really help the child learn to not do that. It's not like saying, 'Don't do that again 'cause you could hurt yourself or you could burn yourself'. It's not telling them what to do. (9 yrs)

A smack doesn't make them learn anything except ... they're naughty. (8 yrs)

Another 8-year-old maintained that children 'would say, "I don't want you" ' to parents who 'are hurting ... their own child', and a 12-year-old asserted:

I wouldn't smack because I just don't think it's ... achieving much. It's just making the children feel alone ... bad. You should make them feel that they've done something wrong ... but instead you're acting like a child yourself. You're ... being just as bad as the child by smacking them.

Children may attempt to avoid physical punishment by lying or trying to avoid getting caught. A 10-year-old admitted:

You wouldn't tell the parent that, 'Oh, I did it deliberately', you would keep it inside and say, 'Oh, I did it for an accident'.

Ineffectiveness enhances risk of escalation

The minimal effect of soft smacking, children observed, increased the likelihood of physical punishment escalating in intensity and frequency, particularly if physical punishment is the parent's preferred disciplinary response. They described how smacks can become more and more painful:

If they hit again it might be harder. (10 yrs)

You can smack ... softly until they get used to it and then you can do it a little bit harder. (8 yrs)

An 8-year-old predicted:

When I'm older I'd only smack if I'd really need to. If they did something really bad ... I'd prob'ly smack them next time they did it. If they did it again ... I'll smack twice as hard: 'If you do that again I'll do something worse'. If you're a smacking person, and that's all you do ... you could start from a kinda tap and get harder and harder until as hard as you can.

Some children described excessive physical punishment:

Sometimes they go overboard. (12 yrs)

They got very upset and frustrated and they've whacked their kids probably harder than they should have. (13 yrs)

Effectively learning violent conflict resolution

Children who have been physically hurt to force their compliance may learn to adopt physical means to resolve conflict:

> It's giving the message that it's okay to smack. (12 yrs)

> If a child has been smacked ... they think, 'Oh, I've been smacked, so I can easily go and smack that kid. It's not wrong.' (11 yrs)

The irony of modelling hurtful behaviour to punish hurtful behaviour was apparent to children, as was parents' hypocrisy:

> Smacking is ... teaching them that they ... hurt someone and now they're getting hurt for hurting someone, which is just completely ironic and just stupid. It teaches the child that it's alright to hit someone if they don't do what they think. (12 yrs)

> Smacking is bad. It's sort of teaching, making us wild like dogs ... like they'd never smack criminals. [Adults] try and set us apart ... saying we're important, we have rules, and they kinda break them. (10 yrs)

When asked if children should be smacked on some occasions, an 8-year-old replied:

> No, well 'cause it hurts and just 'cause they did something wrong doesn't mean they [parents] should do something wrong too.

Children who had not been physically punished were particularly critical:

> It will prob'ly just make them angrier ... thinking that ... violence is a way to sort things out. (12 yrs)

> [They are teaching] their children to hurt others. (10 yrs).

Many participants perceived physical punishment as a parental flaw. Children recognized that physical punishment demonstrated violent means of resolving conflict and could encourage children to avoid it by not getting caught or lying rather than by adopting better behaviour. Children could also foresee that milder physical punishment might almost inevitably escalate in intensity given its limited effectiveness, particularly as children grow older and bigger.

Conclusion

Research suggests that people who have been physically punished as children may not label the act of assault as abusive (see, for example, Bower-

Russa *et al.*, 2001). Environments that condone physical punishment favour a perception of it as normal rather than as an anomaly more aptly described using words or labels that highlight its inappropriateness and incivility. While very severe physical responses to children may readily be described as violence or abuse, physical punishment more easily attracts euphemistic 'weasel words' such as 'smack' and 'spank', as we highlight in the following chapter. Such words are reserved only for violence directed at children with a view to condoning and perpetuating its use. In this chapter, some participants were convinced of the effectiveness of physical punishment, while others perceived it to be ineffective or effective in undesirable ways. Both adults and children recognized the potential for it to escalate in severity. Children thus remain susceptible to unnecessary harm (see Chapter 10).

As noted in Chapter 3, whether sanctioned physical punishment is considered as child abuse will depend on how it is defined, and a consensus of opinion, either professional or public, as to what constitutes child abuse remains elusive. Some people contend that hitting children is always intolerable, yet others consider hitting children with belts and sticks to be reasonable (Goddard, 1995a). Some professionals who work with children tolerate or even endorse physical punishment (see for example Ashton, 2001; Chan *et al.*, 2002; Taylor and Redman, 2004). Like lay people, some professionals make judgements based on their own childhood and parenting experiences. Arguably, professionals' personal beliefs and attitudes should not be allowed to influence their practice (Taylor and Redman, 2004). Hitting a child's bottom or punching a child's face 'may simply be different parts of the same distribution' (Roberts and Roberts, 2000, p. 262), and even if this applies in only some families, changing professional attitudes that stem from culture rather than children's rights to safety should be prioritized (Chan *et al.*, 2002).

7

The subjugation of children through language and physical punishment

Introduction

Goddard observes that words 'have the power to describe, to define, to expose and to change' (1995b, p. 38). Language, moreover, is a powerful means of demeaning, excluding, stereotyping and misrepresenting people (Else and Sanford, 1987). In Western culture, language has contributed to the oppression of women, older people, people with disabilities, people with psychiatric illnesses or social diseases, people whose skin colour is not white, non-English speaking people, homosexuals/lesbians and children (Saunders and Goddard, 2001). Language has also played a major role in changing attitudes toward oppressed and vulnerable people and has led to their enhanced regard and treatment (Cameron, 1985). Kempe *et al.* (1962) recognized the power of words when they described physical child abuse as 'battered-child syndrome'. In a 1981 address to the European Committee on Crime Problems, Kempe said that he had used 'moderate' scientific terms such as 'non-accidental injury' and 'inflicted wounds' without impact so he chose to use emotive, provocative language to draw overdue attention to the vulnerability of small children entrusted to their abusive parents' care (cited in Cobley and Sanders, 2006, p. 17).

Language reveals much about children's position in society, the rights they are accorded, and the esteem in which they are held in society. In this

Physical Punishment in Childhood: The Rights of the Child, by Bernadette J. Saunders and Chris Goddard
Copyright © 2010 John Wiley & Sons, Ltd.

chapter we complete our language analysis, through an exploration of language associated with the sanctioned physical punishment of children, and language used to refer to children and to characterize childhood.

The power of words associated with the physical punishment of children

Garbarino (1996) maintains that hitting children is one of the foundations of child abuse. He and other writers (Howitt, 1993; Saunders and Goddard, 2005; Straus, 2000) emphasize the 'power of language' (Garbarino, 1996, p. 158) in both maintaining acceptance of physical punishment and potentially changing attitudes, beliefs and behaviour. Howitt suggests that the words 'chastisement', 'over-chastisement' and 'corporal punishment' all carry built-in justifications, and appear to be motivated by good intentions: 'it is "good" for the child and has a rational purpose' (Howitt, 1993, p. 43). Justification, he argues, is absent from the term 'physical abuse'. By definition, 'abuse' is the 'cruel and violent treatment' of people or animals; an 'unjust and corrupt practice' (Pearsall, 1998, p. 8). Similarly, as the words 'violence' and 'assault' commonly describe unlawful, irresponsible acts that are unacceptable in humane, civilized societies, adults rarely choose these words to describe parental physical punishment. Yet Graziano and Namaste observe that with the exception of war, self-defence and police law enforcement, 'No human interactions other than adult–child interactions carry ... social supports for the unilateral use of physical punishment by one party to another' (1990, p. 450).

The media's choice of language

The media have played a major role in many child protection issues in Australia and around the world. Indeed, we have argued that the media may 'have more influence on child protection policy and practice than professionals working in the field' (Goddard and Saunders, 2001a, p. 1). The media also maintain a powerful influence on the community's knowledge about, and attitudes to, children and child abuse (Saunders and Goddard, 2003; Tucci *et al.*, 2001). While media coverage can have a positive, mobilizing effect (Goddard and Liddell, 1995; Saunders and Goddard, 2003), language chosen by the media can also create and reinforce social constructions of childhood which deny the child 'personhood, dignity and respect' (Saunders and Goddard, 2001, p. 445). The child may be portrayed as an object and thus 'less than a subject' (Goddard and Saunders, 2001b,

p. 30) resulting in the minimization of children's painful experiences (Goddard and Saunders, 2000).

Media reports of children's experiences of physical pain and even injury at the hands of their parents may reinforce perceptions of parents' responses to children as reasonable and defensible. An emphasis on parents' burden of responsibility for children, and on parents' perceived rights to discipline as they see fit, often characterizes media coverage. This was evident in Australia, for example, when a 'helpless mum' was convicted, under 2001 legislation limiting physical punishment in the state of New South Wales, for whacking her 'toddler' across the head (Goldner and Taylor, 2004, p. 17). The UK press has also been 'vociferous' in its support of the government's reticence to 'interfere in family life' (Foster and Gingell, 1999, p. 189). Rather than using the power of words to advocate for children's rights and protection from assault, the media in places such as the US, UK, Australia and New Zealand appear to regard physical punishment not only as a parent's right but as a source of puns and humour. This small selection of recent headlines is instructive:

Smacking ban slapped down by Westminster. (*South Wales Echo*, 2008, p. 2)

Advocate for spanking whips up furor in area. (Tu, 2008, p. B1)

Spanking law won't hit where it really hurts. (Gelzinis, 2007, p. 8)

All this whipping to stop smacking is wasting time. (Hopkins, 2007, p. 16)

Give the NSPCC a clip around the ear, somebody. (Hume, 2003, p. 18)

Smacks take a beating in UK. (Hickley, 2001, p. 18), and

British get to bottom of child discipline. (Hall and Ward, 2000, p. 10)

The media have the power to foster well-informed debate that can have a positive impact on parent–child relationships. However, often the media trivializes children's physical punishment, effectively stifling serious attempts to move forward on this issue.

Euphemisms

In countries which sanction parental physical punishment, debates about its legitimacy inevitably elicit strong emotional responses. Many if not most parents have been both 'victims' and 'perpetrators' of parental violence toward children, and the language used to describe disciplinary actions has an impact. Words and expressions may be chosen to minimize the nature and intensity, and to reflect value judgements about the acceptability, of a disciplinary action. The literature on physical punishment abounds with euphemisms and carefully selected terminology that serves to justify or condone its use. Euphemisms may have the effect of normalizing parental physical punishment, which may then contribute to its intergenerational transmission (see Chapter 9).

Terms such as 'a light smack' or 'a tap' on the hand or bottom may euphemistically refer to a child's first lesson that violence is an acceptable means to achieve ends or to resolve conflict. Straus (1996) quotes Montague, an anthropologist, who contended more than 60 years ago that 'spanking the baby may be the psychological seed of war' (*Boston Sunday Globe*, 5/1/41). All eight non-violent societies described in Montague's (1978) book, while very different from one another in other ways, adhered to non-violent, positive responses to children's misbehaviour. In contrast, as noted in Chapter 5, many children in countries such the US, UK and Australia may be hit by their parents before their first birthday. Euphemisms such as 'loving taps', 'little smacks', and 'a good spanking', may minimize both the nature and the impact of physical actions directed at children (Leach, 1999, p. 13). Burnette's comments are illustrative. Hardly any children, she maintains, 'never deserve a lick ... if a toddler runs into the street and endangers himself and others, a lick or two ... is appropriate. ... Only a few licks ... to the legs or buttocks using the hand or a small object that will not harm the child' (Burnette, 1997, pp. 5–6).

Garbarino, on the other hand, argues that comforting expressions such as 'a good licking' should be removed from people's vocabularies. He suggests speaking about '"assault against children as punishment" ... "assault as discipline"', and he challenges people to 'come right out and say "I favour assaulting children – for their own good of course"' (1996, p. 159). Straus (2000) highlights the extinction of words and expressions that justified unequal relations between people of different races and between males and females. He argues that child protection workers ought to use words such as 'hitting' and 'physically attacking' that condemn physical punishment. Use of the word 'violence' to describe physical punishment was influential in Germany, where physical punishment was banned in 2000. The word 'violence', Bussmann maintains, aptly describes unacceptable responses to people. He suggests that describing physical punishment as 'violence' helped change people's perceptions of its validity (Bussmann, 2004).

Minimization of physical violence toward children

Language contributes to the blurred boundary between acceptable and non-acceptable disciplinary responses to children, which enhances their exposure to harm. Whether actions are considered to be 'violent', 'abusive' or 'child abuse' may depend on the variables in the situation, such as the age of the child, the reason for the punishment, and moral judgements about the acceptability of physical punishment as a means of discipline. All but three of the 40 adults in this research thought that descriptors for physical punishment influence whether it is used by parents as a means of discipline. Language can be misleading, and minimization through language 'affects your interpretation of what … has actually happened' (police officer). One parent observed that parents may predictably choose language that plays down the seriousness of physical actions that they inflict upon their children:

> To minimize what they'd done is a very human type of thing to do. (parent)

Euphemisms make it easier for parents to physically discipline children, and to feel satisfied that what they are doing is socially and morally acceptable:

> If you use the right language it sounds okay. (parent)

A police officer observed that children may be '"smacked" to the point where their whole bum is bruised'. A psychologist similarly remarked:

> People can very easily justify a slap … or a tap of the bottom. … Yeah, how hard is that bloody tap? Whereas 'belt' and 'thrash' are more emotive words … people will avoid them.

Social workers commented:

> A smack makes it sound like it isn't really anything … it has no impact. Assault makes it sound like it's an abuse … an illegal action. It might be the same action but using those two different words can make an enormous difference in terms of condoning it or giving permission.

> [The word] 'smacking' … minimizes the abuse … There are a group of people who actively minimize what they are doing … and use the term 'smacking' to avoid confronting what they are doing.

Yet, within this context, children's choice of words to describe physical punishment may be judged by adults to be unreasonable:

> Some kids go, 'My parents beat me' … and they describe getting a 'smack'. (police officer)

Minimization may also be achieved by choosing descriptive words, such as 'just', 'little' and 'good', and adverbs such as 'really'. A parent asserted:

> [Calling it] 'a little smack' ... is trying to minimize the importance of it.

A psychologist recalled parents saying:

> A slap is 'just a slap' ... it's not going to hurt them.

A social worker maintained:

> If people say, 'Oh, I just gave him "a little smack" on the legs' ... it can mini-mize the impact on the child.

Children also adopted words that played down and normalized violent adult responses:

> I see kids who are just so spoiled and annoying ... I think someone should give them 'a good slap'. (13 yrs)

> I get physical punishment a lot. It doesn't 'really' hurt me any more because they've done it so many times. (10 yrs)

Framing physical punishment as 'discipline' and 'lawful correction' rather than violence or assault serves to enhance its normality and acceptability:

> Smacking your child with an open hand ... is abusive [but] it doesn't con-stitute child abuse as defined in the legislation. (social worker)

> If a parent believes that slapping a child means assault and they think that ... legally you're not allowed to assault people, then they may feel that is a course of action which is not available to them. (parent)

> Assault ... has criminal consequences. ... It is likely that if we start to use the word 'assault' parents would be wary of using hitting and smacking as a form of physical discipline. (social worker)

Another social worker remarked that if a child who had been 'smacked' was reported to protective services:

> You would struggle to get them to take some action. ... Within the legal definition of child abuse or harm, there is some difference ... but ... I think physical punishment is abusive to children.

A teacher was concerned that:

> Language does a lot to condone the use of some abuse that is kind of seen as not abuse because it is defined as 'physical punishment' ... using the term 'discipline', 'physical discipline' [suggests that] it's somehow teaching that child.

A social worker similarly commented:

> If a parent's using physical discipline it hurts the child ... if they are saying it's discipline, it is not discipline, it's not to teach the child it is hurting the child.

Other participants observed that:

> If you define even a smack as an assault ... it might make people ... it would certainly make me think about it in a different way. (parent)

> Smacking is part of discipline so ... if you started, say on the TV ... saying that it is actually physical abuse ... over time people would see that as a physical abuse. (health worker)

> To talk about ... assault of children ... is very confronting. (social worker)

A social worker contended that the word 'maltreatment' is also minimizing, and primarily reserved for violence against children:

> I have an issue with the word 'maltreatment' versus 'assault'. ... Protective services still call it maltreatment whereas I don't think it is ... if a child is assaulted they are assaulted ... if I punch an adult, I have assaulted them. If I punch my child, it is called 'maltreatment'. ... It is a real watering down.

Objectification of children through language

Language choice also reveals adults' attitudes toward children and children's inferior status in society. A social worker commented that 'there's still a perception in society that children are little objects'.

Participants' language choice appeared to reflect and reinforce children's subjugation and objectification. Adult participants often referred to children as 'it':

> Punishing a child, and using a physical means to punish it ... that's why it got the bruise. (health worker)

> The child just wants to not ... behave in a way that the parent would like it to. (police officer)

> You'd like to take that kid and rip its ears off ... child got a slap from its father ... a child knows that it's done something. (grandparent)

However, reference to an adult as 'it' did not occur; the plural 'them' or 'they' was preferred:

> If I punch an adult, I have assaulted them. (psychologist)

> An adult has already reached the point of maturity and they have their individual values. (parent)

Children also referred to themselves and other children as 'it':

> The little child gets threatened and *it* doesn't feel comfortable with its parents anymore ... (10 yrs)

> The ... child hurts more ... because it's small. (9 yrs)

> The child will probably get embarrassed that it's getting hit. (8 yrs)

Children appeared to have adopted adults' perceptions of children as less of, or less than, a person; objectified to the extent of being the only people in society who may be habitually and unquestionably coerced by physical means to act in ways that are pleasing to adults.

Children's status in contexts that sanction physical punishment

Ratification of the UNCRC (1989) carried a commitment to raising awareness of its principles (Jones, 1999). It is thus notable that only 12 of the professional participants in this research had read any part of the UNCRC, and only two of the 31 child participants had even heard of it.

Children's positioning in society

Participants' comments suggested current perceptions of children and children's place in society. Children, it appears, may be perceived and treated as not yet adult and not quite people (Jenks, 1996), resulting in differing standards of treatment and respect. Children can expect to be hit by adults to reinforce their subordination:

> When you are chastising children physically, you are not equals ... you are that child's superior. (grandfather)

> What's communicated to a child when ... they're physically disciplined by a parent is that your rights are limited ... I have more rights ... to exercise my control than you have a right to be safe. (psychologist)

In this context, a social worker asserted:

> With physical discipline in childhood, it just makes ... childhood an insignificant stage of human development. Childhood is disregarded completely.

A health worker's recollection of a hospital incident was thought-provoking. Children, she observed, may expect to be hit 'because they've been naughty whereas an adult certainly doesn't':

> You develop boundaries as you get older … I saw an adult smacked by one of the nursing staff. … I felt absolutely so mortified for the poor lady like I thought it was so embarrassing. She started crying, the poor lady. It was awful. It was quite an indignant thing. I think that's the whole idea when you smack a child, it's not the hurt it is the humiliation I suppose that goes with it.

When hit by larger, more powerful adults, children are not only degraded but physically endangered, and objectifying language in reference to children further serves to reinforce their vulnerability and powerlessness:

> A child is so helpless … has no way of protecting *itself*… the adult has so much power over the child. There's no way the child can hit back. (social worker)

> A child will always, will inevitably feel that they have less power, authority, influence in their relationship with an adult. So if an adult is assaulting them, hitting them, hurting them … it further emphasizes that position of power-lessness and the child is unable to defend themselves because they're not only feeling smaller than the adult, they are made to feel bad about themselves by the action of being hit. (social worker)

Many adults held strong convictions that supported and maintained children's subordination and designation as 'property within a family'. Parents, a police officer asserted, are 'the boss':

> Children have to do what they're told. … You shouldn't need to, like, whack them all the time. It is just an option.

> People say you can hit your own child because that is yours, that is property … but you haven't got the right to hit anyone else's children. People shouldn't hit any children. Adults have a belief that children are theirs to shape the way they want and that may include physically punishing them. (social worker)

> Some families … have a view that a child belongs to them and they can do whatever they want to them and nobody should have any right to intervene at all, that they're an appendage. (social worker)

Another social worker reiterated a typical parent-to-child monologue or adult thinking process to illustrate this characteristically unequal relationship:

> 'I'm the adult and you're a child and you'll do what I say … I'll make you do it by force.'

Significantly, 22 of the 40 adult participants perceived the act of an adult hitting a child to whom he or she is unrelated to be worse than the act of a parent hitting his or her own child. This appeared to be connected to a persistent view of children as parents' possessions. Seven adults saw the two acts as the same because hitting children is wrong. On the other hand, seven of the 21 professionals considered hitting one's own child to be worse because of the emotional bonds between parents and children and the likelihood that hitting may be a recurrent event. A health worker couldn't 'see a justification for a stranger meting [out] punishment to a child'. However:

> That child is never going to see that adult again ... whereas it's quite likely that what we see in public, the discipline by parents, there's a vast amount more that goes on at the home.

Children are forced to live with this 'domestic violence' – arguably a term that encompasses all violence between family members. When perceived as property that can be 'fixed' and shaped to adults' requirements, children may be 'reasonably' physically punished as parents see fit, including granting other adults permission to hit their children. A parent recalled a neighbour saying:

> 'If [my child] is naughty, you can smack her' ... and one day she did something really naughty ... and [my neighbour] said, 'well smack her, she's in your house. ... I tried and I just can't smack somebody else's child, not for the life of me. In another incident ... her husband ... quite a big, tall man ... smacked [my son] for touching something of theirs. I got really upset. He scared the living daylights out of him, and I just thought that's fine when the kids know what the rules are but they don't always know the rules in another person's house.

As parents' possessions, children may also be denied claims to fairness and justice. A police officer maintained:

> If they're not yours you shouldn't be hitting them ... if it is not a discipline thing then it is unacceptable. You shouldn't be hitting kids. ... Someone big hitting someone little ... it's not fair, it's not right. It's like an adult hitting an old person. It's just not on and they get treated more severely.

Similarly, another police officer stated that 'no one has the right to assault another person', yet she contended:

> Just because an adult has left a bruise on a child I don't necessarily see that as being child abuse. No, it could still be seen in the context of physical discipline.

However, she continued, if an 'independent' person who has no relationship 'hit a child I would consider that to be just as bad as an adult hitting an adult':

> If it's a parent–child relationship then … they have the right to hit the child.

Perceptions of children and their rights and responsibilities

As observed in Chapter 2, perceptions of children in the English-speaking world are ambiguous and uncertain. Care and concern for children appear to coexist with indifference and intolerance. A psychologist commented:

> We are too busy, too distracted. People who … couldn't quantify how important their children are to them … get their children to Scouts, so they … can be babysat for an evening … get them to some other activity somewhere. They don't have to have anything to do with them. That is sad.

International agreements on human and children's rights are ratified, and selective attention is paid to children's rights, yet the treatment and respect afforded to children are in many ways wanting. In discussions about children's physical punishment, children were portrayed by some as, at best, less than angels but also as devilish and even evil. One adult recalled:

> [Getting] whacked across the legs once or twice because I certainly wasn't an angel.

A grandmother recalled giving her son 'a good smack on the leg or the bottom. [He was] a very naughty boy … a little devil'.

A parent described her middle child as 'very wilful', and said that after physical punishment 'the demons seem to leave [child] for a good five or six months'. The same parent observed that 'looking into the eyes' of children who have never been physically disciplined, 'they are not endearing. …One little person is almost evil'. And another grandmother talked about her child and grandchild:

> I've got … the grandchild from hell. He was a little devil … and he's become the most obnoxious child now. [My daughter] was a little devil.

In a similar vein, parents described children as:

> A bit wild. … The twins were wild. They were like my brother.

> The little boy behind us, he's just wild. If he was my child he'd get a whack for sure.

> From ... threeish when they're starting to get very wilful until six ... you
> know you'd have to be a real saint not to hit them sometimes.

Another parent described his child as 'a tetchy little bugger when he was
growing up', and a professional described:

> A child who had ... a number of slaps on the side of the head ... he had
> been, in mum's terms, 'a little shit all day' and, from her description, she is
> probably right.

To gauge current notions of children and childhood, participants' perceptions of children's rights, and parent–child relationships were explored.
Most adults acknowledged children's entitlement to care and protection.
Children need people they 'can rely on' (teacher). They need 'a secure living
environment' (social worker), 'protection, food, clothing, education' (health
worker), 'privacy, dignity' (grandparent), 'constancy' (grandparent), 'positive feedback ... self esteem' (social worker), 'a happy childhood' (parent),
'to feel safe ... emotionally looked after' (police officer), 'to grow up ...
non-threatened in that environment' (parent), and consideration 'of their
needs, their age, developmental state ... modelling ... appropriate ways of
behaving' (social worker).

Some participants emphasized that childhood is a time of little or no
responsibility, with freedom of expression and fun. Childhood is about not
living 'in fear', having 'a sense of innocence and wonder of the world'
(teacher), 'a happy, normal, fun kind of life' (police officer). 'Kids have got
a right to be kids' (social worker), to 'opportunities to develop who they
are' (psychologist) and a social worker commented: 'I wouldn't see kids as
having formal responsibilities ... to be good or be anything'.

Some adults concentrated on children's entitlement to become 'civilized',
fully developed, moral human beings. Obedience to adults appeared to be
closely linked to this process, though some parents accommodated challenge. 'Children have a duty to basically obey their parents' (teacher).
'Parents do have to make decisions ... be the boss. Children will make
mistakes [but] you try and cut down on that' (parent). Children have to
'learn what's right and wrong and ... there's consequences ... be taught to
make decisions' (police officer), 'develop into healthy, positive human
beings ... who can make positive ... relationships' (psychologist), 'reach
their full potential' (social worker), 'live by the rules of the household where
they are able to challenge those rules if they think they are not fair' (psychologist). A parent said 'they have to try and learn about the world, try
and become human ... being human is very much about having values,
about deciding things', and a social worker commented 'they need to have

routines ... to understand how people conduct themselves, where the limits are, how those limits are enforced'. Parents have to 'guide their behaviour and ... mould it so that it becomes acceptable' (teacher), and 'you need to ensure that the children really understand ... house rules and ... society's rules' (parent).

In contrast, some adults emphasized children's entitlement to respect as persons. Children need to be accepted, loved and given 'space and freedom' (parent), 'to feel they matter' (parent), to 'push the boundaries ... the same rights as I'm entitled to' (parent). Children deserve 'some give and take on both sides' (parent), to 'be treated as a human being ... as an individual with their own rights rather than as belonging to somebody else' (social worker), 'to say what's acceptable and what's not' (parent). A social worker said children need 'people around them who care, respect, value and love them. [They need to] be listened to and have their beliefs and feelings heard'. A health worker observed that as children 'get a little older' adults should be willing to 'accept them as another individual in the household'. Parents need to 'talk to them, listen to what they have to say and compromise' (parent), 'support and encourage ... being open and honest' (parent), 'treat children with the same sort of respect that you'd want to be treated' (parent), consider them 'as though they are someone else's children. They shouldn't relate to them as objects in terms of ownership ... treat them with respect and dignity ... not abuse the child's trust' (teacher).

Many parents thought that children should love and respect them, but reciprocal respect did not appear to be in all parents' thoughts. Children need to be 'open with their parents, ask for what they need ... tell their parents what might be going on for them, afford [parents] some level of respect. Children should listen ... although they may not agree' (parent), 'have respect for relationships. They challenge you, but how it's done, that's the most important thing' (social worker), 'relate in a warm loving way to its parent' (social worker), 'relate to the way parents relate to them' (teacher), 'be friendly and loving ... respect our space ... our views and opinions' (parent). Another parent said children should demonstrate 'certain standards of behaviour'. Ideally, 'ways of behaving ... should be agreed upon within a family, and children [should] behave in a way that fits in with that and be respectful of the other members of the family'.

Other participants emphasized children's responsibility to learn and contribute to 'family life'. This was perceived 'as a growing level of responsibility' (social worker). A health worker said 'as they get older' children should 'have a bit of insight into actions ... not make the same error three times', and a parent said 'children even from a very young age should be well aware of how much work goes into bringing them up, and should be helpful' (parent).

Listening to and respecting the views of children

Children's voices are noticeably silent even in debates about issues that affect them:

> Lots of adults think that children's views, experiences just aren't important. (social worker)

In this context, grandparents commented:

> I don't think a lot of adults see children as individuals who have a unique personality, who have something to say, who deserve to be listened to.

> I don't think it's up to children to express an opinion on physical punishment. ... They're still learning their place in the world.

Social workers observed:

> There is a perception in our society that children aren't worth listening to ... I see children being ignored.

> A number of children ... aren't listened to ... are treated as if they're liars or they're manipulative. A fair spectrum of people treat children like that. ...Children need to be listened to more than they are.

A parent observed that parents 'don't talk to children':

> They are a burden. ... Most parents whinge about their children. They can't even say anything good about them.

A social worker similarly remarked:

> Children are ... seen as a burden... a cost, and there's quite a negative context around children. A lot of media ... and framing of the cost of raising children becomes translated into what adults have to sacrifice ... and that can lead to particular rights and entitlements over children. They can ignore the contributions and voices of children because of that position.

Thirty-eight of the 40 adult participants said that they were interested in knowing what children think about physical punishment, and 31 anticipated that they might be influenced by children's views on this issue. However, the following two comments highlighted significant obstacles to hearing children's voices on physical punishment. A social worker presented the dilemma that a subversive environment may unduly influence a child's opinion, and a responsible adult must consider this:

I wouldn't be … looking at not doing something about kids being hit because … kids think it's okay, because that's their environment.

Another participant actively challenged the prospect of listening to children:

If suddenly you tell me that children in general say 'no, they really don't like being smacked on the bum with an open hand', that would not influence me to stop doing it to my children when necessary. … I'd have to hear something like, 'When I go to bed at night all I can think about is this big horrible adult coming towards me', and then I'd have to have backup to say that those children just never grow up to be normal, healthy adults. (parent)

In contrast, other adults felt 'you learn a lot from children' (parent). One social worker believed that children 'can offer us a whole range of thoughts and … feelings on matters'.

Some adults suggested a need for better communication. They acknowledged children's victimization and powerlessness and children's right to comment on issues that affect them:

The voices of children need to be listened to. We don't tolerate physical violence between men and women. We have worked really hard to empower women to take a stand and have a voice in that dynamic, and the issues are similar between adults and children. [Children] need to have a voice, and they need to have some power and some influence. (social worker)

Children have a right to be heard … children have important things to say. (social worker)

There's that thing of children being powerless. … It's important for children to feel that their ideas and wishes and feelings are respected by the people close to them. (parent)

Children's perspectives may be integral to adult understanding and empathy:

Children love their parents … they don't understand us as we don't understand them. (parent)

Adults should be open to hearing a child's experience of pain and anger. (social worker)

Children do have a right to express their opinion. … It's very important because they're the ones being subjected to [physical punishment]. (teacher)

Children … should be allowed to tell how they feel about physical punishment. (parent)

Professionals maintained:

> As I work with and listen to children … how they make sense of the world and how things impact on them … I question the validity of physical punishment. Children have a right to be heard. We need to know what messages children are getting from being disciplined. (social worker)

> If parents did listen to children, they would probably find other ways to sort out situations. [It] would be a powerful thing to hear how children actually feel because we are always hearing from the adult's perspective … it might help adults to rethink their values. (teacher)

> In my work with children over a long period of time I am aware of … what it feels like … from physical punishment right through to abuse. A lot of adults would change their point of view if they could actually hear the impact that it has. If you ask a child, 'How do you think you should have been punished for that?', they will come up with much better ideas. (social worker)

> Some parents might be surprised to know … that's the effect [physical punishment] has on a kid that I love … so they may respond to those emotions. (teacher)

Children reflect upon their status and vulnerability

Some children talked about their humanity as an aspect of themselves that they perceived to have in common with adults. When asked why children are important, an 8-year-old replied, 'because I'm a human being'. A 13-year-old observed that:

> Sometimes adults find it hard to admit that children are humans too and … intelligent too … I think sometimes adults find that challenging and don't want to believe it so will try and turn children into cutesy pie little innocents; even people my age, which is really stupid.

Significantly, this 13-year-old later made a comment that suggested that children may adopt adults' perceptions of them as less than persons:

> I … don't think it's appropriate for [my parents] to physically punish me any more … 'cause I think I am becoming a bit of a person, not a child anymore.

Children may attribute this lesser status and power to their phase of mental and physical development, and to their dependency on adults and subsequent vulnerability:

Children probably don't smack adults because adults have more power. …They can get really mad and swear … and stuff. … Children can't do anything like that because they don't have enough power. We have to do what they say. Adults can … hurt them. (8 yrs)

Children acknowledged power plays in children's relationships with other children. However, when asked whether it is appropriate for children to smack other children, the above 8-year-old replied:

No … 'cause the children that are getting smacked think, 'I'm not as good as this guy I'm just inferior' and the guys who smack them are thinking, 'I smack people … I can rule everything'.

When asked if a parent smacking a child was in any way similar, he replied:

Yeah … parents, they know they're superior to children.

Inequality and double standards

Children were conscious of one standard or expectation for adults and another for children, and some perceived this as unjust:

I reckon adults should be treating children pretty much the same way [as adults are treated] … [A child hitting an adult] is just something that doesn't happen…it's just something that … no one thinks is okay. (12 yrs)

I feel slightly subordinate to adults … I think you should respect all people, and not just somebody because they're … adult. About my age you get a bit old to be smacked. … A parent–child relationship is just unequal. Children have to put up with … following rules, and face the music when they don't. (13 yrs)

When asked what stops children or young people from smacking adults, the above 13-year-old replied, 'children just have a bit of respect'. Indeed, when asked what sort of things you have to do because you're a child, children indicated that adults expected them to 'be respectful to adults' (11 yrs). In most children's minds, hitting adults is unquestionably wrong but adults whom children respect and admire hit children:

If my parents … say, 'Do it now!' I will do it now. (10 yrs)

When asked if it is ever okay for children to smack adults, the same child replied:

> You might get in trouble ... it's not right to hit an older person.

The unfairness of adults' disrespectful responses to children was troubling to children who felt that respect should not be uni-directional:

> Your parents ... wouldn't want you to smack them 'cause they're older and it's like that saying, 'Respect your elders'... It's sort of like what they should do to us. Like they should respect their children for what they've done, not just smack them. (11 yrs)

And a 10-year-old bemoaned:

> Respect their elders, I really hate that ...why respect your elders ... what's the point of respecting your elders when they're just like them ... like racism?

Children commented upon their limited rights:

> It's what keeps us apart, adults are more important than children. (10 yrs)

> We do have some rights, not many though. Adults have many more. (9 yrs)

When asked whether it is ever okay for children to smack adults, an eight-year-old replied:

> It's like a right for kids not to ... it's alright for adults, not for kids. It's like a law for kids not to smack adults. The adults are bigger and more stronger ... and they'll get really mad, so the kids won't do it.

In this context, a nine-year-old advised that for children: 'It's best ... to do what we're told'. When asked if it is ever okay for one person to smack another person, she replied: 'Yes ... like if they've done something bad' but when asked if it is ever okay for a person who's not a child to be smacked, she confidently replied, 'No'. Other children asserted:

> Smacking is not wrong as long as it's a punishment ... to hopefully teach right from wrong. (16ys)

> Parents should sometimes be allowed to smack children ... because they've got to like learn what they've done wrong and like know that you're not allowed to do that. (10 yrs)

> On the spur of the moment parents smack a child. That's alright. (10 yrs)

Physical punishment maintains adults' power over children. A 16-year-old described a smack as:

A form of punishment to put the child back in line … being a child, you usually do what you're told.

And a 14-year-old justified physical punishment but:

[N]ot to the extent of like bruising them and making them bleed, just like a little clip behind the ear or whatever … just to show who's boss really.

Given a choice, four of the 17 children interviewed individually felt that they would rather be an adult than a child, and a further two were undecided. Several of these children wanted to be 'teenagers' or 'early 20s'. Reasons for preferring adulthood included:

You get to go out … can't wait till I work. I wanna drive … design my own house. (12 yrs)

Buy me own smokes … have like freedom. (14 yrs)

To drive and … get a job. (12 yrs)

You can see R-rated movies and go to nightclubs. (9 yrs)

Most children presented reasons for embracing childhood like getting 'attention' (10 yrs); living 'longer … doing things that adults can't do… because they're too big' (11 yrs); having 'freedom … more fun … mum and dad complain a lot about being old' (12 yrs); seeing 'a future' (13 yrs); 'restricted freedom … not have responsibilities, big responsibilities' (16 yrs); and getting 'to play more' (8 yrs).

However, many children felt that adults disregarded their opinions. A 13-year-old observed:

Adults have basically more power. They have a greater say. They are more respected in the … community. It really frustrates me when … I will have an opinion but I can't do much with it. Like if a kid writes a letter to the paper, everyone will think, 'Oh how cute', but they won't really read it.

Many children also felt that adults communicated inadequately with children, especially about matters that affect them:

It's not fair for parents to just have a say in what they think and kids not. (12 yrs)

I try to say something and my parents just don't listen. (11 yrs)

Kids don't … get a chance to talk. I think they have the right to have their say. (12 yrs)

Children should have the right to say something to their parents about getting smacked ... finish what they're saying to their parents instead of them saying, 'Don't talk back to me', and ... smack them. (11 yrs)

Children as chattels

Many child participants saw themselves as both belonging to parents and powerless:

Parents have a right to smack you ...'cause you are their kids. (11 yrs)

If adults [have] physical contact with someone, like punching 'em, it's against the law ... they could go to jail, they could be charged with assault. And that's exact same for smacking. But ... if you're a kid, and it's in the house, it's okay because they're your kids. If you are a kid, it doesn't really matter ... you barely have any say. (10 yrs)

Maybe ... you could employ a law that says children can't be smacked. But some parents might not obey that law because they know no one can see them doing it. (12 yrs)

A 12-year-old highlighted shifts in attitudes but observed that parents usually hit children

when no one else can see, so they keep their reputation. Some people are starting to see that that's not the way and ... other people ... just wanna keep doing it, but they don't wanna get in trouble so they just do it under cover.

Faced with a disadvantageous position, some children nevertheless reticently voiced at least a partial objection to parents' use of physical punishment. Twelve-year-olds suggested:

Parents have a little sort of right to because to them what you've done is bad ... but I think it is wrong that they do it.

It's wrong to smack because ... if anyone else did it then they would have done child abuse. So really in a way they don't have much of a right.

An eight-year-old proposed:

Parents shouldn't smack unless they really have to but ... parents can do whatever they want now ... unless it's something bad.

Revelations that parents may extend permission to other adults to hit their children further confirmed children's vulnerability:

> Say you're living with your grandma then maybe they'd smack you ... because they're like part of your family. Your family might give someone permission to smack you. (11 yrs)

> It's usually either the father or the mother or someone in the family, or if they're getting minded sometimes it could be the babysitter ... and some-times it might be a friend's dad because they've been given permission. (11 yrs)

Within their family environments children were aware of their unequal status and the lack of respect afforded to them as children. Children were aware of double standards, and some children expressed a view, either forthrightly or hesitantly, that this inconsistent treatment was unjust, and an affront to children. Other children did not question this unequal treat-ment, complacently accepting their lesser status and entitlements as parents' belongings. Children expressed dismay, moreover, that parents often silenced them by stifling their attempts to express their opinions.

Conclusion

The potential for language both to subjugate and to uplift children's status is apparent in this research. Advancing positive attitudinal and behavioural change may depend in part on at least encouraging adults to use language that more accurately describes and more clearly discourages abusive responses to children.

8

The effects of physical punishment

Introduction

Physical punishment affects children as victims and parents as perpetrators. Indeed, much of the literature on physical punishment focuses on or debates the immediate and long-term effects. While there is apparent agreement that it would be unethical for research purposes to set up a control group of children who are physically punished and another group who are not, many arguments supporting physical punishment rest on the premise that it is not harmful. In contrast, opponents of physical punishment tend to base their arguments first and foremost on the unjustness or immorality of violent responses to children (see Chapter 10), but also upon its negative effects. In this chapter, both sides of the debate about effects are presented along with the research participants' insights.

Cultural context and physical punishment

Korbin stresses that it is essential to consider behaviour within its cultural context. Particularly significant are 'the socialization goals of the cultural

Physical Punishment in Childhood: The Rights of the Child, by Bernadette J. Saunders and Chris Goddard
Copyright © 2010 John Wiley & Sons, Ltd.

group, the intent and beliefs of the adults, and the interpretation children place on their treatment' (Korbin, 1981, p. 205). A society's cultural beliefs about physical punishment, the views of particular ethnic and religious groups, and the perspectives of individual families may all be significant influences on both children's perceptions of physical punishment and its impact (see for example, Bartkowski, 1995; Deater-Deckard *et al.*, 2003; Ellison and Bradshaw, 2009; Lansford *et al.*, 2004; Stacks *et al.*, 2009). In cultures and families where physical punishment is considered acceptable, its effects on victims and witnesses may not be the same as in environments where it is contentious (Parke, 2002; Socolar, 1997). Konstantareas and Desbois found that preschool children approved of physical punishment if their parents normally used it and the context was a parent asserting their authority in response to a perception that the child was 'naughty' (2001, p. 485). These children nevertheless empathized with other children's embarrassment when physically punished in public. Parents' altruistic motivations together with their children's understanding and acceptance of physical punishment may mitigate adverse long-term effects (Deater-Deckard and Dodge, 1997; Deater-Deckard *et al.*, 1996; Lansford *et al.*, 2004). In loving environments, the 'caring message' might 'buffer' its adverse impact (Lansford *et al.*, 2004, p. 802). On the other hand, children may perceive physical punishment as a frightening experience involving erratic parents who have lost control (Lansford *et al.*, 2004). Parents who physically punish children are often angry, uncontrolled and remorseful (Graziano *et al.*, 1996; Straus, 1996).

Adverse effects may result from physical punishment alone, from a negative attitude to the child, or both (Miller-Perrin *et al.*, 2009; Socolar and Stein, 1995; Vostanis *et al.*, 2006). Hyman (1990) contends that even when a positive home environment lessens the impact, physical punishment always has a negative effect on a child's self-concept. Some argue that it is the primary reliance on physical punishment as a means of discipline (rather than its occasional use as one method among many other non-abusive methods) which may be detrimental to a child's development and later adult functioning (Power and Chiapeski, 1986). Any discussion related to the longer-term negative impact must, however, acknowledge the difficulty of separating the impact of other factors in the child and the child's environment (Gershoff, 2002a), such as minimal or no parental warmth, poor parent–child attachment, hostile parenting and inconsistent child management and monitoring (Bauman, 1996; Cohen, 1996; Miller-Perrin *et al.*, 2009).

Physical punishment may co-exist with child abuse, as currently defined. Children may live in families characterized by multiple forms of violence and possibly criminal activity (Stanley and Goddard, 1997; 2002). Physical punishment may occur with verbal aggression or with reasoning (Baumrind *et al.*, 2002; Gershoff, 2002a; Larzelere, 2000). Parents differ in how often they resort to physical punishment, its severity, the emotional state they are in when they use it, and whether it is part of a repertoire of disciplinary responses. These variations will have an impact upon the 'child-mediated processes' stimulated by physical punishment and the possible outcomes (Gershoff, 2002a, p. 552). An Australian longitudinal study of over 481 babies aged from seven months to 36 months found that the 'consistent and cumulative predictors of early externalizing and internalizing difficulties ... were parent distress and negative parenting practices' (Bayer *et al.*, 2008, p. 1172).

Physical and verbal aggression together may produce more damage than either physical aggression or verbal aggression alone (Ney *et al.*, 1994; Vissing *et al.*, 1991). Adverse impacts on children may also be more likely if children are both witnesses to and direct victims of physical violence (Hughes, 1988; Hughes *et al.*, 1989). Parke (2002, p. 598) asks the question: 'What impact does witnessed punishment of a sibling have on children's outcomes?' He comments that research tells us little about this experience or about children's thoughts in relation to the types and frequency of physical punishment that they receive compared to their siblings. Mullender *et al.* (2002) document children's accounts of cuddling together when violence between their parents occurs. Children act in various protective ways to shield each other from the violence. Adults are inclined to overlook 'child–child links' (Blanchard, 1993; Mullender *et al.*, 2002, p. 212).

The immediate and long-term impact on children

As hurting a small child seems intuitively wrong (Leach, 1999), parents may delude themselves that physical punishment is not painful. Parents' inclination to be violent towards their children raises questions about parent–child relationships and highlights a discrepancy between the ideal nurturing, protective parent and the reality that parents hurt, even injure, their children (Graziano, 1994). Behaviour modification is unlikely to result unless the parent-inflicted pain is 'severe enough to last for some time in which case harm is arguably done' (Turner, 2002, p. 198). Parents, as Philip discerns, frequently hold unrealistic notions about the nature of a 'gentle tap', and their children will not surprisingly disagree with their conceptions (1996, p. 185). In research by Smith *et al.* (1995), 85% of mothers who had smacked their one-year-old children and 40% of mothers who had smacked their four-year-old children believed that they had not hurt them.

Given these apparent contradictions, Holden (2002) proposes that studying physical punishment from the perspective of children rather than adults is of paramount importance. In recent times, children around the world have revealed that physical punishment causes physical and emotional hurt, resentment, confusion, sadness, hate and humiliation. They may feel angry, apprehensive, anxious and fearful (see, for example, Dobbs *et al.*, 2006; End All Corporal Punishment of Children, 2009; Saunders and Goddard, 2008; Willow and Hyder, 1998).

In relation to longer-term effects, Straus (1994; 1996) points out that individual research studies may appear inconclusive about the detrimental effects of physical punishment. However, he maintains that cumulative evidence suggests that physical punishment may (at least in part) be responsible for depression and suicide, violence and crime, masochistic sexual relationships, alienation, reduced income and physical abuse. Some will dismiss or dispute these 'harmful side effects' as they may be delayed and may occur only in some recipients of physical punishment (Straus, 1996, p. 340).

Larzelere (1996; 2000), a proponent of limited physical punishment, completed two analyses of peer-reviewed journal articles investigating the effect on children of 'non-abusive' parental physical punishment. The results of the two analyses were very similar. In 2000 he reviewed 38 articles written between 1995 and 2000 which focused specifically on 'non-abusive' or 'customary' parental physical punishment, typified by 'a two-spank procedure to the buttocks'. The review of research studies found beneficial outcomes in 32%, detrimental outcomes in 34% and the remaining 34% produced mixed outcomes. Physical punishment was found to reduce non-compliance in all of the studies in which it was investigated. Seven studies found that physical punishment enhanced the subsequent effectiveness of non-physical punishment such as 'time-out' and reasoning. Larzelere argues that the better effect of more gentle disciplinary responses should safeguard against 'disciplinary problems' wearing down parents' caregiving capabilities (2000, pp. 207–8). The detrimental outcomes of physical punishment evidenced in the studies included increased numbers of 'externalising problems' such as unsociable behaviour, 'mental health problems' such as diminished sense of self, heightened aggression, and 'emotional problems, and lower competencies' (Larzelere, 2000, p. 208).

Larzelere's second review, like the first one, indicated that older children suffered more detrimental effects than children under the age of six years. Detrimental outcomes were connected with frequent (one to three times a week) and severe physical punishment. Beneficial outcomes tended to occur 'when physical punishment was used non-abusively, not too frequently, primarily as a back-up to milder disciplinary tactics, and flexibly'

(Larzelere, 2000, p. 209). One study (Strassberg *et al.*, 1994) found that the 264 children who had been 'non-abusively spanked' prior to attending kindergarten were more aggressive than the 11 children who had not been physically punished.

Larzelere (2000) also reviewed the findings of studies that compared the effects of 'spanking' with alternative means of discipline. He concluded that, for four- to six-year-olds, 'nonabusive spanking' could be compared favourably to six alternatives. Four alternatives worked as effectively as 'spanking' children aged six to nine. Grounding was confirmed as a preferable disciplinary approach to teenagers. Larzelere disputes the argument of Graziano *et al.* (1996) that evidence suggesting the equal effectiveness of 'spanking' and alternative means of discipline supports the prohibition of 'spanking'. He maintains that, when confronted with challenging child behaviours, parents should be able to choose amongst, and alternate between, several alternatives including 'spanking' – just as people may choose between various pharmaceuticals that have been proven to be equally effective but may affect individuals differently, or be used as a back-up.

Gershoff, who opposes physical punishment, completed a meta-analysis of 88 studies between 1938 and 2000, and identified eight 'constructs' that may be associated with the impact of corporal punishment (2002a, pp. 541–2). She concludes from her meta-analyses that physical punishment was related to one positive outcome: immediate compliance, and associated with ten undesirable outcomes:

> [D]ecreased moral internalisation, increased child aggression [and] delinquent and antisocial behaviour, decreased quality of relationship between parent and child, decreased child mental health, increased risk of being a victim of physical abuse, increased adult aggression [and] criminal and antisocial behavior, decreased adult mental health … increased risk of abusing own child or spouse. (Gershoff, 2002a, p. 544)

Gershoff (2002a) cautions that parental physical punishment may not be the definitive cause of detrimental effects but it may increase their likelihood. She acknowledges other factors that may be of equal or greater influence, such as the child's characteristics, parent–child interaction patterns, marital conflict, social support and cultural factors. She recognizes the complexity of the parent–child relationship and the unlikelihood that physical punishment would alone account for children's behaviour and development.

Gershoff (2002a) draws attention to deficiencies in the research designs of much of the research included in her meta-analyses, particularly retrospective rather than prospective data. However, Baumrind *et al.* criticize Gershoff's conclusions because she includes 'severe and excessive levels of hitting in her operational definition' of physical punishment (2002, p. 584). They suggest this resulted in findings which arguably cannot apply to debates about whether normative physical punishment harms children and whether mild to moderate physical punishment should be banned. Holden, in contrast, concludes that Gershoff's findings reflect increasing evidence that physical punishment 'does no good' and may indeed harm children (2002, p. 594). Gershoff's (2002b) response to Baumrind *et al.* (2002) includes statistics from the 1995 US Gallup survey of over 900 parents which found that over 25% of parents hit children between the ages of four and eight with implements, and therefore severe hitting ought to be considered 'normative spanking'. As previously noted, severe or even fatal child abuse may occur through escalation and may be an unintended or accidental outcome.

The impact of physical punishment on parents and witnesses

The physical punishment of a human being affects not only the victim but others in some way connected. Newsom *et al.* (1983, p. 235) refer to 'social effects' of punishment. The most obvious 'social effects' of the physical punishment of children are parents' remorse, regret, guilt and even subsequent distress (Durrant *et al.*, 2003; Gough and Reavey, 1997; Graziano *et al.*, 1996; Jones *et al.*, 1987). The issue of physical punishment may also be a point of contention in marital conflict (Dobson, 1992). Further, as described in Chapter 5, both children and adults who witness physical punishment may feel, among other reactions, distressed, powerless and threatened.

For some parents, physical punishment is 'natural, normal, harmless and necessary. The use of the label "physical punishment" seems to legitimize and sanitize the intended action, minimize its significance and trivialize any suffering associated with it' (Davis, 1996, p. 294). These parents may feel a sense of satisfaction, righteousness and even relief after physically punishing children. They may understand children's distress as validation of physical punishment's effectiveness rather than seeing it as a response to pain and hurt feelings from which caring parents would normally attempt to protect their children. On the other hand, research suggests that many parents feel that resorting to physical punishment is wrong and they would prefer to use alternative methods of discipline (see, for example,

Coleman and Howard, 1996; Graziano *et al.*, 1996; NSPCC, 2002). At the same time, in societies that sanction physical punishment, parents who choose not to use it as a method of discipline may be labelled deviant and feel that they have to keep their decision to themselves or else face criticism and pressure from family and friends to conform to societal norms (Deitz, 2000).

Physical punishment's effect on parents

Seventeen parents always, sometimes or occasionally regretted using physical punishment as the physical or emotional effect on their child was not intended or anticipated:

> I usually regret it … I usually feel that wasn't the right thing to have done.

> I always felt bad about it afterwards, and … it didn't seem to bring about the change that maybe I thought was needed in the child. Sometimes they got so much more upset, and took a long time to settle … to feel better.

> They needed it but I felt terrible … I thought … 'I shouldn't have done that, I should maybe have talked to them. There must be another way besides smacking them … because it's physically hurting them'. I regretted it.

Some parents apologized to their children, particularly when they recognized that the child's behaviour was secondary to their own feelings of tiredness or stress:

> I … always apologize … particularly if I'd really lost it, and we would always have a hug. Perhaps … I was tired and really it wasn't their behaviour alone. I'm always emotionally drained, upset over the whole thing.

> I regret having been violent … when I lost it … because it wasn't appropriate, and I had to apologize because I had gone over the top. But … you can't be perfect, and you have to be prepared to apologize to your children because you are modelling imperfection.

Parents felt 'guilty':

> There are lots of better ways to solve behavioural problems than to use physical punishment.

Grandparents recalled feeling:

> Awful … I always did regret it, I always felt guilty, I remember saying I won't do that again.

> Sometimes when I'd think maybe he didn't deserve to be smacked because I was tired, stressed ... I did apologize ... I felt very emotional then and guilty for doing it. I'd lost control.

Moreover, some parents felt 'sick', physically and emotionally unwell:

> I felt very upset and ill.

> Just awful, like out of control, realizing parent control ... it was a real message to me that I was over the top and ... I get a gut feeling [my child] would know I was out of control too.

> Very bad ... upset ... I actually felt ... how I felt as a child even though I was the one who was meting out the discipline.

> I feel bad, polluted ... sometimes I think 'I did that a little bit too hard'. They'll get really upset and I'll get really upset and ... it's horrible.

> I don't like doing it. I don't know if it hurts. It disappoints me that it has to get to that ... I've felt bad. (parent)

This parent tried but found it very difficult not to resort to physical punishment:

> Usually I just yell a lot and then I lose my temper and ... I feel terribly disappointed in myself ... I thought that I could manage things better ... that there were other strategies. I should be more self controlled ... and I've failed.

Some parents felt justified yet they were angry because they perceived that their children's behaviours compelled them to use physical punishment. A grandmother said she felt 'satisfied'. A parent hoped that she 'got the message across' and others acknowledged:

> I don't feel good about it ... I'm probably more annoyed than anything else that it's got to that stage. I don't think I've regretted it.

> I have always regretted ... that it had to come to that, but ... I don't remember being dissatisfied with the outcome ... it generally worked.

For pinching his two-year-old, one parent felt 'bad ... very guilty ... but she has learnt from it'.

Frequent use of physical punishment may desensitize parents to its effects:

> It was something that I did and I got a result ... I certainly wouldn't have felt good ... but I don't think it really affected me.

It appears that parents who would normally empathize with their children's pain or distress ignore the impact of physical punishment:

> If she cried, perhaps I would be a bit sad ... it depends. If I was too busy and preoccupied with something ... her crying wouldn't have mattered.

Other parents felt:

> Lousy ... and ... think 'I shouldn't have done that' ... Other times I feel very satisfied, very vindicated, that I've finally got my point of view across, even if I had to resort to that.

> Partly justified and ... partly annoyed that I didn't have any alternative strategy in my bag to pull out to use ... it needed a response and ... you always regret it on a level. I don't think that it's appropriate to hit children.

> Most times ... really awful ... but there have been a couple of times when, not that they deserved it ... but I had given them every possible out.

Professionals' insights

On parents' attitudes to physical punishment

Until recently, children have rarely been asked how parental physical punishment affects them, and parents may have little insight into its impact on their child. Societal approval may discourage parents from considering its effects.

Social workers commented upon parents' limited insight into how physical punishment affects children:

> Physical punishment is one of the most tolerated actions on the part of adults and the impact of it on the child ... has never been understood.

> It hurts. Maybe ... as an adult you don't know how much it hurts. I am absolutely certain that my mother would have had no idea of the impact of it. Because, otherwise, why would she do it? I don't think people are ill-intended ... people just need to know.

Another social worker revealed that children tell her they 'hate' physical punishment, that it 'hurts' and 'makes them sad'. A psychologist lamented:

> The saddest part is when they talk about how bad it makes them feel about themselves ... their perception of why they are being hit ... how they are a bad person and ... unloved.

On the parent–child relationship

Professional participants drew attention to children's dependence, powerlessness and vulnerability in the parent–child relationship, and many were concerned about the impact of physical punishment on this relationship. Social workers observed that the parent–child attachment places the child 'in a very vulnerable position and trusting of their parent'. When a parent hits a child, it has an impact 'on their trust and on their relationship':

> It's worse for a child to be hit by a parent because that child has to go home to that person every day and that person is there for their nurturing and their understanding of life. (social worker)

Children have described abuse as 'being let down by those with whom they are in an emotional relationship' (Mason and Falloon, 1999, p. 9). When physically punished some children in this research questioned their parents' love and care. Moreover, children found apologies difficult to accept given parents' position of responsibility and their decision to use physical punishment while in that position (see Chapter 9).

Parents' insights into how their children feel

Parents' perceptions of the effect of physical punishment upon children were wide-ranging. Twelve parents thought that their child feared physical punishment:

> They are fearful of me in full flight yelling … I am big.

A teacher acknowledged her son appeared:

> Cross at me … shocked … There's times when I yell … and his look in his eyes. I guess there's a real fear there that he thinks I might be going to do more … become physical.

Parents admitted not knowing how their children felt:

> I'm not sure if I know how they feel.

> She must have hurt a little bit … I suppose that is not all. I don't know how she would have felt. She probably did fear it.

Seventeen parents had threatened to use physical punishment prior to using it, and 14 felt that the threat of physical punishment sometimes, often or always resulted in not having to use it. A health worker said her children are fearful, 'because I threaten them, and they know … I could do it'. Some parents acknowledged that the child may be physically hurt, otherwise 'you have to question why the hell you are doing it in the first place'.

Others maintained that physical punishment should not cause physical pain:

> A smack … is just to say, 'Stop!' … I don't think a smack should cause pain … it should just give them a fright … a bit of indignation. They get embarrassed by it.

Parents described children's distress:

> [He was] really upset … he must have felt betrayed … the look in his eyes, the tightening up of the body, the crying even before … one could do it.

> Sadness and going off to their room, and … being quiet for a while. They looked scared.

> Initially she cried but … hopefully [after pinching her] her boundaries will be more understood … I do think she fears physical punishment. Another method that her mother uses is threatening to hit her.

Despite children's signs of distress some parents dismissed fear as a response:

> Upset, indignant. … They don't fear it. It's more like … 'you wouldn't dare'.

> They cry … get upset then … get over it quickly. There's nothing to fear … they say 'don't smack me.' I don't know why.

Parents felt children's anger:

> They feel angry, hard done by … quite distressed. They tell me, 'don't do that, I didn't like that'.

> He was angry … I don't think he was thinking like, 'Oh I deserved that'. I don't think that entered his head.

Some parents minimized the physical effects of physical punishment, suggesting that children experience humiliation and remorse more than pain of any significance:

> I'd like to think that they would also feel annoyed that they let it get to that stage. They have tried to go outside [the limits] and they've been caught. They shouldn't have that fear because that's not a normal trait in this family … if … they have just kept pushing and pushing … suddenly bang. It's not premeditated … I would be disappointed that it's got to that. I think they would feel the same.

> [My child] is always remorseful afterwards. It seems to take [physical punishment] before [child] can admit being in the wrong. She wouldn't do what she does … if she really feared physical punishment.

Children may feel a combination of emotions. Parents perceived that children felt:

> Hurt, frustrated, angry, upset.

> Angry and hurt. They say, 'Don't hit me, don't smack me' … they act in a way that is frightened … they might try and run away.

Children can be:

> Upset, very upset and often I think it's not the physical punishment it's because they can see I'm so angry. Very often he … will say 'I'm sorry I was bad … I'll try' … sometimes they will say, 'that wasn't fair'.

The effects of physical punishment: children's voices

Only four of the 17 children interviewed individually agreed with the adult expression 'a smack doesn't really hurt'. Children talked about 'really hard' hitting that 'hurts a lot':

> It really, really hurts and they may understand or they may not. Sometimes it leaves red marks, it's that hard … I don't like being smacked on the bottom because when I sit down it hurts … I feel sorry … I wish it never happened. (9 yrs)

> It hurts … feels very painful. … If you've done a worse thing, then the smack will be hard. If you haven't done something that wrong, the smack won't hurt as much. (10 yrs)

> It can sting a bit and then be nothing, or it can be a bit of a problem for … another hour or two … if you poke it, it's, 'Ow!' [I feel] either angry or sad … generally both. (13 yrs)

Children shed tears and felt a range of emotions.

> Even if a smack's not very hard it can still make someone cry and be angry. (11 yrs)

> When my mum and dad … smack me I just like mumble under my breath rude words to 'em and stuff … a couple of tears like come to my eyes and … I just go in my room. (11 yrs)

> If you've been a bit naughty … and your mum slaps you on the bottom … like you'd think, 'Whoops!' … The extreme is when a kid gets hit quite hard and … they're emotionally really upset by it. (13 yrs)

[You feel] shocked and then you feel down. (12 yrs)

[They feel] really scared and just run away ... like into their bedroom and slam their door. They start to cry... (8 yrs)

[I'm] hurt and ... makes me feel bad. (8 yrs)

[I'm] more angry inside for them hitting me. Often it hurts a lot and I often get a red mark, and so I'd start crying even more. (12 yrs)

Some children were inclined to be destructive when parents hit them:

They feel like they wanna smash something or ... kick the wall or break something. They just get a lot of anger build up. (11 yrs)

Children may also want to retaliate:

You feel really mad and ... you feel like hitting them back. (8 yrs)

A 16-year-old acknowledged that when hit at home he felt 'a bit embarrassed' as well as 'a bit sore', and a 13-year-old felt that physical punishment may complicate guilt feelings that stem from behaving foolishly or inappropriately: '[I felt] guilty 'cause it was a really dumb thing to do but ... I was upset ... just distressed basically'.

Several children contrasted their poor treatment with the better treatment of animals. An 11-year-old said that physical punishment was like 'being squashed ... I reckon animals are more well treated. In some cases... It just makes you feel like you're a nothing, you're a cockroach.

A 12-year-old similarly said:

Being smacked is like being treated like something very little and not important to the rest of the world.

Children claimed that physical punishment may curb children's natural inquisitiveness and curiosity, essential to positive development and learning:

The good things about being a child is like you get to have fun...The bad thing about being a child is you get smacked ... when you shouldn't. (8 yrs)

When asked whether physical punishment should be a part of childhood, children replied:

No ... being a child gives you a chance to explore new worlds ... things that you've never seen before. (8 yrs)

> With smacking ... it makes you think your doing stuff wrong. They wanna explore but sometimes they do something wrong when they explore and ... smacking sends something to their brain that makes them not to want to explore. (9 yrs)

Parent–child relationships may be adversely affected:

> No one likes you any more and ... you feel hurt, more than physical ... inside. (12 yrs)

> You go off and cry ... get it all out of your system ... [I feel] very heartbroken, sometimes ... I just blurt it out all in my books, I just write down, 'Oh, you did this'. ... They've hurt my feelings for one. They've kind of let me down, 'cause I really trust ... 'cause they're taking care of me, and then as soon as you get hit, you think they're breaking your trust ... and then your heart just goes down and you get very sad. (10 yrs)

> If [parents] smack the child and then say, 'I'm sorry' and ... all that rubbish ... it will tell the child ... they still like me right now.
>
> *Principal author: So when you've been smacked the parents don't like you?* Um, that's what most children think. (12 yrs)

Children may have diminished regard for parents who resort to physical punishment:

> If parents smack their children then their children are gonna feel a lot weaker and be less able to say what they think ... and ... they're just not going to feel as good about their parents. It hurts ... children's feelings and physically, and I wouldn't want my children to feel that way against me. (11 yrs)

> I wouldn't smack my children because I want them to learn how you should respond to people ... and I don't think a smack would make them ... um, realise. Even if it did, then I don't think I should because I would hurt them and they would think that I'm a bad parent. (9 yrs)

Some children expressed confusion, questioning why parents who purport to love them also physically hurt them:

> They think it's okay to smack you ... like your family is trying to hurt you. (12 yrs)

> I know they could love you but it kind of makes you think that they don't like you ... and it hurts you. (8 yrs)

> It hurts, you're actually getting hit ... it would like hurt you emotionally ... because it's your parents that's just hit ya ... like your parents are people that

you love most … they just smacked ya. I feel really upset and depressed. (14 yrs)

Children may feel unloved:

The child thinks he…or she's not loved. (11 yrs)

You don't feel loved. (11 yrs)

I feel … they don't love me anymore… (14 yrs)

Children feared being hurt again:

You feel scared … you feel like shaking and like you shouldn't do that again 'cause you'll get another smack … you … feel really, um, sad. (8 yrs)

[They feel] scared 'cause they know how it's gonna hurt. (10 yrs)

Another child acknowledged his fear and raised important questions:

[There's] pain … hitting you … and you're sort of frightened when you bounce back. Why intimidate them … make 'em more angry and just scared and … quiet [and] unhappy? It is wrong … because it intimidates them and hurts them. They get really emotionally scared. (10 yrs)

An eight-year-old described children's fear and reticence to challenge parents:

Children are getting hurt and they want to say to their parents, 'Stop smacking me, this hurts' but they can't say it 'cause … if you look in their parents' eyes they kind of like give 'em a warning not to do anything else wrong.

Some children who had been physically punished felt dominated, intimidated, subordinate to adults, less than a person and unimportant. A 13-year-old described children feeling 'defiant and self protective' because adults 'have control over you. There is … helplessness … with being a child'.

Children were conscious of, and threatened by, the physical size and power of adults. Eight-year-olds observed that children get smacked:

Because they're little.

Parents are basically jus' like the boss.

When asked why children don't smack adults, other eight-year-olds replied:

Adults think they're superior and they'll just ... do something bad to the children.

Children probably don't smack adults because adults have more power. ... Adults can smack children whenever they want.

Other children commented:

They are more tougher than the kids and they'll do an even harder smack ... and it'll hurt more. (10 yrs)

A lot of children are scared of their parents. Like my dad, he's a lot bigger and stronger than me ... I know when I'm going to be hit 'cause you can see anger in their eyes. You feel worried ... you're going to be hurt, how you're going to get away from being hit. (14 yrs)

[They're] intimidated by the parents ... children can't fight back. Children are smaller and their parents have ... freedom with ... smacking children. They can get away with it. (12 yrs)

Children compared parents to 'bullies':

Smacking is like bullying. It's similar because one's the victim and one's the bully. The bully, who is the equivalent of the parent, is not getting hurt but the victim, or the equivalent of child, is getting hurt. (8 yrs)

We're too small and if you smack an adult you feel like, 'Oh no they can ... bash me up, they can cut off my pocket money, they can take away pets and my toys'. They have too much power and you can't really stand up to them whereas ... a bully ... in a playground, they're not much older than you and you at least have a bit of a chance. (11 yrs)

In this context, the threat of physical punishment may act as a powerful tool to enforce compliance:

Smacking is not good ... the little child gets threatened and it doesn't feel comfortable with its parents anymore. (10 yrs)

Smacking should not be a part of childhood 'cause it would frighten them. (8 yrs)

This 16-year-old described his anger, distress and sense of injustice after being hit, but his comment suggests that children's fear may coerce the outcomes for which parents aim:

You're just sore for a while, you can't sit down ... it's like a grieving period. First you're angry ... upset and you try and break things ... sometimes. Then you think, 'Oh it's unfair,' and you think, 'If he'd have done that he …'. Then afterwards … depending on age, you'd think, 'Oh I shouldn't have done that, I won't do that again, I won't get hit'.

Changes in children's behaviour may be motivated by intimidation and fear of pain:

> You just don't want to be hurt. (12 yrs)

> If they've … got severely punished … then that might happen again. (12 yrs)

> Some people will try and intimidate their kids with hitting … and sure they'll be good but is that what you wanna be doing with your kid, intimidate them so they're good … hit them … an' yell at them? [They feel] frightened. (10 yrs)

In individual interviews, 12 children said threats of physical punishment prompted them to obey their parents. They knew that it would hurt. Two children were less motivated because:

> I don't think mum and dad would touch me because if my mum did, I'm a lot stronger than my mum, and my mum's got a buggered shoulder. (14 yrs)

> I get physical punishment a lot … because they've done it so many times it doesn't really bother me any more. (10 yrs)

The impact of being hit in public

Children described the humiliation of being smacked in public. Many children disliked strangers observing their tears and physical signs of embarrassment:

> It really puts them down and humiliates them. (13 yrs)

> You're blushing, you don't feel so good, and … you wanna hide … you wanna revenge sometimes. (9 yrs)

> If you start crying you're embarrassed 'cause like there's heaps of people around. (9 yrs)

> At home … they don't feel very embarrassed with themselves. The child's feelings get hurt when they get hit in a public place. They say, 'Oh God, did mum have to hit me here, you know, where everyone can see me?'

A child, aged 12, who had not been physically punished, remarked:

> The child will probably get embarrassed that it's getting hit and, also, um prob'ly fairly angry or might want to cry. If it's a public place … they probably won't want everybody watching.

Some children appeared to be resigned to being smacked at home but they considered a smack in public to be rude or bad parental behaviour:

> In shopping centres … it is like embarrassing for the kids, and rude to hit if you're at someone's house. (10 yrs)

An eight-year-old felt that hitting a child in public is: 'like making people think that parents are bad … and rude…', but smacking a child is not rude at home 'when no one else is watching'. Children also expressed concern that their parents may be judged unfavourably if they are seen smacking their children:

> In public places … it makes you look like bad parents … the kids get really embarrassed and start crying. (14 yrs)

> Parents get a bit embarrassed, their kids being smacked in front of other people. (9 yrs)

A 10-year-old presented an unusual perspective. He condoned what he called 'meaningful smacks', hitting children 'on the spur of the moment', and to protect them from danger. He added that being hit in public 'makes children less afraid of parents'.

Parents may not know how children feel

Thirteen of the 17 children interviewed individually found the adult expression, 'It hurts me more than it hurts you', hard to fathom, and did not agree. A few children were aware of parents' emotional upheaval when they purportedly felt they had to hit children for the child's own good. Some also sensed parents' feelings of shame and self-disappointment when they hurt their children in the heat of the moment. However, most children clearly refuted adults' assertions that physical punishment doesn't really hurt. Indeed, some children perceived that adults didn't know how they felt:

> The adult's not getting the pain. (11 yrs)

> Some people really feel pain, especially children, and what an adult may think is soft, a child could think is really sore. And the adult can't judge how hard to hit the child before it's just hard enough to make the child think about what they've done. (16 yrs)

An 11-year-old remarked:

> They wouldn't feel the same way about smacking if they knew how their kids felt.

Another child suggested that children could say to parents:

> Imagine if someone a lot stronger than you smacked you, how you would feel … it really hurts.

A child, aged 10, conceded that it is wrong 'in a way' to smack children because:

> The child feels really sad inside, and maybe the parents don't know how the child feels.

And a 12-year-old maintained that adults have forgotten what it feels like to be hit:

> Last time the adults prob'ly got smacked was when they were a little kid and they wouldn't know what it felt like. I mean if I went up and smacked them, then they'd know, but children don't normally go up to their parents and go, 'Stop behaving like that!' and smack them.

Some children tried to conceal how they felt

Like some of the adult participants, some children remarked that to reveal the physical and emotional impact of physical punishment would be giving away too much:

> If my parents … smack me … I just turn around and laugh at 'em, even if it hurts, 'cause if they think it doesn't hurt me they won't smack me anymore. I'm not one that will let out my emotions. I'll jus' keep them inside and pretend nothing's ever happened. (14 yrs)

A nine-year-old said he felt 'sad, very, quite sad, like you gonna cry but I don't'. And a 10-year-old said that when his mother smacks him, his brother cries, and

> I'm just, like … 'it didn't even hurt that much'. I don't cry. He does … I just don't feel the pain. Sometimes I feel sad or angry at the person.

Having been hit, some children felt it would be inappropriate for others to suffer a similar experience. Twelve-year-olds said:

> I wouldn't want to smack 'cause I know what it's like to be smacked.

> Even if the children get smacked then they don't have a right to smack back.

Some children wanted an apology:

> You feel like you're alone and all you want is a cuddle and you want them to say, 'I don't want to do it again. I'm sorry for smacking you', and you usually feel pretty down for the rest of the day. (11 yrs)

Children described feeling hurt and in some degree of physical and mental pain (see also Dobbs and Wood, 2004; End All Corporal Punishment of Children, 2009; Willow and Hyder, 1998). They felt shocked, sad, angry, dejected, disliked, embarrassed, depressed, regretful and let down by their parents. Some children felt unimportant. Others felt insecure and fearful of being hit again. Some children defiantly hid their feelings from parents. Some felt parents may be too distanced from them to understand how they feel. Children revealed that physical punishment may lower children's estimation of their parents. It may also curb children's spontaneity and curiosity.

Children's observations of how physical punishment affects parents who use it

Parents may normalize physical punishment

Physical punishment may be so habitual that it has no impact on parents:

> They probably feel maybe a little bit sad, have a bit of regret but … if they do it regularly, it would probably be fairly normal. (12 yrs)

> They can sometimes just not feel anything … they've convinced themselves they did the right thing or … they could just feel absolutely like really horrible that … they might of like really hurt their child and they really wish they hadn't done it. (12 yrs)

Parents may feel justified and satisfied

Some children saw physical punishment as something that parents responsibly administer to children who deserve it if they overstep boundaries or behave inappropriately:

> Usually they don't feel sorry. They think, 'Well he deserved that'. (10 yrs)

> Sometimes they feel better in a way, and bad because they might think like that was the wrong thing to do or … my dad normally feels like, 'That'll teach you a lesson'. (11 yrs)

A ten-year-old felt:

It depends on their point of view whether smacking is good or bad. If they didn't really want to, but they thought they had to, it'd probably feel kind of guilty. And if ... they'd felt that they got the child to listen ... well they're not proud but, I don't know a word to describe it.

A 16-year-old observed parents' relief:

[That] the action has stopped ... and a feeling of ... guilt that it had to come to that and they didn't really want to do that but it's fixed [the children] up now and hopefully they won't need to do it again ... it hurts the adult emotionally that they have to resort to that.

However, children also sensed that parents who smack children may not feel good about having to resort to hitting:

It might hurt the mother or father to have to do it ... like their feelings. (10 yrs)

They don't really want to smack them because they're your child ... you want to look after them and you don't really want to smack them. (10 yrs)

An eight-year-old said that parents:

Feel more bad with stuff inside like they don't want to smack but they do because like the child needs to be taught a lesson ... [Mum would] feel ... like not wanting to and feeling bad inside because she did it.

Ten of the children interviewed individually maintained that parents apologized after physically punishing them:

After I've been smacked ... I go into my room. After a while mum feels sorry ... and she comes in. (8 yrs)

They usually do think that it's the wrong thing to do and sometimes ... they tell me, 'Sorry'. Sometimes ... they just can't bring themselves to say it. (11 yrs)

They usually tell me sorry ... they didn't think before they did it ... 'cause they are angry at you. (12 yrs)

When my mum ... smacked me she just sort of sat there for a minute stunned, looking at her hands sort of shaking an' went paper white an' then sort of looked at me an' said, 'I'm sorry, I'm really sorry'. (12 yrs)

In this context, children demonstrated empathy and respect by thinking about parents' and others' feelings. A 10-year-old observed that his mum and dad retrospectively thought about why they hit him and 'it upsets me, so I think about it'.

Other 10-year-olds said on the subject:

> I don't think parents should smack … because it hurts the kids, and it upsets the adults.

> Hitting … my parent … it's not right. They're the ones taking care of me and doing the right thing, maybe sometimes, but you shouldn't hit a person. Parents might have the same feelings as us. They might think maybe the child doesn't like us. It's my only parents that I only have, and if they think that, 'Oh, my child is hitting me because she doesn't like the way I'm handling her'. It kind of hurts their feelings too in a way.

Parents may feel sad, bad and guilty

An 11-year-old said her dad felt 'sad for hurting his only daughter'. Another child said:

> My mum says … they don't want to have to hit … they feel like sad … they've actually hit them. When they see the kid crying they don't feel very well. They just feel like they're gonna cry … in pain it hurts the kids more, but in the brain it hurts the adult more, in the mind. (10 yrs)

Parents who love their children may, children suggest, realize that it was wrong to hurt them:

> They would feel bad 'cause they just hurt somebody and … disappointed in themselves. (8 yrs)

> It prob'ly hurts … their feelings because they feel bad smacking their kids. (11 yrs)

> They smack and … think to themselves 'What have I done?' They feel awful. (9 yrs)

> They're probably unhappy 'cause they've had to smack and didn't want to. … They would feel bad … guilty … for actually hurting their own child. (9 yrs)

A 10-year-old recalled after one incident 'Dad … was really upset'. He had 'headaches', 'bad dreams' and felt 'sick'. A 13-year-old talked about an incident when dad hit her sibling and 'for two weeks afterwards … it hurt every time he swallowed because he was so angry with himself'. She went on to observe:

Mum feels angry and ... dad feels upset with himself ... because they got annoyed ... frustrated ... angry. They'd be very happy if they had no occasion to smack their child.

Conclusion

Many parents acknowledged feeling remorse, guilt and regret after physically punishing their children. Parents also described feeling physically unwell and emotionally distressed, sometimes because they were disappointed in themselves for having resorted to a violent means of discipline. Others felt self-righteous, justified, angry or indifferent – believing either that their children knowingly provoked physical punishment or behaved in a manner that compelled physical punishment. Rationalized in this way, rather than being moved by children's reactions, some parents interpreted children's distress as validation of the effectiveness of physical punishment (Davis, 1996). Parents in this research did not, however, recall feeling good after using physical punishment. Many parents acknowledged that their children appeared to fear physical punishment, and were hurt and angered as a result.

Children's sensitivity to their parents' feelings and the impact of physical punishment on their parents is remarkable. This research suggests that children may be more concerned about parents' feelings and rights than parents are about their children's feelings and rights. Conscious of how parents felt after physically punishing them, many children expressed confusion about parents' continued use of physical punishment when it elicits negative and unproductive emotions. The persistence of physical punishment is explored in the next chapter.

9

The persistence of physical punishment

Introduction

In this chapter we ask what motivates parents to punish children physically and, in contexts where physical punishment continues from one generation to the next, how it is explained and justified. We begin by considering various parenting styles and some theoretical understandings of the reasons why physical punishment persists today. We then present the perspectives of the adults, families, and children from this research.

Motivations and rationales for physical punishment

Parenting styles

Three 'controversial and polarised' perspectives on physical punishment have been identified: 'the anti-corporal punishment position: "violence begets violence"; the conditional corporal punishment position: "no blanket injunction warranted"; and the pro-corporal punishment position: "spare the rod and spoil the child"' (Benjet and Kazdin, 2003, p. 197). Parents' motivations and rationales for using or not using physical punishment will

Physical Punishment in Childhood: The Rights of the Child, by Bernadette J. Saunders and Chris Goddard
Copyright © 2010 John Wiley & Sons, Ltd.

be determined, at least in part, by which one of these perspectives they adopt or lean towards.

Parenting practices are 'multi-determined' by 'individual, historical, social and circumstantial factors' (Reder, Duncan and Lacey 2003, p. 6). As Belsky and Vondra (1989) observe, parenting is influenced by the adult's and the child's personality, and by the personal, social and political context within which the parent–child relationship forms. The parent's childhood experience, personal relationships, social connections and employment status have an impact upon their disposition and sense of well-being, which then affects the child's development.

Baumrind identifies three common parenting styles, described as 'authoritarian', 'permissive' and 'authoritative'(1966, p. 887). These parenting preferences derive from cultures categorized as 'hierarchical', 'individualistic' and 'egalitarian' (Giles-Sims and Lockhart, 2005, p. 197). 'Authoritarian' parents expect children to obey their commands and failure to do so incurs punishment, including physical punishment. From an 'hierarchical' cultural perspective, 'unequal humans with various short-comings require improvement through expert guidance'; 'socially flawed' children must learn correct behaviour from adults in authority (Giles-Sims and Lockhart, 2005, pp. 199, 202). In contrast, 'permissive' parents place few demands on children and avoid limiting children's behaviour. Self-regulation and self-interest characterize an 'individualistic' cultural orientation (Giles-Sims and Lockhart, 2005, p. 199). 'Authoritative' parents support their children and encourage their children's independence but respond to their children's behaviours in a consistent and firm manner. An authoritative parenting style may be promoted in Western societies to develop independent, emotionally secure children who are socially and intellectually competent. Adherents of an 'egalitarian' culture see humans as largely equal and 'unmarred by natural flaws destructive of social harmony' (Giles-Sims and Lockhart, 2005, p. 199). Given the 'multi-deter-mined' nature of parenting (Reder *et al.*, 2003, p. 6), however, parents' responses to children in individual families may vary, exhibiting features of more than one particular style of parenting.

Australian research suggests that parents often adopt a parenting style which combines induction (an authoritative approach) and power asser-tion (an authoritarian approach) (Kolar and Soriano, 2000). Parents may initially attempt to reason with children before yelling at them or enforcing time-out. As a last resort, children may be physically punished. This escala-tion in the intensity of parents' responses to their children also cleverly diverts responsibility for the physical punishment from the parent to the child. Having explained disciplinary intent, parents empower children to regulate punishment 'by controlling the behaviour on which punishment is contingent' (Baumrind, 1996, p. 828).

Particularly in Western cultures, physical punishment may be at least explained, if not justified, with reference to pedagogy, intergenerational transmission, catharsis, and temperament (see, for example, Gough and Reavey, 1997).

Pedagogy

Many parents will typically justify their right to resort to physical punishment 'as a means of promoting responsible, appropriate and safe behaviour, which ultimately furthers the welfare of the child' (Spink and Spink, 1999, p. 27). Parents often provide pedagogical reasons for physical punishment or 'virtuous violence' (Straus, 2009, p. 1315). Physical punishment may be perceived as an aid to a duty, bestowed on parents by society or God, to teach their children correct, or acceptable, behaviour as opposed to behaviour that is deviant or inappropriate (Bartkowski, 1995; Ellison and Bradshaw, 2009). The biblical quotation 'spare the rod and spoil the child' (Proverbs 13:24) fits this rationale comfortably (Kazdin and Benjet, 2003). The use of physical force to communicate that hitting is wrong may not be seen as contradictory.

Implied in this rationale is an entrenched belief system. Punishment ought to be considered carefully and administered in a determined manner (Baumrind, 1996). The child is to be taught a lesson; one that will be remembered. Moral arguments, and arguments based on the efficacy of physical punishment abound: physical punishment is 'toughening and character building … the world is cruel, learn consequences early' (Wissow, 1996, p. 815). Moreover, it is effective because young children, some argue (see, for example, Ginn, 1996), do not respond to verbal reasoning and dangerous misbehaviour must be stopped quickly (Wissow, 1996). Research suggests that belief and practice tend to be highly correlated (Durrant *et al.*, 2003; Socolar and Stein, 1995).

Such beliefs may stem from religious sources and affiliations (Bartkowski, 1995; Ellison and Bradshaw, 2009), from parents' experiences of physical punishment in childhood (see, for example, Capaldi *et al.*, 2003; Gagne *et al.*, 2007), and from a perception that desirable responses, such as immediate compliance, were achieved when parents last used physical punishment (Gershoff, 2002a; Larzelere, 2000).

Intergenerational transmission

Salt observes that 'humanitarians' regard the 'flogging' of men, women and children as 'an abomination' (1905, p. 82). It is perhaps most damaging to children, he contends, because their 'ethical sense is more liable to be permanently confused and distorted by a lesson in personal violence as a substitute for moral persuasion'. Moreover, it will almost certainly instil in children 'a tendency to act in a similar manner when the conditions are reversed' (Salt, 1905, p. 82). It appears that the 'values and behaviour of each new generation towards its young in turn forge the functioning of the next society' (Solheim, 1982, p. 153; see also Zeiher, 2003). People who have been punished physically as children often retain a positive perception of its usefulness (Capaldi *et al.*, 2003; Gagne *et al.*, 2007). Thus, people who received physical punishment as children may be more inclined than other people to use physical punishment on their own children (Capaldi *et al.*, 2003; Conger *et al.*, 2003; Hops *et al.*, 2003; Scaramella and Conger, 2003). Multiple factors may, however, impinge on the likelihood of repetition.

Why some victims of abuse become perpetrators while others do not remains unclear (see Egeland, 1993; Kaufman and Zigler, 1989; Medley and Sachs-Ericsson, 2009; Pears and Capaldi, 2001; Zuravin *et al.*, 1996). Some insight into intergenerational transmission is provided by social learning theory, which suggests that abusive disciplinary practices are modelled by parents and imitated by children (Bandura, 1973; Muller *et al.*, 1995). Also, future behaviour may arise from one's personal experiences of physical punishment together with one's perception or judgement of those experiences. Byng-Hall (1995) uses the term 'family scripts' to describe current behaviours prescribed by a belief, attitude, expectation or past experience. 'Scripts' can be adopted or rejected. For example, in response to an aversive discipline as a child, parents may decide not to respond similarly to their own children. This may result in novel, more lenient forms of discipline. Byng-Hall cautions, however, that when stressed, the parent 'may replicate exactly the same ferocious discipline, sometimes saying and doing precisely the same things as his or her parent did' (1995, p. 43).

Longitudinal studies of intergenerational transmission of aggressive parenting styles reveal that when children experience and observe aggressive parenting directly they are likely to discipline their own children in an aggressive manner and this may result in their children behaving aggressively (Capaldi *et al.*, 2003; Conger *et al.*, 2003; Hops *et al.*, 2003; Scaramella and Conger, 2003). Several factors may interrupt the cycle. Compliant children who are not 'highly reactive and emotionally negative' may reduce both parents' anxieties and stress levels and parents' tendencies to automatically replicate their own parents' aggressive parenting (Scaramella and Conger, 2003, p. 420). Children may be more cooperative and emotionally positive if they experience authoritative rather than authoritarian (Baumrind, 1966) harsh parenting, and children's development of aggressiveness may be curbed by their interactions with people other than their parents. Moreover, when children become adults they may learn non-aggressive parenting skills from partners, professionals, friends or other relatives (Capaldi *et al.*, 2003).

Research suggests that some parents who have been physically punished and who physically punish their own children welcome opportunities to learn about alternatives (Garvey *et al.*, 2000). These parents perceive physical punishment to be ineffective, are aware that they could hurt their children when they are angry, and do not want their children to be punished physically. Parents in the study by Garvey *et al* (2000) who continued to administer physical punishment to their children did so when under stress, with little knowledge of alternatives, and because they believed physical punishment was effective and valued by their culture. Victims of physical punishment perhaps most likely to perpetuate its use are those who experience 'sub-abusive' discipline; potentially injurious but not serious enough for them to reject it (see Ball, 2009; Bower and Knutson, 1996).

Adults commonly contend that physical punishment did not harm them. To admit that it might be harmful would imply some self-criticism, particularly if they use physical punishment on their own children. It would also imply criticism of the adults' parents (Straus, 1994; 1996). Approval of physical punishment is closely related to having experienced it (Deater-Deckard *et al.*, 2003; Gagne *et al.*, 2007). Deater-Deckard *et al.* (2003) confirm from their longitudinal research involving mothers and adolescents that convictions about effectiveness and harmlessness are probably integral to its transmission from one generation to the next. Notably, Hyman found that parents who had experienced physical punishment as children and had chosen not to hit their own children had, by putting 'themselves in the shoes of the child experiencing the pain, frustration and anger of being hit', developed empathy with their children (1990, p. 42). Gagne *et al.* (2007), on the other hand, found that people who remembered suffering severe physical punishment were less likely to favour it but not necessarily unlikely to use it.

A significant contributing factor in intergenerational transmission is the continuing acceptance and sanctioning of its use both legally and socially. Graziano *et al.* (1996) observe, and this research confirms, that even children suffering the immediate effects of physical punishment, such as distress, hurt and anger, accept physical punishment as their parents' right. Unless challenged, children may claim the same right when they become parents.

Simons *et al.* (1991) propose four pathways that may lead to the transmission of harsh parenting: the endorsement of a 'parenting philosophy' that condones physical force as a means of discipline; the development of an aggressive personality as a result of being disciplined violently; the spontaneous and thoughtless imitation of violent responses to children's behaviours; and the replication of living conditions that produce stress which results in physical punishment. Parental stress that motivates physical reactions to children may be produced by characteristics of the environment (Belsky, 1980; Burrell *et al.*, 1994; Connelly and Straus, 1992; Woodward and Fergusson, 2002), parent characteristics (Belsky, 1980; Woodward and Fergusson, 2002) and behaviours of the child (Belsky, 1980; Engfer and Schneewind, 1982; Holden *et al.*, 1995; Woodward and Fergusson, 2002; Woodward *et al.*, 1998). These pathways are not mutually exclusive. Chen and Kaplan (2001) found that constructive parenting techniques are also passed from one generation to the next through modelling of authoritative parental behaviour and the development of positive modes of personal interaction.

Catharsis

Stressed or angry parents and parents with unrealistic expectations are more likely to have authoritarian and negative attitudes toward children, and to use harsh physical punishment (Deater-Deckard and Starr, 1996; Holden *et al.*, 1995; Regalado *et al.*, 2004). An individual parent's tendency toward aggression (discussed below) has been found to increase the use of physical punishment as a means of discipline, as has hostility and conflict between parents which results in a 'climate of negativity' (Jouriles *et al.*, 1991; Korrel *et al.*, 2003, p. 20). Taylor and Redman (2004) state that some medical professionals perceive smacking as valvular because it provides adults with a legitimate, controlled means of expressing their anger and may thus curb parents from resorting to other forms of abuse (Alcorn, 2000; Price, 2000). Others have satirically contended that adults should have access to the same 'safety valve' in response to irritating colleagues and other adults (Vaidya, 2000, p. 261).

   Peterson *et al.* (1994) found that challenging behaviour by children that threatened parents' sense of control (for example, defying or disobeying a direct command) provoked the most anger, which in turn often resulted in physical punishment of an intense nature. Similarly, Graziano *et al.* (1996) found that physical punishment most often occurred when parents were angry and children were disobedient, challenging parental authority and dominance. Sibling disagreements and household damage less often resulted in physical punishment. Research suggests that tolerance of parental use of force against children is high if parents are reacting to children's disrespectful provocation, stirring parent's emotions or threatening parental power (Kelder *et al.*, 1991; Ruane, 1993). Davis (1996) observes that ignored parental threats may both facilitate and serve as justification for parents' physical aggressiveness toward children. A child who ignores a warning may be deemed more deserving of the assault. Physical punishment motivated by parental catharsis is especially worrying as physical punishment, 'like most assaults and homicides, is usually impulsive, done in anger and often regretted' (Straus, 1996, p. 837).

Physical aggression towards a child often reflects the parent's emotional state rather than a considered response (Cohen, 1996). An inconvenienced, unprepared, tired, frustrated or depressed parent (see, for example, Shay and Knutson, 2008) may have minimal tolerance of normal childhood behaviours such as crying, spilling food or drink, toileting accidents or waking up at night. The desired effect of permanently stopping such behaviour is unlikely to occur (Gershoff, 2002a). Consequently, levels of violence toward a child may escalate. In the US, Starling *et al.* (2007) studied 630 cases of deliberately inflicted skeletal trauma in 194 hospitalized children, aged between 0 months and 13.9 years. The average age of children injured by identified males, predominantly biological fathers, was 4.5 months while the average of children injured by identified biological mothers was 10 months. Injuries resulted from aggressive handling, pulling, twisting and squeezing children's bodies and limbs. Starling *et al.* speculate from their findings that 'skeletal trauma and traumatic brain injury may have different triggers'; excessive irritation at a baby's crying may motivate inexperienced parents to shake the infant whereas 'fractures' may result from 'the frustrations of everyday parenting … changing soiled diapers … unrealistic expectations … toilet training and toddler negativism', increased mobility and independence (2007, pp. 997–8). Environments that are cold and critical further heighten the risk of abuse (Little, 1995).

Temperamental disposition

Research suggests that harsh parental discipline may lead to a 'hostile personality' in victims who, as a result, will behave aggressively to their own children and to people in general (Simons *et al.*, 1991). This predisposition toward aggressive behaviour may be learned, as suggested above, or it may be an inherited trait, and the complex interaction of genetic and environmental factors in the possible transmission of aggressive behaviour is significant (Di Lalla and Gottsman, 1991; Gulbenkian Foundation Commission, 1995; Jaffee *et al.*, 2004; Lynch *et al.*, 2006; Simons *et al.*, 1991). The Gulbenkian Foundation Commission notes the impossibility of determining the degree to which temperament is innate as opposed to a product of the environment, particularly the parent–child relationship. A child's moods or behaviour can prompt parents' 'rejection or inappropriate treatment …

which can in turn increase any potential for violence' (Gulbenkian Foundation Commission, 1995, p. 40). An aggressive personality, whether inherited or learnt, may be tempered or stimulated by factors in one's environment; for example, family, peer group or cultural influences.

Whatever the origins of an aggressive personality, research suggests there is a greater likelihood of severe parental physical punishment occurring in response to verbal and physical aggression (Engfer and Schneewind, 1982; Herronkohl *et al.*, 1983, cited in Muller *et al.* 1995; Smith, 1984). The aggression may be directed at parents, at siblings, at peers and at others. Children, with behavioural problems, whom parents find difficult to control may be subjected to more physical punishment (Gershoff and Bitensky, 2007; Holden *et al.*, 1995; Muller *et al.*, 1995).

Multiple forms of violence co-exist in some families, with a resultant increase both in the dangers to which some children are exposed and the physical, emotional and behavioural impact upon them (Stanley and Goddard, 2002).

Why use physical punishment? Adults' perspectives

From some adults' perspectives, physical punishment 'asserts an appropriate authoritative structure between a parent and a child' (social worker) yet from the perspective of others it reflects:

> A lack of bonding, empathy and understanding ... poor control of parents' own feelings, and downright disrespect. (social worker)

A health worker observed that professionals who work with children form 'polarized groups'. For some 'there is no indication for physical discipline, no matter what'. Others say 'there will always be indications for physical discipline and that becomes the territory of the parent'. The remainder feel that 'occasionally there might be a last resort indication for doing that'.

Very few parents in this research felt there was 'no indication for physical discipline'. Some parents did, however, break 'the cycle':

> Physical punishment wasn't an experience of mine I wanted my children to have. It's just a promoted ... kind of ... violence that I didn't want my children to hold.

> It wasn't effective or respectful ... I don't want children to ... have that experience. I think about what children are experiencing when they're being physically disciplined.

I don't believe in physical punishment … I don't believe any one has the right, even parents … I don't use it with my children.

Professionals observed that some parents who were physically abused as a child make 'up their mind that "I will never lay a hand on my child"' (social worker). Indeed, a police officer noted that some people 'can be absolutely against any form of physical discipline' because they believe 'physical discipline is physical abuse'.

In a society that sanctions physical punishment parents may be motivated to use it because, as one social worker pointed out, 'it's just tolerated and accepted in society'. A psychologist suggested it is tolerated because:

> We don't engage in conversations which say this is not helpful to kids. Parents are more likely to use it when they are stressed … but they are only able to think that it's possible to use it because it's acceptable in the community. I might walk into a shop and be really, really stressed waiting in a line but I'm not going to punch the people out, because it's not acceptable. If you're frustrated with children … it's acceptable to hit them.

Parents who physically punish children may 'think they have the right to smack' (teacher). Social workers commented:

> Physical punishment requires a pre-existing belief that that way of operating is okay … 'it's a good thing to do. Children don't learn unless they experience this sort of punishment or discipline.' It's embedded in their value system … their rights as a parent.

> I grew up in a culture where physical punishment was sanctioned so … I understand it being acceptable and I don't necessarily see it as cruel. When I hear 'it doesn't do any harm, it didn't do any harm', I understand where they're coming from so that influences me from being as black and white as I might be otherwise.

Entrenched behaviours and value systems tend to resist challenge:

> It might just be a day-to-day part of your life, 'Violence is the way that problems were solved with me, that's the way they are going to be solved with you'. (health worker)

> Parents say, 'it's all I know and that's what everyone around me does. That's what happened to me … I turned out okay, so that's an effective way'. (social worker)

> A lot of parents have relied on 'it happened to me, therefore it is okay … I can do it with my kids', even though there might be people in their peer

groups who are advocating other ways. So there is a lot of ... history. (social worker)

It's ... upbringing ... it's an acceptance of the use of physical action as discipline. I haven't come across a situation where a person has not been physically disciplined as a child and then chooses to use it. (social worker)

Parents who approve of their childhood physical punishment may espouse its use:

I just wish that some parents would not be so against physical punishment. ... If I'm not against it, and after my childhood, why are other people?

In terms of my own childhood ... would I question the discipline that was put to me? ... No.

A grandparent described physical punishment through three generations. He recalled a feeling of 'catharsis' when 'thrashed' as a child. 'At times' he 'had a feeling of having been purged of some sin and made cleaner, and more accepted again'. As a small boy, he remembered:

I had a very rusty little truck, and I looked in the shed, and ... there was a tin of paint. I painted the truck ... I got a thrashing ... put over the knee and given a few. It had to be done ... I pinched my dad's paint.

Then as a parent:

When I had a kid over my knee I would invariably count the number of blows to his bottom ... often five, usually 10.

As a grandparent, he said:

If a child repeatedly refuses to do what he is told, he is going to get hurt for his behaviour. Recently, I took two grandchildren to our bush block [plot of land in the country]. One was about five, the other two. I said, 'you have got to be able to see me wherever you are'. And they got out of sight ... I gave a verbal blast, and I reinforced it by putting [five-year-old] over my knee ... five slaps on the bum. The younger child took a great deal of notice. So it achieved some good. There was another occasion ... with another grandson ... in the car. I told them to shut up several times. In the end I stopped ... dragged one boy out and I put him over my knee. Ten smacks on the backside ... tossed him back in the car and said, 'now sit down there and behave yourself'.

This grandparent revealed:

My daughter is coming to the conclusion that ... she is going to have to thrash my grandson some time. He is being very puerile.

Some participants recognized a cycle of physical punishment, sometimes despite disapproval:

> When I had ... hit any of my children I always felt terrible guilt ... I would be thinking, 'God, I am just like my mother'. (teacher)

> When I smacked ... it was like I felt I had lost control and was like my father. (teacher)

A social worker who had been physically punished as a child described having had a recent miscarriage and being extremely stressed. She described the shock of physically punishing her child only once and said that hitting her child was not 'premeditated ... I can remember being absolutely horrified and having to leave and go outside and take a breath'.

Physical punishment may be the only form of discipline that some parents have either experienced, know of, or value. Half of the 26 parent participants who had physically punished their children had felt bereft of alternatives. Social workers observed:

> It's simply a learnt behaviour, that's the way the parents were brought up, that's the way that they bring up their children ... there's a lot of intergenerational transmission of values and disciplinary practices that people really don't know any alternatives to.

> If parents have a history of their own physical abuse that has been unresolved ... and consequently their problem solving skills are well developed [or entrenched, they] resort to violence because they don't know of any other means.

A teacher recalled parents saying that they were motivated to punish physically because it was 'the only way I could make him stop ... give him a good slap' and 'the only thing I could do that got him to settle down ... the only thing that works'.

> It's the way children learn, it's what they see as being acceptable ... 'I got belted and it never hurt me'. By virtue of the fact they say that, it did hurt them ... they have not been presented with other options ... in a feasible light. Parents will say, "well what else do you expect me to do? How else are they going to learn? Talking to them doesn't help, so that's all I've got". (psychologist)

> A lot of parents do not have the skills to be able to talk to a child. Physical punishment is the way it's done, nothing else works in their setting. That's the method that's tried and true. (health worker)

In this context, some parents try hard not to use physical punishment but cave in:

> I've got friends who've tried very hard not to smack their kids but they have. One friend would say, 'I've tried absolutely everything'. Once in a while a smack is the quickest way of dealing with it. (social worker)

> They fight a lot physically ... it drives me to distraction. We've done talking about it, explaining, taking away privileges, fun things they like to do, no television. I've tried just taking no notice. Eventually they go on until someone gets hurt ... I have yet to find a strategy that works. (parent)

Sixteen of 24 parents punished their children physically for pedagogical reasons. Many parents thought that physically punishment for undesirable behaviours would encourage appropriate and acceptable behaviours: teach children to 'know what's right and wrong'.

> [To] teach children what they'd done is incorrect ... you wouldn't do it for any other reason. (parent)

A social worker remarked that parents who hit their children commonly say that their child 'needs to learn'. Another social worker recalled:

> I have condoned the use of physical punishment as a way of discipline and ... minimized it. I thought it was not only acceptable but that that was the way to teach children to grow.

Some parents felt unable to reason with a young child, and there were also elements of retributive intent, 'an eye for an eye', where children are meant to learn by being treated in the same way that they may have treated others. A parent who pinched his daughter said:

> I wanted her to recognize that she was causing pain to other people.

And a health worker empathized with a friend who said to her child:

> 'This is what happens when you bite'. ... The teeth marks on that little child was awful. She was trying to teach the child. [My son] bit someone once and I said, 'Hey look!' [and bit him] but I didn't hurt ... You are trying to teach them ... give them an idea.

Only four of 25 parent participants denied that feelings of anger and tiredness were factors motivating physical punishment. Parents frequently hit children without forethought or self-control:

> I don't think too many dish out a slap when they're in a calm frame of mind. (grandmother)

You are not in control ... you haven't thought through other options. (teacher)

Sometimes you'll hit the kid ... and if you came back a week later to that moment again, you wouldn't hit them, but ... in that moment, things just happen.

Professional participants similarly recalled many parents saying '"I had had it" ... "I was at boiling point [feeling] frustration, anger, feeling almost desperate"', and a health worker talked about an incident where 'dad gave [three-year-old] quite a wallop ... the father lost it. It was awful.'

Children who parents perceive to threaten their sense of power and control may arouse extreme anger. Parents will say, 'I was furious ... the kid made me so angry' (social worker). In this context, a health worker empathized with some parents:

If I have had a really shitty day at work or I am horribly tired ... your threshold for reacting is very, very low indeed. Why does that then translate into physical responses? ... You start to feel relatively impotent. The other methods of getting the message across aren't working ... frustration. ... 'Because he didn't do what I told him to do' ... 'I had asked him five times', or 'I just had a shocking day and everything had gone wrong and I just lost it.'

For some parents, physically punishing a child can be cathartic; one social worker described it as 'getting rid of your own frustration'. A parent, for example, admitted that physical punishment is 'to show my feelings ... my distress. It's because I'm cross.'

Justifications for using physical punishment

In a potentially life-threatening or injurious situation, fearful or angry parents may spontaneously hit children:

I was concerned that the child would get hurt if she did what I told her not to do.

A police officer recalled parents explaining that children:

[Had] got close to the heater or 'I saw [child] going to the car'. ... Some parents are really scared ... hyped up and they've whacked them when they're in that state. They lose the plot and cross the line because they are scared about what would happen.

Restraint, along with an explanation, is not perceived as a better option, according to one social worker. Parents will say:

> 'A small child is not going to relate to a long explanation of why they can't go near a heater' ... 'It's just a little smack' ... 'You have got to do that to stop kids running out on the road'. [Such] arguments would be self-justifying.

Many parents contended that some children sometimes 'need' physical punishment as their challenging behaviour extends beyond acceptable or tolerable levels:

> There's a place for physical discipline ... some children seem to require it ... to need that as a means of seeing their boundary.
>
> [Our friends'] kids can run riot ... and the mother says, 'don't do that' and the child keeps doing it for the next half an hour. Well I'm sorry, in our space, get real!

Physical punishment for behaviours that are perceived as extreme were also readily justified:

> They have to do something really bad to get a smack. (parent)
>
> Sometimes they need a smack that hurts. ... When kids have been really, really naughty people comment like, 'that child needs a bit of a smack'. Most people smack their children. (health worker)

In this context, some parents felt compelled to hurt their children:

> There have been times when I wished I didn't have to do this. I just feel that I have to smack her. (police officer)

To really hurt children, some people will even justify physical punishment with implements. Clinical experience led a social worker to comment 'there is still a sense that, as a last resort, using something to hit a child is reasonable'. Physical punishment with implements was condoned as

> appropriate if they have done something really very bad and they need to be punished. I was physically punished ... with an implement and I certainly respected my parents and I would never say that I was physically abused. I think some implements are more appropriate than others: the wooden spoon, the belt. (police officer)

From a professional perspective, the same police officer observed:

[It's] the first thing that parents grab because they know that if they use their hand it's gonna hurt their hand. They might get a better effect by using something ... not necessarily injuring the child but ... it would scare the child more because an implement is going to hurt them.

Often parents' feelings of stress or frustration, and consequent use of physical punishment, were attributed to a child's annoying behaviour; something the child was saying or doing:

Parents often believe they are disciplining a child because of the child's behaviour but ... often it's a response to their own stress. (social worker)

The child's behaviour may be developmentally normal or attributable to physical or mental disabilities over which they have no control, rendering them particularly vulnerable (see O'Reilly, 2008). Children whom parents perceive to be challenging are more likely to be physically punished (Alizadeh *et al.*, 2007; Holden *et al.*, 1995; Muller *et al.*, 1995; Watkins and Cousins, 2005), as these professionals observed in their work with families.

[Parents say] 'she talked back' or 'she wouldn't stop crying' ... those kind of frustrated things. ... Disposition in the child ... children who are ADHD [Attention Deficit Hyperactive Disorder] ... perhaps they are more difficult children to be with. That's a factor. (social worker)

Being a parent when the babies are so young and you are so lacking sleep and they're crying and crying ... you get really frustrated. Most parents know what it is like. ... They are not realizing that they are going to hurt their poor babies. (health worker)

A police officer was accustomed to parents blaming their children for the physical punishment they had received. She disputed parents' explanations but simultaneously used language that objectifies children. Reference to children as 'kids' may also be demeaning and inappropriate (Saunders and Goddard, 2001):

The kid is not being naughty. The kid is doing whatever you have allowed it to do since it was this big. You have created the problem and now you are having a tantrum and are smacking them out of the tantrum, not smacking it because you are trying to educate it. You have failed big time.

Some justifications for physically punishing a child stemmed from arguments about human nature:

> We're just all human beings and you can smack your child. I've smacked my kids when maybe I could have dealt with it better. Being realistic about how difficult it is to be a parent at times ... we're not perfect, none of us are. (social worker)

> We're not talking about saints here, we're talking about ordinary people who get aggravated ... impatient ... tired, who haven't got as much money as they might want. And the kids are nagging you for something ... and you say, 'not now ...', and then they keep it up and keep it up. 'Shut up!' [smack]. We're human. (grandmother)

A social worker felt that some parents' temperamental disposition may result in them being 'unable to manage anger and frustration ... there's a predisposition to violence'.

A teacher said:

> It ... can be that their frustration level is pretty high and they're just not coping, so it's some sort of immediate response.

Physical punishment is often perceived as justified when other attempts to enforce a child's compliance have failed:

> You'll try everything ... and it will go on again and you've got to make a stand ... it's the last resort. (grandmother)

> If all other means had been exhausted and it was done in a controlled, measured way that didn't leave marks or injuries ... as a last resort it is okay. In every other way, these families are seen as responding to their child's needs in a really appropriate way ... it is more about frustration and anger and exasperation. (social worker)

> You have got a few screaming kids hanging off you ... it is pouring, and you just need to get those kids into the car. In terms of a last resort sometimes a smack is necessary. (teacher)

> Being violent ... is the last resort. I've run out of doing the nice word bit ... the subtle soft threats and withdraw[n] the minor privileges. (parent)

Parents described inconsistent motivations and rationales for physically punishing children. Explanations fell into two categories: child-deficit arguments, such as teaching children lessons in desirable behaviours, and cathartic, parent-focused arguments, such as maintaining power and control, asserting parental rights, and releasing negative human emotions. Physical punishment motivated by anger, loss of control, and parents resorting to what was done to them as children appeared predominant. Controlled, rational, child-centred physical punishment seemed more of an adult-empowering myth than a reflection of reality. Some parents, however, had little or no knowledge of alternatives that were equally effective, or more effective, than physical punishment, especially as a last resort and to enforce a child's immediate compliance (see Lyons, 2000). Physical punishment was valued and justified.

The primary reason that physical punishment is used may be that it is legally and socially sanctioned, and remains largely unchallenged as a parent's right in relation to the children they believe they own and can discipline as they please (Gittens, 1998). Minimal knowledge of effective alternatives, along with the absence of incentives to respond to children in more respectful ways (Leach, 1992), may contribute to intergenerational transmission of physical punishment. On the other hand, parents who have some knowledge of alternatives to physical punishment and who hold a view that children have a right to physical integrity, and to be treated in a respectful and positive manner, can disregard the physical punishment 'script' provided by their parents.

Parallel stories: childhood reflected in adulthood and mirrored in the next generation

Family members from 10 families and from two or three generations within those families shared their experiences of and views about physical punishment. All but two families used physical punishment as one method among other means of discipline, and all adult participants in the 10 families had experienced physical punishment. All of the 16 child participants from the 10 families presented as well cared for and loved. Six of the 13 children who had been physically punished felt that they would use physical punishment as parents. Social learning and intergenerational transmission of parental behaviours were clearly evident in family members' comments, as were indications of parenting practices being 'multi-determined' by the parent's and children's individual characteristics, the parents' marital and family relationships, the parents' education and occupations, and the social context that sanctions physical punishment (Reder *et al.*, 2003, p. 6).

The comments of one father and two of his children demonstrated the influence of one generation's attitudes and behaviour on the next generation, and lent support to research suggesting the significance of disassociation in transmission of abusive behaviours. Disassociation serves to minimize abusive experiences, possibly increasing children's tolerance of pain, and weakening parents' ability to empathize with their children (Singh Narang and Contreras, 2000). This father was motivated to use physical punishment because 'it happened to me ... and I'm reasonable ... it didn't do me any harm'. He recalled:

> Nine times out of ten dad used a slipper to hit us ... the threat of it kept you on your toes, you didn't want it to happen. I didn't want to cry ... I wasn't going to show that it hurt. I've got a brother who's exactly a year younger ... and he used to jump around all over the place ... I don't like hitting my kids. I don't know if it hurts. It disappoints me that it has to get to that ... I have felt bad.

Both parents in this family physically punished their children. Like their father, two of the children tried to control their reactions to being smacked. When asked how he felt when smacked one child replied:

> Well sad, very, quite sad, like you gonna cry but I don't. (9yrs)

The other child similarly responded:

> When Mum smacks us, [sibling] is like crying, and I'm just like ... 'It didn't even hurt that much.' I don't cry. He does ... I just don't feel the pain. Sometimes I feel sad or angry at the person. (10yrs)

Interestingly, their 12-year-old sibling commented that when physically punished:

> It shows how much more you are upset if you're crying.

She was more like their mother, who admitted that she sometimes cried after physically punishing her children.

Family characteristics

All of the family members in each of the families who participated in this research presented as caring and supportive of other family members. The families could be divided into two main types. In a Type A family both parents used physical punishment and in a Type B family neither parent used physical punishment. Type A families could be divided into two sub-groups: Type A (child-deficit) families and Type A (parent-focused) families. In the Type A (child-deficit) family subgroup, the parents presented as motivated to use physical punishment predominantly for pedagogic reasons. In the Type A (parent-focused) family subgroup, parents were primarily

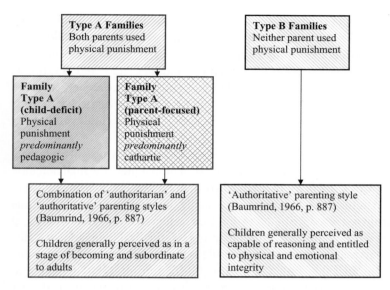

Diagram 1 Characteristics of Parenting Type A (child-deficit), Type A (parent-focused) and Type B Families

motivated to use physical punishment for cathartic reasons. Type A families appeared to combine authoritative and authoritarian parenting styles (Baumrind, 1966, p. 887), with physical punishment a valued disciplinary option. The parenting style of Type B families could be described as authoritative (Baumrind, 1966, p. 887). Physical punishment was not used.

Family Type A (child-deficit)

Six families (identified by the pseudonyms Bates, Collins, Ibis, Forrest, Grant and Harvey) could be described as Type A (child-deficit) families. Parents in these families used physical punishment predominantly for pedagogical reasons, to set boundaries and to modify children's behaviours. Stress and mood swings did, however, affect their responses to their children.

Alyson Forrest held slightly different views from other Type A (child-deficit) parents. Despite being intent upon using non-violent means of discipline, she admitted:

> I just yell a lot ... lose my temper and ... I feel terribly disappointed in myself. I thought that I could manage things better ... that there were other strategies.

Whereas Alyson would support a total ban on physical punishment, Family Type A (child-deficit) parents typically did not favour a ban. Children in Type A (child-deficit) families appeared to be perceived as subordinate to adults. Acceptable behaviours, children's boundaries and parental expectations were clearly defined in these families and, when necessary, enforced by physical coercion. Sam Bates, aged 16, observed that a smack is 'a form of punishment to put the child back in line ... being a child, you usually do what you're told'.

Type A (child-deficit) parents believed that children provoke physical punishment, and these parents made physical punishment the final outcome if children overstepped pre-established boundaries. Parental threats were used by parents to both facilitate and justify physical punishment. Threats and warnings also contributed to children feeling that they were 'bad' or at least behaving badly and thus deserving of physical punishment. This works effectively for parents who would rather not feel totally responsible for the pain that they inflict on their child (Baumrind, 1996). Children in Type A (child-deficit) families could expect to be hit if they pushed their parents' boundaries too far; particularly if parents were angry, tired or stressed. The following in-depth description of the Bates family serves to illustrate a characteristic Type A (child-deficit) family.

The Bates family

The Bates family comprised parents Jeremy and Pamela and three children, Sam (16yrs), Kris (12yrs), and Logan (9yrs). As children, both parents had been physically punished at home and at school. While Pamela judged her own upbringing to have been harsh, Jeremy contended that neither being hit at home nor strapped at school did him any harm. Pamela's decision to physically punish her children, despite condemning her own experience of physical punishment as a child, made her an exception to previous research (Hemenway *et al.*, 1994; Hunter and Kilstrom, 1979):

> I just wish that some parents would not be so against physical punishment ... if I'm not against it and after my childhood, why are other people?

In contrast, Jeremy's decision to punish their children physically supported research findings that suggest that people who perceive non-injurious physical punishment to have been deserved are unlikely to consider physical punishment to be abusive (Bower-Russa *et al.*, 2001; Bower and Knutson, 1996; Herzberger and Tennen, 1985; Rodriguez and Sutherland, 1999). Jeremy observed:

> In terms of my own childhood ... would I question the discipline that was put to me? ... No.

As parents they were committed to non-injurious physical punishment as an appropriate and effective response to children's persistent misbehaviour. Indeed they, along with some other parents in this research, commented that parents who do not physically punish their children may be perceived as deviant and irresponsible. Pamela asserted that 'physical discipline is … relating to that child's well-being' and after physical punishment:

> The demons seem to leave [child] for a good five or six months. I know people who have got children … who have never been physically disciplined because the parents don't believe in it. You can almost see through [the children's] body language and looking into their eyes. They are not endearing … one little person is almost evil.

Jeremy explained:

> I'm not a violent person by nature. Being violent … is the last resort … a case of saying, in a very strong way, that you [child] have pushed the bounds. You have challenged this house to that point and this is the reaction we're gonna have. It's now a case of that is totally unacceptable. … In this household, where there has been continuity for 20 years and the meeting of minds, they know full damn well that if I was to smack them there is no point running off to [mum]. … She'd say straight away, 'You probably deserved it and you're lucky I didn't get to you first.'

Nevertheless, there were occasions when Pamela regretted using physical punishment:

> Sometimes I feel lousy … and think, 'I shouldn't have done that', and other times I feel very satisfied, very vindicated that I've finally got my point of view across, even if I had to resort to that.

In this context, the privacy of the home and non-interference in their parenting decisions were highly valued. Jeremy stated that he 'really wouldn't give a damn what the Australian attitude is'. Similarly, Pamela declared:

> Parents should have some kind of ability to discipline their children … like a smack on the bum. It's a sad day that the government bans it completely. I just can't even imagine what would happen then.

The Bates parents' motivation for using physical punishment was primarily pedagogical:

> Discipline is if your intent is to teach. To punish is … to harm the child. My husband and I see our responsibilities towards our children … to teach them, pass on our moral points of view. (Pamela)

However, at times both Pamela and Jeremy resorted to physical punishment when angry and tired, and because the children had been defiant and ignored warnings:

> They have tried to go outside [the limits] and they've been caught. If they have just kept pushing and pushing … suddenly, bang. It's not premeditated … I would be disappointed that it's got to that. I think they would feel the same. (Jeremy).

Living in contexts where physical punishment is seen as a normal parental response to transgressions, parents and children in Type A (child-deficit) families were inclined to consider physical punishment to be deserved and justified when warnings had been ignored. Adults who were abused as children have rationalized their abuse in a similar way (see, for example, Buntain-Ricklefs *et al.*, 1994; Knutson and Selner, 1994):

> If you're warned, and if things are laid out to you why you shouldn't do it, and … the consequences if you do continue doing it, then physical punishment is fine. (Sam)

> My dad … he says 'don't answer back', and then you mumble. Then they say, 'don't answer back, I heard that', and then you mumble again, and they get very annoyed and they get up and give you a smack … answer back and then they're gonna get very, very angry. (Logan)

Pamela and Jeremy admitted that Kris had been the most challenging of their children and had been subjected to more physical punishment than Sam and Logan. Kris was perceived to challenge parental authority and this, as research suggests, resulted in more frequent and severe physical punishment (Gershoff and Bitensky, 2007; Holden *et al.*, 1995; Muller *et al.*, 1995).

Neither Pamela nor Jeremy believed that any of their children feared physical punishment, but they acknowledged that threats were sometimes or often effective. All of the Bates children claimed that they were smacked only after being warned or threatened. They had a sense of natural justice; something which several children in this research considered important. Kris, unlike Sam and Logan, considered smacking a child to be wrong. Yet all three children thought that parents should sometimes be allowed to smack, and that their parents used physical punishment to teach them right from wrong:

> If it's discipline they've done it on purpose … so there is no reason to say sorry. That smack was done to help the child realize that what they had done was off. Parents are just putting morals into them and reinforcing them. A

smack is not wrong as long as it's a punishment … to hopefully teach right from wrong. (Sam)

Just something that the parent does, everyday life … it's just sort of natural … it's going to happen because they just done something bad. (Kris)

It's okay to smack when you're about five and older. They shouldn't smack their children for no reason. They should think for a while [but] … if children continue to do the same thing … then smack. (Logan)

Kris and Logan did not plan to punish their own children physically. Kris said, 'I'll be sending them to their room', and Logan said 'I'll just tell them again', rather than hit them. Their older sibling, Sam, like their parents, perceived physical punishment to be an indispensable method of discipline, especially as a last resort:

If it gets to the point where [my children have] been warned and threatened and there's no other resort, they haven't reacted to the removal of material objects, I think I would have to resort to that … I'm all for it but not with an object and not on the spur of the moment.

In relation to the intergenerational transmission of physical punishment, a possible explanation for the differences among the Family Type A (child-deficit) siblings is that Sam appeared to have adopted Pamela and Jeremy's parental reasoning and had not disapproved of their parenting. This confirms the observation by Deater-Deckard *et al.* (2003) that adolescents may endorse physical punishment. Indeed, Sam appeared to use his parents' arguments to justify physical punishment, supporting the findings of Graziano *et al.* (1996) that even children who are hurt and distressed as a consequence may perceive it as a parent's right. On the other hand, Kris, the middle child, may have decided that the greater amount of physical punishment that he had received was not the experience he would want for his children, supportive of Hemenway *et al.*'s (1994) and Giles-Sims and Lockhart's (2005) research. On the other hand, children who are cognizant of their parents' benevolent pedagogical intent may nevertheless conclude that physical punishment is not necessary to achieve the same goals. They may realize that alternatives are equally effective and are a more appropriate response. This explanation could be explored further in future research.

Family Type A (parent-focused)

In Type A (parent-focused) families, parents typically punished their children physically as a means of expressing emotions such as frustration, anger, annoyance and tension. Physical punishment in these families is often a first resort rather than a final attempt to achieve children's compliance. The Denton family typified a Type A (parent-focused) family.

The Denton family

The Denton family included parents Nadine and Ralph and two children, Parker (13yrs) and Jamie (10yrs). This family attributed physical punishment primarily to the release of negative emotion, without any suggestion of a child-focused pedagogical motive. Nadine and Ralph appeared to consider it to be a legitimate means to express and relieve frustration and annoyance. Nadine said she physically punished her children:

> To show my feelings … my distress … it's because I'm cross.

Ralph admitted that he felt:

> Bad, polluted. Sometimes I think, 'I did that a little bit too hard'. They'll get really upset and I'll get really upset and … it's horrible.

Both Nadine and Ralph had received physical punishment as children, and their comments suggest that social learning may have influenced its perpetuation. Notably, Nofziger claims that her study provides 'the first confirmation' that a parent's self-control influences the development of children's self-control (2008, p. 218). Nadine said that when her mother hit her as a child 'it was just loss of temper, just … feeling pushed to the limit'. Ralph commented:

> My dad's rule of thumb was never hit a child unless in anger … there's some logic to it. It would have to be heat of the moment, passionate.

Neither Ralph nor Nadine acknowledged a connection between their parents' responses to them as children and their own parenting responses. Parents may resist attributing their parenting behaviours to intergenerational transmission because this detracts from parents' sense of autonomy to act in independent ways (Gough and Reavey, 1997).

Ralph and Nadine did not perceive that either of their children received more physical punishment than the other. Both parents commented that when they punished their children physically it was always because they did not know any other way, they were angry, tired or stressed, and their child provoked them:

> Sometimes … you'll hit the kid … and if you came back a week later to that moment again, you wouldn't hit them but … in that moment things just happen. (Ralph)

Nadine acknowledged that 'excessive aggravation on the part of the children' motivated her to hit her children. She reasoned that:

> If you hit 'cause he's driven you absolutely insane, I can't see that being an issue.

Ralph acknowledged that he sometimes reacted impulsively and violently and then regretted his actions. Both parents' behaviours supported findings that violent reactions to children may be motivated by parental emotion (Cohen, 1996; Rodriguez and Green, 1997; Straus, 1996). Nadine recognized that her children probably feared physical punishment, and that her threats to hit were sometimes effective. Ralph claimed that he never threatened to hit and he, unlike Nadine, would accept a total ban on physical punishment.

The Denton children emphasized children's lesser status, vulnerability and experience of intimidation; supporting children's comments in Mason and Falloon's research (2001; 1999). Jamie commented:

> I don't think it's appropriate for them to physically punish me any more ... 'cause I think I am becoming a bit of a person, not a child anymore. (13yrs)

Parker described an incident in which their father used physical punishment:

> He didn't really hurt me ... but I was very scared an' you don't like your dad doing things like that ... it's not nice like having your father ... who's mean ... not a nice thought that you can't rely on him. (10yrs)

Yet both Jamie and Parker contended that parents should sometimes be allowed to smack their child, again confirming the findings of Graziano *et al.* (1996) that children may perceive it to be a parent's right:

> From my experience, adults would at some stage get frustrated enough to ... shake or slap them. It's just a bit letting out feelings ... just when they're really, really angry. (Jamie)

> On the spur of the moment parents smack a child ... that's alright ... Mum just gets really angry, and so does dad. (Parker)

When asked whether they thought that they would smack their own children, Parker thought:

> I might now an' then on the spur of the moment but I'll try not to.

And Jamie said:

> I can imagine getting frustrated and slapping them. I don't think I could imagine hitting them really hard, um ... I mean it's hard to know how annoyed you can get.

A possible explanation for this anticipation is that children who are physically punished for purely emotive reasons may recognize that, when they are parents, they too could succumb to emotion-driven physically punitive responses to their children. Alternatives may be perceived as less effective outlets for the release of pent-up emotions, such as anger and frustration (Alcorn, 2000; Ginn, 1996; Price, 2000). This explanation could be further explored in future research.

Family Type B: Physical punishment is not used

The Ayres, Egan and James families could be described as Family Type B authoritative families in which physical punishment was not used. Discipline consisted predominantly of reasoning and negotiation, backed up by star charts, time-out or removal of privileges, and was motivated by child-centred boundary setting and positive reinforcement of desirable behaviours. The James family included a foster-mother and her two foster-children, both of whom had received counselling for their abuse. Her biological children were older and had left home.

The children in Type B families had a strong sense of children's rights to physical integrity and a belief that parents should never be allowed to smack their child. These children did not intend to punish their own children physically. The following in-depth description of the Egan family serves to illustrate a typical Type B family.

The Egan family

In this family the maternal grandmother, Eileen, mother, Elise and Jess (10yrs) were interviewed. Eileen had punished Elise physically as a child, and Elise had witnessed and been distressed by such punishment of her sibling, particularly by her father:

> Dad was giving my younger brother the strap ... I got really distraught, saying 'stop it, stop it'.

Elise nevertheless described her upbringing as generally happy:

I look at my childhood as … a majority of happy times with a caring and loving family. Physical discipline wasn't a regular occurrence. My parents wanted to instil right from wrong in us and it was the only way that they knew how to discipline.

Elise had attained tertiary qualifications in early childhood studies, and had decided not to use physical punishment to discipline her own children. Her husband had been raised in a family that did not use such punishment and he had not used physical punishment on their two children. Elise declared:

I don't believe in physical punishment … I don't believe anyone has the right, even parents. Even though there was the use of physical punishment as a child I don't use it with my children … I just wish people could realize that there are other ways.

Jess was aware that children in other families are punished physically by their parents, and she argued against it:

That will teach their children to hurt others … it's easier to talk so then you can like settle it.

Jess did not anticipate physically punishing her children:

If they don't do what they're asked, I will probably speak to them sternly and I might have a system like pocket money or a star chart.

Significantly, Jess's grandmother Eileen had been influenced by her daughter Elise's ideas about discipline and they both would accept a total ban. Eileen commented:

I must admit I did smack my kids and I deeply regret it. I would never, ever do it again … if I had my time over. I don't think an adult should hit a child.

It may be that a decision not to use physical punishment as a means of discipline is more likely to be implemented in families where (a) at least one parent has not been physically punished, (b) parents have been educated about alternatives and about child development, and (c) parents hold similar views that physical punishment is undesirable and unnecessary as a means of discipline.

In contrast, in the Bates Type A (child-deficit) family, both parents had similar beliefs about the usefulness of physical punishment so the parents' responses to their children were reinforced by each other. On the other hand, in another Type A (child-deficit) family, the mother, Ann Forrest, was less committed to the legitimacy of physical punishment than the father, and both parents acknowledged that the mother was more influential in relation to decisions about their children's discipline. Consequently, it is perhaps more likely that the use of physical punishment as a means of discipline would be discontinued in this generation and also in the next. One partner's views about, and experiences of, physical punishment may influence the other's. Two Forrest family children did not intend to use physical punishment when they were parents and the other child didn't know whether he would. This process of influence and the subsequent use or non-use of physical punishment in a family warrants further exploration.

Links are clearly apparent between behaviours experienced and observed in families, attitudes communicated in families, and the repetition of these attitudes and behaviours in the next generation. Discontinuation rather than repetition of attitudes and behaviours appears to rest on a conscious decision. Continuity of physical punishment across generations appears to occur easily when it is not questioned as a reasonable response to children, regardless of its effects or its effectiveness. Discontinuity appears to be easier if individuals make a decision based on knowledge of alternatives and a judgement that physical punishment is disrespectful to children and a denial of their rights as human beings. Continuity may still occur, however, if parents are particularly stressed or out of control and they resort, without forethought, to what they observed and experienced in childhood.

Parents' perceptions of children appeared to differ in families that use physical punishment and those who decide that physical punishment is unacceptable. Children in families who used physical punishment appeared to be regarded as subordinate to adults with developing but inferior capabilities – not quite people, irrational, and a source of annoyance. In contrast, children in families where physical punishment is not used appear to be regarded as small people who in many ways are not unlike adults. Children were respected as reasonable human beings whose capabilities were different but not less important than adults' capabilities. Adults are also 'becomings' (Hengst, 2003) who, at times, behave inappropriately and irrationally. It appears that children who are not physically punished may be given more opportunities to participate in decisions, to explain their actions, and to negotiate consequences. Power in families that did not use physical punishment appeared to be negotiated with, rather than exerted upon, children. The support of a partner in either continuity or discontinuity may be a significant factor worthy of further exploration.

Why do parents use physical punishment? Children's views

'Teaching you to be good'

Children may understand childhood as a time to learn to act responsibly and behave better. For some children this means having to endure physical punishment. Thirteen of the 17 children interviewed individually thought that parents sometimes or often use physical punishment to teach their children right from wrong. Parents, an eight-year-old observed, are 'teaching you to be good'.

Children associated being punished physically with doing something 'bad', 'wrong' or uncontrolled; behaving in ways that affected their parents:

> It happens ... when the child's bad and ... if the adult is at a time when that is affecting them. (16yrs)

> Sometimes they just can't handle themselves, they just go wacko and ... the parent has to ... just smack. (10yrs)

Parents, children maintained, do not want their children to carry 'bad habits' into adulthood so they are punished physically 'for a good reason' (12yrs).

> Because they've done something wrong. And it makes them so they don't do something again. (8yrs)

> You get a feeling that was pretty bad, and you think mum or dad's going to get really pissed off about that. You know pretty well that physical punishment is what is going to happen. (13yrs)

The smack causes pain that is meant to be remembered as a deterrent:

> If you're like very naughty they might give you a smack to definitely not do that again, and the smack will remind them to not do it again. (9yrs)

A 10-year-old maintained that parents:

> Say ... through the hit, 'don't do it again' and the only way to stop parents smacking is children doing the right thing.

An 11-year-old said 'parents can't just ... let 'em be naughty an' keep letting them do it', and when asked if smacking was the only way to stop children from doing it, he replied, 'yes'. Other children maintained:

> It's their child. They don't really want to smack the child but they have to. It's the only way the child will learn. (9yrs)

> If I did it on purpose then yes maybe they could give me a smack. They have to do something to stop them from doing it, so if they smack them, they will think, 'oh no, if I do this again they will smack me again'. (10 yrs)

A 12-year-old felt that parents 'prob'ly felt bad for smacking … but maybe that was the right thing to do'. And a 16-year-old observed:

> If the adult does smack the child usually it's for a good reason … they're just putting morals into them and reinforcing them. A smack is not wrong as long as it's a punishment to hopefully teach right from wrong … to steer you in the right place.

Another child proposed that a calm parent and an explanation increase the educational value of a smack, which is 'not a big deal':

> Kids have gotta learn … you have got to explain to the kid what is wrong … what are the problems … and if all else fails just say, 'well, I'll slap you again if you do it'. It only really teaches them a lesson if it's controlled. (13yrs)

A 16-year-old argued that if children 'don't get hit or smacked you tend to keep on doing it because you think it's okay'. When asked if it was necessary to smack or hit as an aid to learning, he replied, 'if it's within reason'. To explain 'within reason', he continued:

> I used to hit up my brother and sister when I was little … I'd get a bit rough so I'd get hit. I think it only took me two hits to realize that I shouldn't be doing that.

Some children saw physical punishment as an act of love:

> [Some parents] don't really know how to love someone like without having to punish them. (12yrs)

> A smack is so wrong and right because they should be smacked and they shouldn't be smacked … they should be like tapped, just like a smack, because they've done the wrong thing. You give them a tap love, like it's a tap but it's like love. (8yrs)

> I don't think parents like hitting their children … it's like their own flesh and blood that they're hitting and they love that person to death. The only reason they do it is because they love them so much. They don't want them getting hurt or in trouble. (14yrs)

Children valued procedural fairness, and some understood that physical punishment could be a final consequence of their inappropriate actions; a last resort:

> It's wrong to smack ... I would only do it if I really had to. (8yrs)

> When you weigh up all the pros and cons of smacking, smacking is wrong ... but sometimes it's the only way after warnings and threats have been made. (16yrs)

> They might have done something really, really naughty and sometimes just banning things ... doesn't actually make them stop. But ... if dad smacks ... it will make them not do it again. (12yrs)

This 12-year-old also observed that sometimes parents are:

> In such anger that they don't think before they move ... but other times, when [mum] gave us a warning ... she'll hit us, which I think's fair because she told us to stop and we didn't so it's our fault for not stopping. They know that they're going to get smacked because they've been doing the wrong thing.

A 16-year-old engaged in the following conversation:

> *Principal author: Should parents sometimes or never be allowed to physically punish their children?*

> Child: If it's a repeated offence then I guess yes, sometimes.

> *Principal author: Do you think parents think about whether to smack a child before they smack or do they smack first and then think about what they've done?*

> Child: Here [at our house] it's always been think about it if the action's been that bad ... It's just a better way to do it ... then you're not emotionally drained afterwards with the guilt.

> *Principal author: Do you think parents would rather not smack or physically punish their children?*

> Child: The majority would not want to. They know that it will hurt the child physically and it will hurt [parents] emotionally ... but if they are threatened or warned, then ...

> *Principal author: Do parents ever say they're sorry after they've physically punished a child?*

Child: If it's discipline they've done it on purpose ... so there is no reason to say sorry. That smack was done to help the child realize that what they had done was off. ... If you're warned, and if things are laid out to you why you shouldn't do it, and the consequences if you do continue doing it, then that's fine.

Unruly, annoying children need physical punishment

In individual interviews, six of the 17 children felt that a 'smack' could be a good thing for a parent to do. Children readily presented arguments as to why parents should physically punish unruly, annoying children who 'sometimes need it' (14yrs).

> I see kids who are just so spoiled and annoying, and just have no interest in anyone else. I think someone should give them a good slap. (13yrs)

> It's wrong to smack ... a child unless you really, really have to, [like when they] do something against what you say ... like maybe hurting someone. Me and my cousin always want [my cousins] to get smacked because they don't get any discipline. My uncle goes like, 'you've got one more chance' and he keeps doing that for the entire day. (11yrs)

> Sometimes people have got ADD [Attention Deficit Disorder] and they get out of control ... and practically the only way of controlling them is smacking 'em. (11yrs)

Some children recognized that parents may consider a smack to be the quickest, most effective response to misbehaviour. A 16-year-old asserted:

> Sometimes adults say I've just given him 'a good smack'. That implies that they've really hit them hard. It also sounds as though they hit them within reason ... because the act that they did was that bad that they needed to be fixed. A quick fix was just to hit them.

Cathartic motivations

Parents' release of negative thoughts and emotions often drive their responses to their children. Children may be physically punished either more severely than a parent may have intended or unjustly because a physical response to a child may have occurred without forethought or self-control. Many children described parents in a temper:

> It's just like a rush that goes through your body when you smack someone. You feel better. They get a bit scared sometimes. They think they might have hurt you badly. (11yrs)

> It's basically just frustration … like it's a bit … punishment but I think it's just a bit letting out feelings [as well] … just when [parents are] really, really angry. (13yrs)

All of the children perceived that parents are sometimes or always angry when they punish them physically:

> The adults … get all mad and then they start smacking the children. (9yrs)

> A lot of parents just do it out of anger [and] might not know what they're doing when they hit them. They smack first and then think about what they've done. They stop and they realize they just hit one of the people they've loved most in the world. … I've got a really, really bad temper. I know if I hit someone I don't really think about what I'm doing first. I just go ballistic and I hit. (14yrs)

> Parents smack kids a lot … adults have got quite an aggressive temper. They get very angry … they can't control their temper so they just hit. (10yrs)

> I don't think Mum meant to hit … she just got over angry and smacked and didn't mean to hurt … 'cause they're in such anger … they don't think before they move. I don't think a lot of parents want to smack … it just happens like all of a sudden. (12yrs)

Children also described spontaneous physical punishment. An 11-year-old observed that when children's behaviour 'gets onto your nerves too much you smack' and, for a 13-year-old's mum, smacking 'is just a reflex'. Children recounted that parents:

> Smack and then the thing the child's done should only deserve a [telling] off and then they think …'what have I done? It's not done something so bad.' They feel awful. (10yrs)

> Wouldn't do it to hurt the child … some grown-ups only stop and think after they've done it. (8yrs)

> Smack first and they think about what they have done … because they can't control their temper. (10yrs)

> Got very angry at what the child's done and don't have time to think. They just hit the child. (12yrs)

Five of the 17 children interviewed individually thought that physical punishment only occurs when the parent is tired, stressed or angry. Eleven children thought that sometimes children are physically punished because parents are tired.

> Often they just get really tired and if you're doing the same thing like over and over again they just lose their temper. (10yrs)

> When they come home from work they'll feel like really tired, stressed out. You don't want to get your parents angry ... they just hit the child. (12yrs)

> If they are tired and the kid is being really annoying they might just hit them. (10yrs)

Children also recognized that sometimes parents smack children out of fear or concern for their safety:

> I might smack my children but ... prob'ly won't 'cause I know how it feels to be smacked. Maybe if they run away ... I might smack 'em and say 'don't do that again ... I was worried'. (12yrs)

> If they were running away ... you'd smack 'em to stop 'em ... or if they were near a cliff, you know, in danger and say gonna run across the road. They should only be really hitting them in the spur of the moment things. (10yrs)

Intergenerational explanations

Many children saw physical punishment as a learnt, cyclical response to children:

> Smacking will teach them to smack and then it would just keep going. Their parents might have smacked them ... and they think that's okay. (10yrs)

> It's just a type of discipline that most people do, and most people don't know that it can go through from generations to generations and how bad it really is. (8yrs)

> As the children get older they start to smack their children and then ... it just keeps going on and on through generations. (9yrs)

> It's like the pokies [poker machines]. It's addictive ... people have been doing it for so long ... you just do it. (11yrs)

> My mum smacks me but she probably got it from her mum. Parents are teaching you a bad lesson ... kids might copy what your mum's doing to their own children. (9yrs)

However, some children observed that parents have a choice:

> Parents have the choice of smacking or not, and they chose to smack ... they were prob'ly smacked when they were children and they think it's still the right way. (11yrs)

If people got smacked when they were kids then they could either ... just follow their parents or if they don't like it, then they'll just not do it to their kids because they know it's bad. (11yrs)

It's giving the message that it's okay to smack. It's just a big cycle ... people are gonna get smacked until someone finally doesn't smack in your family. (12yrs)

Ten of the 17 children interviewed individually anticipated that they would 'smack' their own children:

[Parents] smack you ... that's what I would prob'ly do if I had kids. (9yrs)

You probably won't think ... before you act ... like your parents have been smacked before as well, and their parents didn't think about it, and so you just do it before you think about it. (12yrs)

Some children associated smacking with the release of emotion. An 11-year-old anticipated smacking children:

Only if they don't be good ... it gets to your nerves too much.

Another commented:

I can imagine getting frustrated and slapping them. I don't think I could imagine hitting them really hard, um ... it's hard to know how annoyed you can get. (13yrs)

And when asked if she thought that she'd smack her children, a 10-year-old replied 'I might now an' then on the spur of the moment but I'll try not to'.

Some children associated smacking with a parent's responsibility to modify children's behaviours and therefore felt that it was probably what they will do when they are parents:

If I have to hit I will ... like if they do something badder. (8yrs)

Other children commented:

Maybe if they are not behaving well, if I had warned them, you know, with my voice ... and they still do it, maybe I'd smack them. (10yrs)

If it gets to the point where they been warned and threatened ... I think I would have to resort to that. I'm all for it but not with an object and not on the spur of the moment. (16yrs)

Of the six children interviewed individually who did not intend smacking their own children, three had never experienced physical punishment. However, some children planned not to punish their own children physically, given their recent experience of pain and emotional distress:

> If I smacked my children they won't be happy ... I don't reckon it's very nice 'cause it hurts them and I know what it's like to be hurt ... I don't want my children to be hurt. (9yrs)

> I don't think I'll smack ... if I have kids because I've experienced it and I don't like it ... it hurts. (11yrs)

> My mum stopped smacking me at around this age. Now she only smacks me if she really, really, really, really needs to, but that's not very often ... I don't think I'd smack my children because it would make them smack their children and their children would smack their children, and their children and their children, so it would go on and I really don't want that to happen. (8yrs)

Children who had not experienced physical punishment did not consider adopting the practice. Twelve-year-olds commented:

> I'm not brought up like that.

> It's fairly cruel to be smacking, um, since the people will probably grow up thinking that it's right to do that ... that telling them off or something won't get the message through, and they have to physically hurt them.

Many children described physical punishment as a norm which occurred because parents experienced it as children or they considered it to be quick and effective. Parents may also hit, children explained, because they don't know any other means of discipline or simply because they are allowed to.

A number of children who had been punished physically in an apparently loving and supportive environment appreciated the pedagogic reasons and the disciplinary continuum that their parents had made clear to them. Children also acknowledged the responsibilities that parents had, and the pressures that parents were under, and they rationalized parents' hurtful and disrespectful responses to them. Parents put 'morals into them' (16yrs) and didn't 'want them getting hurt or in trouble' (14yrs). This link has been noted in previous research focusing on the cultural contexts in which physical punishment occurs (Deater-Deckard *et al.*, 1996; Lansford *et al.*, 2004; Larzelere, 1996), and may explain why children may suffer minimal, if any, long-term effects of physical punishment. Some physically punished children nevertheless clearly expressed that there were better ways to discipline children without hurting them. Many recognized that parents hit them when they were angry, tired, and sometimes out of control. Like European-American children (Larzelere *et al.*, 1997), some children recognized that parental physical punishment is parent-focused, dismissive of children as people, and has the potential to escalate in severity.

Conclusion

Children revealed remarkable insights into the intergenerational transmission of parental reasoning and disciplinary behaviours. Children who had been smacked made connections between their parents being smacked as children, their parents smacking them, and the likelihood that as adults they may in turn smack their children. Children who had not been punished physically appreciated that parents had a responsibility to guide and place limitations on their behaviour. However, this was always achieved by non-violent means, and these children did not intend to use violence as a means of achieving compliance or resolving conflict with their own children: 'I've been brought up to sit down and talk' (12yrs). Children observed that parents have the choice whether to use physical punishment as a means of discipline and, in children's eyes, some parents unwisely choose to use it. It is significant that children know parents have a choice. This research suggested that making a decision, rather than spontaneously responding to children without forethought, may be a key factor in breaking such intergenerational cycles.

Children's contributions to this research suggest that it is adults' differing perceptions of children as a group or class rather than the characteristics of individual children in families that appear to determine how respectfully children are disciplined. Willow and Hyder (1998) made a similar observation. Mayall contends further that '[t]aking children seriously as people leads to shifts in thinking' (2000, p. 248). In the next chapter we consider the morality of physical punishment.

10

The morality of physical punishment

It's not the law that makes me feel that it's the wrong thing to do. It's more a morality kind of issue. It is degrees ... it's saying it's alright to give them a smack but it's not alright to hit them with any force, it's not alright to use a stick. ... I'd probably go with it's not acceptable, no means, no smacks even if it leaves no mark. (parent)

Introduction

Children have been characterized as 'becomings'. Yet, as Hengst observes 'under the current conditions of all-embracing and rapid social change, people of all ages and generations are "becomings"' (2003, p. 127). This recognition that adults are also 'becomings' challenges constructions of childhood that confine children to a lesser stage of evolution during which they become adults or achieve personhood. In Mason and Falloon's (1999) research, young people aged between 11 and 17 years strongly emphasized the perpetuation of structural inequality through children's devaluation and exclusion from adult society. Significantly, a fundamental tenet of children's rights arguments is recognition that children and babies are people (Newell, 1989). Moreover, children ought not be considered 'silent

Physical Punishment in Childhood: The Rights of the Child, by Bernadette J. Saunders and Chris Goddard
Copyright © 2010 John Wiley & Sons, Ltd.

objects of concern' because they have feelings and views of their own (Cobley, 1995).

Morality and legality are in many ways intertwined:

> [W]e may appeal to morality to tell us what the law ought to be, so we may appeal to the law as providing a pointer to sound thinking in the moral sphere ... the law has been changed in response to changes in 'popular morality'. But equally, law can influence the way people think in the moral sphere. (Cane, 2002, p. 14)

In this chapter we consider the morality of punishing children physically. We present participants' views on current legal responses to physical punishment and on law reform. Children's comments on alternatives, and their ideas about channels through which to communicate children's feelings and views, are also presented.

Is physical punishment morally justifiable?

Lord Shaftesbury maintained that 'what is morally right can never be politically wrong, and what is morally wrong can never be politically right'. At least three arguments appear in the literature positing reasons why physical punishment, even if it could be proved to be effective and harmless, is morally unjustifiable. The first argument contends that to cause people unnecessary pain is wrong and an affront to their human right to bodily integrity. Being a child and being hurt should not be synonymous (Daro and Gelles, 1992). Indeed, Freeman argues that 'distinctions between ordinary safe smacks and inhuman or degrading punishment' are 'morally bankrupt' (1999, p. 132). He implores us to envisage 'legislation which allowed husbands to smack their wives but withheld from them the power to use an implement!' (Freeman, 1999, p. 132). People's attitudes, he contends, are not changed 'by half measures'; laws can encourage people to behave morally even in relationships between parents and children, and adults must forgo their 'habit of hitting children because it is wrong ... as it is wrong to hit adults' (Freeman, 1999, p. 139).

The second argument suggests that physical punishment is morally unjustifiable because it is disrespectful to children who, like adults, are people. Newell contends that 'hitting people is wrong – and children are people too' (1989, p. ix). The third argument highlights children's vulnerability and dependence on adults, and proposes that children deserve at least equal, if not greater, protection from violence than adults. Saidla contends that positive human evolution depends on adults choosing not to hurt children because 'it is their right as individuals to grow to adulthood with their dignity intact', to reside 'in a world without fear of harm from their caretakers' and to be recognized as people 'who deserve our respect' (1992, p. 82).

It is difficult to justify physical punishment as a legitimate approach to child-rearing given that it has little association with desirable behaviour change. It fails, Carey (1994) contends, to improve children's mental abilities or moral reasoning, and children are not flawed because it is not used. Similarly, Mount (1995) outlines four arguments against physically punishing children, all of which appeared in participants' contributions to this research. The first he calls a 'human rights' argument that proposes that children have citizenship rights, and should be treated the same as other people; the second rests on the inability of physical punishment to achieve desired outcomes; the third emphasizes the links between physical punishment and child abuse; and, finally, physical punishment may contribute to adverse outcomes such as increased aggression and criminal behaviour. Others have contended that even if the latter three arguments failed entirely and physical punishment was proven to be effective, decisions regarding the use of physical punishment ought to rest not only on effectiveness but on parents' consideration of how ethical and humane it is as a response to children (Parke, 2002). Indeed, Freeman maintains that physical punishment 'teaches violence' and today's 'victims' will turn out to be 'tomorrow's violent criminals' (see also Margo and Stevens, 2008). Prohibiting physical punishment, Freeman argues, 'could thus be justified on utilitarian grounds' but 'even if it could be shown that it acted as a deterrent, it could not be justified on moral grounds' (1999, p. 139).

Adults' perspectives on current law and law reform

Given these moral arguments, continuing debates about possible long-term effects of physical punishment, and gradual law reform throughout the world (as outlined in Chapter 3), we explored participants' understanding of law related to physical punishment, the impact of this understanding on their attitudes and behaviour, and their views on law reform.

Confusion and misconceptions about lawful correction

It was apparent that at least some people in the state of Victoria were unsure about the legality of physical punishment, and some perceived community dissension about physical punishment:

> I think the nature of society today is that you are dead scared to physically punish your child. (grandparent)

> I thought you weren't allowed to in Australia, I thought that was the law. (parent)

> A lot of people don't know legally what they are allowed to do. Lots of people are of the opinion that they can't smack their children. You can ... but it has to be reasonable. (police officer)

Professionals who valued clear parameters as guidance, called for legal clarification:

> It should be clear legally what's acceptable and what's not acceptable. (social worker)

> A lot of people just don't know where they stand ... it probably should be clarified. (police officer)

When asked how the reasonableness of physical punishment was determined, a police officer replied:

> We normally sort of weigh up from the kids and from the parents what are the values in the household.

And another police officer made clear that those decisions about what is and what is not legally acceptable physical punishment may be more subjective than objective:

> There's nothing that's black and white in relation to physical punishment and what's appropriate and what's acceptable ... it's too complicated to have clearer guidelines. There are so many different circumstances that can affect the decision as to whether or not a criminal offence has been committed ... whether it's the age of the child, the form of the discipline that's been used ... the behaviour that they're correcting.

In some such cases, 'reasonable marks on a child' will not result in charges:

> [W]here the parents pushed them but they had then fallen off the chair and banged their head. If they had an injury from that we would write it off but if ... they punched them in the head and left a mark they would get charged. (police officer)

Privacy of the home

Some participants observed that the privacy of the home and the current prevalence of physical punishment would make restrictions on its use difficult to formulate and monitor:

It probably should be changed but that's really difficult for legislators. (grandmother)

There'd have to be varying opinion in every single household ... how are they going to administer that? (parent)

Arguments that what goes on in the home is nobody else's business may be used to defend parents' entitlement to raise their children without state interference:

Within the privacy of your own home ... the threat of legal action would affect some people, but certainly not others. (grandparent)

The law can mind its own business ... what happens in the privacy of the home most times people wouldn't know. It would be an absolute disaster if a child got a slap from its father and it was well deserved and then that father is brought up in court. That's going to be more damaging to family relationships than anything. (grandparent)

I really wouldn't give a damn .... what the Australian attitude is ... 'Do I want to have a Swedish model imposed on me? No'. (parent)

It's what feels right for me ... to change a law imposes some people's thoughts on a vast majority and if they wanna go out and use an implement ... at the end of the day, that's their business. (parent)

Though 34 of 40 adult participants thought that current laws that do not forbid implements should be changed, only 19 would accept a total ban on physical punishment. Many parents maintained that parents should have the right to discipline their children however they choose, without outside interference. One parent declared:

I probably would take no notice of it.

Other parents said:

You could make the law but the law wouldn't stand.

We're over-regulated by laws ... I don't like people telling me what to do with my child ... people have to be able to make their own judgements and decisions.

It's up to the parents. Parents have still got the right to say how they bring up their kids, not have the kids telling them what to do.

Concern was expressed that:

Some kids need it ... some kids are way out of hand. (parent)

In this context, some teachers also expressed concern:

> If it was illegal there'd be significant parents who still hit their child, and would be much quieter about it and less likely to be picked up. When there is still a strong attachment between the child and the parents, the involvement of the police is going to freak out the child.

> It would be a hornet's nest if they [banned physical punishment] … people would be dragged up for smacking their kids.

Law reform proposals

Adult participants were generally cautious about law reform:

> I would be quite sceptical … I wouldn't be optimistic. I would certainly be prepared to listen. (grandparent)

They were asked how they would react to a partial ban on physical punishment specifying no implements, only hitting on hands and bottom, not hard enough to leave a red mark. For some:

> That would be a step in the right direction – saying to the public … you don't have any right to be whacking children across the head or using implements. So that would perhaps be better than what's in place now.

Most felt that it would be unacceptable to specify where on the body a parent may hit a child but some approved of specifying the legs, the ankles, the backside, and the hand. Some raised concerns about hitting a child on the face and head, the genitals, and above the waist.

Thirty-five adults would willingly support a law that forbade the use of implements to discipline children. One parent pointed out that hitting children with implements 'would make it very easy for people to just go overboard', and a social worker highlighted intriguing double standards:

> I don't think it's legally defensible to do that to an animal, so why would it be okay to do it to a child?

Other participants' arguments against the use of implements included:

> I don't think you should be using straps … whips or anything on your kids. It's cruelty. (parent)

> To use an implement adds a further element of harshness and pain and power and physical damage to a child. (social worker)

> It is assault. I don't think there is any justification for hitting a child with an implement … any situation where that would be reasonable. (social worker)

> It might be in the rashest moment of frustration and the heat of the moment ... but if you can stop for that split second and actually pick something up and use it to hit a child ... that is just so wrong. (psychologist)

From one parent's perspective, the type and size of the implement, the size of the child and the intensity of the force used are all variables that may be used in arguments for or against the use of implements to hit children:

> So much would depend on the situation, how hard the child is hit, whether it was a big ... or a little wooden spoon. If you've got a big hulking boy of 17 and you hit him with a wooden spoon ...

In a similar vein, many professional participants commented that a parent's physical force alone can be more damaging than using an implement:

> Younger children are much more likely to sustain serious, more fatal, injuries ... it is the intensity of the attack more than what is used to hit them. (social worker)

> Many of the children I've seen ... have been killed with bare hands. An implement hasn't been used ... so I don't know that banning implements is an answer. When you have got the social situations that I see every day, legislation is a waste of time ... I don't know [whether] a child that has been whacked around the legs with a spoon or a stick is worse off than a child who has been whacked around the face with a hand. (health worker)

Questions about limiting physical punishment to actions that did not leave marks on a child produced the following rather worrying, but probably realistic, comment:

> That would be a bit hard, to leave a red mark, or not leave a red mark, that would be almost impossible ... If it gets to the stage of bruising it's a different matter. (grandparent)

Several participants felt that it would be unjust if the law prohibited or limited physical punishment as it is an inevitable human response (an idea that is also discussed in Chapter 9). Professionals remarked:

> We're just all human beings and you can smack your child. I don't want parents to feel like there's a policeman hanging over their back fence. (social worker)

> The practical part of me says the courts would be so clogged up and the other part of me also says that none of us are perfect either and I ... feel for the frustration that some parents might experience. (psychologist)

Some parents' observations added weight to these views:

> Mother Nature permits us to protect our children from harm with physical restraint, and restraint is sometimes hitting, so I really wouldn't like to see it put into law.

> Parents are likely to hit their children ... to react angrily, and then ... our world would be full of kids taking their parents to court ... and that is wrong. There should be allowance there.

However, 22 adults would accept a law that forbade people who are not blood relatives of the child, such as parents' partners, step-parents and child minders, from physically punishing a child in their care. Arguments against such a law included:

> I don't think it's acceptable for someone else than a parent but ... there might be times where that parent feels it is appropriate. (teacher)

> We're put in the place of the parent many times. The law can get involved into areas where it's really got no business. (grandparent)

> When ... parents used to send their child to me, I used to tell them if they did anything wrong, I will hit them. (parent)

> If you're a step-parent ... I don't think there should be any legal distinction there. (parent)

Twenty-nine adults thought that forbidding parents from hitting children in public places would not be an effective legal change:

> It only means they do it in their house and no one sees it. (psychologist)

> You are pushing it underground. (teacher)

> They can do it at home in secret. (grandparent)

> If they're not allowed to do that then no one sees what's happening. (parent)

> It's more humiliating to everyone but maybe it's better they're not doing it behind closed doors. (parent)

Perceived as parents' possessions, children's physical punishment at home and in public may be considered 'up to the individual parent' (parent):

> If you go shopping you see kids really causing an absolute strain to their parents and if a smack on the bottom can stop ... it's their child. (parent)

Further, some parents justified publicly hitting children who are out of control or in danger:

A slap, well administered, publicly is a last resort. (grandparent)

In the supermarkets ... if they're pulling things off the shelf you might have to give them a little bit of a tap. (grandparent)

That's where they need it most. Ever been to a shopping centre? (grandparent)

If a little girl runs on the road ... of course you're going to smack her. (parent)

In contrast, a health worker felt that a ban on physical punishment in public would be a good idea:

It might make people stop and think and control themselves a bit more.

The following parent's suggestion was more challenging:

The parent isn't likely to be abusive in a public place. Maybe forbid them ... in privacy. They'd have to go out to a shopping mall.

Should physical punishment be banned?

Some participants would not be satisfied with law reform of a limited nature because limiting rather than completely banning physical punishment effectively condones it:

It's a principle thing ... 'cause if you say you can't hit the child [under certain conditions] it's like condoning that it's okay to hit, and I don't believe that it's okay at all. (social worker)

It's all a bit disgusting really to say, 'you can hit them here, can't hit them there' ... 'they're allowed to hit them this much and not leave a red mark'. (parent)

Two-thirds of the 21 professional participants and five of the parents thought that parents should not be allowed to punish their children physically at all. Physical punishment was associated with a society that generally does not demonstrate respect for others.

We should be aspiring to a community that holds as a firm principle respect between individuals ... adult to child, adult to adult, powerful to less powerful. We should be teaching [children] about being empathetic towards peers ... being able to appreciate and understand vulnerabilities in their friends and other children ... that is the basis of parenting. (psychologist)

> There's such a focus in society on [having] a good home ... job ... car ... rather than respecting each other ... nurturing and caring. (social worker)

Physical punishment was seen as a blight on childhood:

> It's awful if a child doesn't have assertiveness. Some kids will be visibly timid in the presence of their parents ... their life just squashed out of them. (parent)

> It shouldn't be part of a child's experience of childhood. (social worker)

> People should not smack or hit anyone. (social worker)

> Physical punishment hurts the child ... physically, emotionally, in every way. (social worker)

> For a lot of children it mars their experience of their childhood. (social worker)

> Nobody deserves to be physically hurt. (social worker)

Many participants thought a non-violent society was something to strive for:

> In an ideal world physical punishment ... shouldn't be part of childhood. (teacher)

> I can understand the influence of having been hit ... I can't understand that with education and support and challenge to that view that people wouldn't want to change that. (social worker)

> Childhood should be a time of great wonder and growth and development and sunshine and tadpoles ... from an ideal world ... smacking's not acceptable and it should be considered an assault ... but society's values and views of smacking isn't at that point. (social worker)

> Ideally physical punishment doesn't have a place in childhood. (parent)

Most adult participants suggested that society's attitudes to the physical punishment of children ought to be changed:

> If they can be taught to bring up their kids by other means ... go for it, a kinder and gentler world. (parent)

> It's good for our development as humans ... to move away from violence. (parent)

> Get rid of this notion that somehow it's okay to hit a child when people wouldn't tolerate an adult hitting another adult ... there is that absurd discrepancy, contradiction. (teacher)

Several professionals highlighted that physical violence of any kind toward children was an infringement of children's rights:

> If they are physically punishing a child they are abusing that child's rights. (teacher)

> Physical discipline is depersonalized so that … it's not a parent hitting a child … it's an act of shaping a child's behaviour. So the outcome is what a parent holds on to when they're hitting rather than what they're doing. No adult has a right to hit a child. Just like no adult has a right to hit another adult. (psychologist)

> [Children have] a right not to be in pain … not to be hit. (parent)

> I have a right not to be hit by anybody at any time and I don't see why a child shouldn't expect the same.

Several social workers emphasized alternatives to physical punishment:

> There is a whole range of ways of disciplining a child that are appropriate and necessary … physical punishment doesn't have to be the integral part of discipline.

> We shouldn't be condoning violent behaviour … parents resort to physical discipline far too readily. If we educate parents they will be more likely to utilize another strategy.

> There has been a real change in people's perception of the law, and what they are allowed and not allowed to do, and people are becoming more aware that it is not acceptable, and yet we know it still occurs. I don't think people know how to respond in other ways. It is harmful in a number of ways to the child, and there are other ways of disciplining.

> There needs to be a balance between going down a justice system track and addressing families' difficulties to change their behaviour. Until awareness is raised about the impact of physical discipline … the emotional harm … the physical harm … what it does to children's self esteem and their ability to relate to people … and [until] parents are given alternative strategies, I don't think that any effective change can occur.

Others felt physical punishment was simply wrong:

> I just don't think people should hit people, full stop. (psychologist)

> It doesn't matter if there is not pain. It is just the act itself. (teacher)

Some contended that law reform needs to carry educative penalties:

> There have to be some kind of consequences. Otherwise … 'who are you to tell me that it's allowed or not allowed?' If you do physically discipline your

child then they have to attend parenting classes rather than a fine. Child-care, kindergarten, schools have a crucial role in monitoring. There has to be a whole logistic way of addressing it. (social worker)

However, other participants felt that for significant groups of parents, law reform that banned or further limited physical punishment would inevitably be meaningless:

I have got no doubt that violence just becomes an acceptable method of solving problems, an acceptable end point of an argument. When life has turned to shit … laws mean nothing. (health worker)

The role of law in stimulating attitudinal and behavioural change

Generally adult participants felt that a comprehensive, multi-faceted approach would be required to bring about changes in community attitudes:

Through community education, through change in the law … there has to be a pretty comprehensive approach. (teacher)

However, participants varied in their opinions about whether law reform should be an impetus for change or a reflection of change brought about by community education and increased support for all parents. Many adults drew attention to the difficulties of parenting, regardless of circumstances. Social workers described being a parent as a 'daily challenge', one of 'the hardest' jobs:

You're not always sure what to do … but you have to think quick and deal with it in an appropriate way. It would be good if parents know about as many methods as possible so they can choose hopefully the non-violent one. (parent)

There needs to be more of an acceptance that parenting is an incredibly difficult job … and that people at times will need help and that doesn't mean that they are bad parents. We should be able to assist them. (social worker)

Nobody lets people know that it's a difficult, specialized job and that you need help, support and education. People don't know that childhood is a particularly vulnerable time of development. They don't just need food, clothing and a roof over their heads … it's a lot more to do with building a child's self-esteem. (social worker)

The lack of non-stigmatizing parenting supports and education was also highlighted:

> I don't think there is enough general recognition that the role of parents is a tough one ... so that the people who are struggling as parents end up feeling like they've got a problem rather than that it's normal, and although there's an increasing number of supports and support services, it's still not enough. Parenting is an important, crucial role and people need information sessions [when] considering becoming parents ... ongoing support and training for people who have become parents ... services available for parenting children at different stages ... and there also has to be financial assistance to allow people to go to those training sessions. (social worker)

> There is an openness to start changing ... it is a matter of doing that in a way that doesn't intimidate ... in a supportive way ... we need to tackle it from the point of view of let's do more of this, rather than let's stop doing that, so that parents are equipped to have other strategies. (social worker)

> [We need] parent education seminars [that] normalize the idea that it is okay to need and want information ... guidance and support as a parent rather than having to be something that is based on a deficit. (social worker)

Underlying problems, such as low levels of education, social skills deficits and financial pressures were seen as important to target and address:

> You take one step back from a child with the injuries and start to talk to them about their life ... at home, what's on the table. A lot of their parents have no respect for the law. A lot of these incidents occur on the spur of the moment. So I am not convinced that [legislation] would change ... behaviour immediately but if there was an effective campaign of selling the idea, and secondly there was a backup or a support service: 'If you are feeling like doing this to your five-year-old, here's what we can do'. ... We just don't have the social supports for this enormous, vulnerable group of people out there. [A ban] might be a goal that we can work towards if we have got educational strategies ... but we are not near it now. [We need to] develop home visiting services, some interested person that they could mentor to ... 'I know my relief is coming tomorrow, I can get through until then'. [For] many people there is no relief ... the high risk group is money very well spent. (health worker)

> More educated parents have more knowledge of alternative disciplinary strategies and parents in a lower socio-economic group have less knowledge of how to manage stressful situations. Education is a fundamental issue and identifying parents who use physical discipline and the factors behind that ... if it's a lack of social support, financial stresses, other stresses, drugs, attack all those, and you'll be halfway there. (social worker)

> We have to make parenting-type education attractive to people ... because they will say, 'you can't tell me how to raise my kids'. Education in terms of how to relate to people is really important ... you can't start that too early. (psychologist)

Parents who have relied on physical punishment as discipline need particular support:

> You can't just whack a law in place because it would be more detrimental. You'd have to have ... training programmes and support networks for when people felt that they couldn't cope. (parent)

> More funding for ... playgroups ... where you see different styles of parenting ... community support agencies. If they were to bring in a law it would need a couple of years of free education and debate, discussion and classes around what else can you do ... rather than just being cheated of their one way of managing their kids. It used to be quite abusive in schools so I don't doubt they could do it. (social worker)

> [Provide] resources and help for people [who] have been used to responding with a smack. Parental support is very important ... not only relating to their parenting, helping them develop as people ... has a flow-on effect. (social worker)

Along with calls for 'legislative change', participants anticipated a need 'to set expectations' through media and key community organizations:

> A mass community awareness campaign underpinned by a whole lot of community-based infrastructure and support services to facilitate that happening ... [and] some work with parent communities in schools. (social worker)

> An education campaign. ... When there's a law, people start to change their attitudes. They have to, they're required to. (social worker)

> Media, through schools ... it's like changing any kind of legislation, if you wanna change the rules you gotta let everybody know. (police officer)

> Run an education programme on television saying, 'Smacking children is bad ... there's other ways of responding'. Start people thinking this isn't a good thing to do. Some people, because of their own peer group, condone each other's smacking. If you can start getting messages into that social group that it's not okay, and there's other ways, you may change some behaviour. If it was illegal ... Hitting is about not coping. We need to be able to respond to people ... by supporting them. (teacher)

Hard-hitting Transport Accident Commission (TAC) campaigns have successfully influenced driving behaviour and curbed road accidents in Victoria, Australia. Similar campaigns were recommended:

Some kind of public awareness campaign springs to mind. TAC ads tend to be really effective. (parent)

First legislation ... lots of huge campaigns like TAC awareness campaigns. Education right from primary schools and ... running parenting programmes and offering more supports to family. (social worker)

There has to be a kind of societal acceptance that it is not the right thing to do. Ads will generate discussion, and a lot of people will disagree totally [but] it is worth the discussion and the angst. (social worker)

Some participants re-emphasized the power of language, as discussed in Chapter 7, to assist community attitudinal and behavioural change:

Explaining to parents that smacking is a form of assault can assist people's awareness of it as something different from the perception that they previously held. (social worker)

Raising public awareness, using terms like 'beating' and 'assault' to make people aware that even what has been considered in the past to be acceptable really is a physical assault. (parent)

Educating and supporting children was also considered integral to breaking intergenerational cycles of physical punishment:

We need to start with the children ... start in the primary schools so that you are actually changing society's attitudes to what is acceptable and what is not. (teacher)

There could be more thought given to how issues of family and parenting could be integrated into the secondary school system. (social worker)

Some kids in intolerable family situations need more lifelines taking them outside the family ... I don't think the law is probably the problem. (parent)

If you were to introduce that law [a ban] in the home, where it is not visible, it can only be through the child ... or brothers and sisters getting to the point where they would report it. You would have to have an education campaign that would advise children, so it would have to go through the school. (parent)

In summary, many professionals in our research favoured a complete ban on physical punishment. However, several professionals prioritized non-stigmatizing social supports and education about effective alternatives to physical punishment above legislative change. The idea of law reform encouraging and promoting attitudinal change was put forward by other professional participants. Importantly, participants generally considered that law reform would need to be accompanied by both parenting education and support to break intergenerational cycles of physical punishment.

Children's reflections on physical punishment, current law and law reform

Most children would not contemplate hitting an adult, yet children know that parents are allowed to hit and physically punish them. Many children accommodate this anomaly with few reservations. When asked why adults don't smack adults, a 10-year-old replied:

> I think it's against the law, isn't it? If you [have] physical contact with someone, like punching 'em, it's against the law. You'd go to jail. And that's exact same for smacking. But if it's in your house, if you're a kid, and it's in the house it's okay because they're your kids.

As with many adult participants, children's views about the legality of using physical punishment on children were often based on their own experiences and what they had heard or observed. A 12-year-old remarked that children normalize physical punishment because:

> They don't wanna think that their parents are doing something sort of illegal almost. It's almost illegal.

Another believed that implements for physical punishment 'haven't been used for ages. They're now illegal' (12 yrs).

Thirteen of the 17 children interviewed individually contended that parents should be allowed to punish children physically:

> Parents probably feel bad for smacking ... but maybe that was the right thing to do. (12 yrs)

> They can hit them with their hands sometimes if they've been a little bit bad ...but don't use an instrument. (9 yrs)

> Parents should be allowed to smack because it's a tough job. (10 yrs)

> Parents should be allowed but ... not to the extent where they bruise and bleed and stuff like that. (14 yrs)

> Sometimes if you do get hit you know that you shouldn't do it any more so that is okay a little bit. (10 yrs)

A 10-year-old disapproved of implement use, but felt that allowing parents to physically discipline children was 'a good law'. Another 10-year-old stated, 'I don't think they should be able to do it'. She added that she would like law reform 'but others may not'. With similar insight some children, even if disapproving of physical punishment, expressed reservations about legal prohibition of physical punishment:

> I think the government should try and encourage people not to smack [but] I think a lot of people would continue on doing that even if they make any laws against it. I think it is a bit drastic … a lot of people would get very angry about it. (12 yrs)

Eleven of the 17 children interviewed individually thought that children should sometimes be punished physically, but they proposed limitations:

> If they need a good lesson maybe … just a little smack maybe might give them a lesson but not a smack that hurts – one that will give them a warning. (10 yrs)

> If you blew up a house or killed someone you should be smacked … if you haven't done something too bad then you shouldn't be smacked. (9 yrs)

Children unanimously condemned implement use. They talked about implements hurting and frightening children more than hitting with the hand. Hitting 'bare skin, will hurt', but:

> When you've got a wooden spoon or something it's like an extension of the hand and it comes in harder and faster and it'll actually bruise and hurt you. (14 yrs)

> It's … even more intimidating than just with your hand … beating with a stick … it's just way intimidating. (10 yrs)

> I don't think a parent should ever do something to a child that's gonna cause any real physical pain … when you start getting into belts, sticks and stuff, that can happen. (13 yrs)

An eight-year-old conceded:

> Parents should only scare them … Like they would say, 'if you do it again I'll like hit you with it', an' then they wouldn't do it again.

Most children maintained that parents shouldn't smack babies:

> They should be a model, a role model to them … they're all new and fresh. They shouldn't be smacked. (12 yrs)

Babies, children observed, have 'sensitive skin' (12 yrs); 'they're just little' (10 yrs); 'they don't know what's going on' (8 yrs); 'it leaves a red mark there for about 10 weeks' rather than 'an hour or a minute' (11 yrs); and 'you could kill it' (10 yrs). Children further asserted:

> I don't think people should be smacked but a baby's body is not like totally developed yet ... so it might hurt them worse than it would an older child. (10 yrs)

> You don't know if a baby was crying ... for some reason ... and you don't know what the baby is trying to say to you. So you say, 'come on, stop crying' and you keep on hitting it and hitting it and the baby will just keep on crying if you hit it. (10 yrs)

> Smacking a baby because it is crying is not going to fix it because they don't have the thought power to think, 'Oh I shouldn't be doing that'. (16 yrs)

> Babies are very fragile and maybe it'll be alright to smack them on the bottom or something but why take the risk? (10 yrs)

Five children thought that it was acceptable to smack a child over 12 years old:

> It depends how bad they are ... yeah, if they do something really wrong. (9 yrs)

> Sometimes, because they've been like really, really, really, really, really, really, really, really, really naughty. (11 yrs)

> They should know better than to go and break the rules. (14 yrs)

> They're older than babies and because they're much stronger than little kids ... it should be okay to do it. They're stronger so they can handle stuff, not as strong as adults. (8 yrs)

A 12-year-old imposed the limitation 'not across the face' and a 10-year-old maintained that with 12-year-olds 'You should talk and settle it'. Other children felt:

> It's just stupid smacking someone 12 and up. (10 yrs)

> It's too old. Parents should be able to control their temper in smacking. Just punish them in another way. (12 yrs)

> You just ground them, you don't smack them. (9 yrs)

> They're old enough to realize what they've done, so maybe there's the punishment to go to your room or minutes off your bedtime ... or something. (12 yrs)

They know what's right and what's wrong, so ... just give them time-out instead of being smacked. (8 yrs)

A 16-year-old declared that physical punishment of older children:

Affects them emotionally as well because ... they've got more of a viewpoint on the world and emotionally things start to happen to them. So I think if a 12-year-old is smacked they might take it in the wrong way ... and that can really affect them.

Some children maintained that it should be 'a rule' not to hit children (12 yrs):

It should be illegal ... to smack their child. (8 yrs)

You shouldn't smack your kids ... they should make the law that you're not allowed to smack. Smacking is wrong and it hurts. (12 yrs)

Smacking should be illegal ... forever, for everyone. It's absolutely ridiculous. (10 yrs)

Other children were convinced that parents should not be allowed to 'smack':

No – 'cause it would hurt them and they could prob'ly like not forget for their whole like whole life and when they're really old and they remember they could prob'ly have a heart attack. (8 yrs)

It shouldn't be done. It doesn't work as a disciplinary method and it just hurts people ... physically and mentally. Just because they made a mistake and they did something wrong they're gonna get punished in like an extreme way. I think it's just not on. (12 yrs)

It hurts very badly ... and I'd just like to say I just wish parents wouldn't do that because I don't reckon it should be right. (11 yrs)

It hurts and just 'cause they did something wrong doesn't mean they [parents] should do something wrong too. (8 yrs)

Messages for adults

If adults heard the conversations that we're having I think that they'd be able to see why smacking is bad and why we shouldn't smack. (8-yr-old in a focus group)

Many children were enthusiastic that adults should learn their views about children, childhood, physical punishment and its alternatives. Some hoped that they could 'help adults see things in a different way' (16 yrs). An eight-year-old commented:

> Since adults are older, they think they know most stuff but sometimes they don't … sometimes they're mistaken.

Children talked about wanting respect, fair treatment, and some recognition:

> Children are our future so they have got to be important. Parents think hitting children is sort of their right. I guess parents have gotta learn to respect children. (13 yrs)

> Parents should respect their children … not smack them. (11 yrs)

> I'd like the adults to actually listen instead of ignoring children's thinking. (12 yrs)

> People should be treated equally the same, like one shouldn't get more than the other in ways of better treatment, like treat them better just because they're older or younger. (10 yrs)

> People have said smacking is discipline but I don't agree with it … I just find it a bit funny, a bit silly … to get a person to do something, rather than talk to them, you have to use physical violence. I just think there might be a better way than doing that. (12 yrs)

A 13-year-old talked about adult disrespect and 'abuse of power' that extended beyond just children:

> There is a problem … with how adults treat children, but then there is a problem with how adults treat adults, and how children treat children. Generally humans don't treat each other as well as they could. Abuse of power can be the issue. (13 yrs)

Children observed inherent contradictions in adults' use of physical punishment as a means of discipline. Physical punishment:

> Hurts when it's getting done to you and hurts both people's feelings. Like the person that hit you thinks, 'Oh I've done the wrong thing … I shouldn't have done that'. The child feels sad and bad and awful because their parents had hit them. (12 yrs)

> The adults feel bad … feel guilty. I don't think it teaches the child much. If it's not making the adult feel good, what the hell's the point of it? I don't think there is any point of an adult punishing a child physically. (13 yrs)

It hurts the kids, and it upsets the adults if they've done it, so it's stupid both ways. It hurts both people. If you're a parent, they're sad, and the kid's sad. It's kinda stupid really. What in the world point is it for doing it? (9 yrs)

It's a bad habit they could get into. If they didn't like being smacked they shouldn't do it to others. (12 yrs)

If they're feeling bad about hitting their kid, they shouldn't be doing it. If the adult was hurting doing it at all, he would stop it. (10 yrs)

Some children wanted parents to think about what it feels like to be smacked:

They should be a role model to them and shouldn't smack them. You wouldn't like it if someone smacked you, so you shouldn't be smacking. (12 yrs)

Children would like adults to know that smacking hurts and they'd like it to stop. You shouldn't smack people. You shouldn't smack children, 'cause it's hurting them. Treat others like you treat yourself. (8 yrs)

Parents whom children looked up to as role models may fall short of children's expectations:

You should make them feel that they've done something wrong ... but instead you're acting like a child yourself. Parents are being just as bad as the child by smacking them. (12 yrs)

They haven't ... obviously thought about it that much because there are ways to punish people that's better because it's actually teaching them not to do that. (11 yrs)

It's just the way you bring your child up. You set the example like ... how they're meant to treat people ... so it's really up to you in what you set as the example. (9 yrs)

The child will grow up with that intention of smacking, [thinking] hurting people is the right thing. They might end up hating their parents because of that. (12 yrs)

I think my mum and dad have like actually matured in a way because they haven't smacked me since I was like four. (12 yrs)

Children wondered why parents physically hurt and distress the children that they love and for whom they want the best outcomes:

I think anyone who has been smacked wouldn't like smacking ... sometimes kids just like run away ... they don't like to face their fears and stuff, and I don't think that they should just smack ya because nothing is as precious as your children's feelings. (11 yrs)

A kid is so impressionable for them to think that sometimes mummy or daddy smacks me … I don't think they are really old enough to understand what they've done wrong basically so I don't think that's acceptable. (13 yrs)

Ideas about alternatives to physical punishment

Child participants had all experienced discipline other than physical punishment. Many children preferred reasoning, and they wanted parents to know that they can discipline them using more effective, non-violent methods:

It's just not the way … hitting, like you shouldn't hit people … because there's a better way of doing things than hurting someone. (12 yrs)

I don't think adults should smack children. They should talk to them … 'cause [smacking] will teach the child to smack. (10 yrs).

It's like a kinda first choice; 'cause some people make dumb first choices … and there is other ways than just smacking. (11 yrs)

Reasoning

These children suggested why reasoning, explanation and discussion are more effective:

Sometimes even for them to say that what you did is really bad. You don't need a punishment because you feel bad enough for what you have already done but it makes you know not to do it next time. (12 yrs)

It's easier to talk so then you can like settle it, and it doesn't like turn into an argument with crying and stuff, 'cause it's hurting. If you can't get their attention maybe like speak a little louder but I don't think you should hit. One of our punishments is, if we're naughty, we either lose some pocket money or lose a star from our star chart. (10 yrs)

They should sit down and talk to them [children] and ask, 'Why'd you do it?'. (12 yrs)

It's better to get growled at than getting smacked. They make you cry but it's better than making you cry and sore. (11 yrs)

Grounding or withdrawal of privileges and treats

Some children suggested removal of things they enjoyed:

If they're really attached to something, taking that thing away from them is just as good if not better than a smack. (16 yrs)

Minutes ... or hours off your bedtime ... ban them from something, say that you're not going to the party. (12 yrs)

Missing out on something, like an icy-pole [ice cream lolly] ... I'd ground them if it's pretty bad ... not let them watch their favourite movie. (8 yrs)

There's no need to smack when there are things ... that are worse that won't hurt ... like they could ground you for a month and stop you from having treats. (11 yrs)

When my brother does something wrong they [parents] try to get him to say sorry, and then they give him his toys back, and if he does it again ... they take it away for a little bit longer until he understands that he has done something wrong. (9 yrs)

Banned from the footy for a month ... from pocket money ... from videos and from having friends over. I'd prob'ly give them a different punishment than smack them. I would prob'ly threaten them or take something off them. (9 yrs)

Curb children's free time

Children noted the effectiveness of alternatives to physical punishment which impose upon children's free time:

Sit them down and talk to them. If my parents said, 'you're not allowed to watch telly for a week', I wouldn't go do [what they didn't want me to do]. But if they said, 'I'm gonna smack you across the bum' ... they'd smack you once and that would be it but telly, it's longer ... [a smack] stops you from being bored. (14 yrs)

Time out, sending them to their room ... banned for a while from TV and playing ... not let them go outside for the rest of the day, or like just let them do their homework when they don't have to. They would be more sad if they were banned from something than getting a smack because like that means they couldn't play their favourite game or something like that. (8 yrs)

Disapproving glances

Knowing they have disappointed or angered their parents may be enough to entice children to behave reasonably, because most children want to please their parents:

I'd just try to punish them by looking at them in a way that they'll know that I'm angry or upset with what they're doing. (12 yrs)

> You could just get very angry at them … I know that works quite often. They just know the look, they know that [the parent is] angry and they won't do it again. (10 yrs)

'Time-out'

Both parents and children may benefit from a temporary period of separation to calm down and review the situation:

> Just say, 'go to your bedroom', or give them a warning … don't smack them. (8 yrs)

> Tell them to go to their room for three hours, and take everything that's fun for them out. (10 yrs)

> You could go to your room for some minutes or an hour if you were really, really naughty … instead of smacking them. (8 yrs)

Grabbing/restraint

Particularly in situations where children are in danger, restraint and an explanation was proposed as a better option than physically hurting a child:

> Tell them off, yell at them … or grab them. Grabbing is a lot easier, a lot better, than smacking. (10 yrs)

Positive discipline

Any discipline that taught positive behaviours and had positive long-term effects may be preferred:

> They should just do something … that would just help the children grow up and be nice. (9 yrs)

Ideas about communication channels

Campaigns and demonstrations

Some children suggested voicing objection to physical punishment through campaigns and street marches:

> Set up a campaign. That won't stop all of it but it might stop some. (11 yrs)

The Aboriginals [had] a walk to make John Howard [former Australian Prime Minister] say sorry. I think we should have a walk ... to say: 'Stop hitting children, it's not doing anything to help the kid'. This is not the way to ... discipline, by hitting a child. Why? Think about it ... any hitting, you can see a bruise but you can't see how it mentally affects someone and they'll carry that right through their childhood, right through their adulthood. (12 yrs)

One child thought that it might be more effective if adults spoke out on children's behalf:

A lot of people think the children are just being spoilt brats ... just asking for too much. I think if a lot of parents spoke out it would be more of an effect. (12 yrs).

Some children suggested that media exposure, advertising, literature and parent education may encourage adults to adopt alternative means of discipline:

Tell the parents not to smack them, putting ads on the television, little booklets in the supermarkets [and] next to the card stand like all the newsagents have. (8 yrs)

Talking to them ... because if they know how other parents treat their children, they may realize that it's wrong to do what they're doing, so they may change. They prob'ly know it's not good to smack ... because they know it hurts. (10 yrs).

A good way to stop parents from smacking their children is to like have it on the news ... like [reporters] going around and talking to kids and seeing what they think about smacking and why they shouldn't do it. (11 yrs)

Adults should be treating children pretty much the same way [as themselves]. They [children] still need to learn though. Give them [parents] methods instead of smacking [Parents] might not think it is wrong; so tell them that it's wrong ... try and encourage people not to smack. (12 yrs)

Conclusion

The literature on attitudes towards physical punishment in Sweden, Germany and more recently in New Zealand, and the success of their physical punishment bans (Bussmann, 2004; Durrant, 1999; Nielsen Omnibus

Survey, 2008), are encouraging in contexts such as the state of Victoria where, as this and other research (Tucci *et al.*, 2002; 2006) suggests, attitudes are moving in the direction of at least limited prohibition of physical punishment. However, while many participants favoured the banning of implements to hit children, further law reform was less well supported. Freeman (2008), drawing on data from Sweden attributed to the ban on physical punishment, allays concerns about prosecutions and the intrusion into families expected to result from a ban. He notes that child assault reports have increased but prosecutions have not, and social work involvement in families has decreased. 'Outlawing corporal punishment', he maintains, 'is more likely to lead to fewer prosecutions, because there will be less abuse, delinquency and violent crime ... corporal punishment teaches violence' (Freeman, 2008, p. 10). However, this research suggests that the privacy of the home and parental discretion in relation to the disciplining of children remain firmly held entitlements.

Children emphasized that if parents are allowed to punish them physically there should be limits: no implements, not on the face, babies and children 12 and over should be exempt, and bruises and injuries should not occur. However, children's willingness to suggest compromises rather than a complete ban is perhaps a reflection of their sense of powerlessness, and their lack of participation in discussions about matters that affect them.

11

An ideal childhood

In this research, a 12-year-old child suggested that if adults parent 'the right way', teach children 'about the world and look after' them, childhood can be 'the happiest time of your life … if treated badly it can wreck the rest of your life'. Another 12-year-old observed that when a child is born he or she is 'all new and fresh' and the child's parent 'should be a role model'.

From the moment of birth, a child's experiences will develop his or her attributes as a person. Children depend on their parents and other adults for love, understanding, guidance and a positive sense of self. Children usually delight in giving their parents pleasure, and most parents cherish their children and are proud of their smallest achievements. Most parents feel concerned when their children are hurt, unwell or unhappy. Why then do some parents who love their children punish them physically and, by so doing, suggest to children that physical aggression may be a means to a desirable end?

Many parents in this research regretted punishing their children physically, and few considered it to be effective or necessary. Being a parent is challenging and can be difficult. It can also be rewarding, particularly when parents are confident in their roles and are well supported by family, friends, communities and supportive services. Children need discipline so that they can learn ways to survive and develop to their full potential. Physical punishment is unnecessary, may be harmful (Gershoff, 2002a), and there are

Physical Punishment in Childhood: The Rights of the Child, by Bernadette J. Saunders and Chris Goddard
Copyright © 2010 John Wiley & Sons, Ltd.

alternatives (see, for example, Durrant, 2007). In this research, children who had not been physically punished could not imagine hitting or hurting children to discipline them:

> I've been brought up to sit down and talk. (11 yrs)

Thirty years ago in Sweden a decision was made to 'use words as arguments, not blows' to 'talk to people ... not beat them', to 'convince ... children with words [not] with violence' (Barnombudsmannen, 2008). In an ideal childhood, physical punishment does not have a place.

Advancing children's perspectives

Suffering physical punishment, and being forced to live with other children's physical punishment at home and in public, may continually reinforce children's perception of themselves as lesser beings. In the preceding chapters we have presented children's comments and insights, together with those of adults. At times, children's voices refute adults' perceptions, such as when adults suggest that being hit does not hurt. Sometimes adults' ideas are child-focused and aligned with children's perspectives; for example when discussing respect, physical integrity and protection from assault. At other times, some adults and children appear strangely in agreement over issues such as parents' right to hit children. This perplexing agreement may stem from children's learned perception of themselves as less than adults. In turn this may be a consequence of being subjected to physical punishment or may arise from awareness that many children are subjected to physical punishment.

The minimization of a person's importance and value to society enables degrading treatment to occur. Historically, children have belonged to parents who have been relatively free to enforce their children's obedience by almost any means. Violence directed at a possession may, from the owner's viewpoint, be considered an acceptable, private matter. Similarities between the way women were once commonly treated and the current treatment of children are not easily dismissed.

Many children in this research described adults' power over children: 'Adults have more power ... we have to do what they say ... adults can hurt' (8 yrs); 'It's what keeps us apart, adults more important than children' (10 yrs); 'If you are a kid, it doesn't really matter' (9 yrs). Children drew attention to the double-edged nature of adult power which heightens children's vulnerability: 'Adults have more power ... they have a greater say, they are more respected in the community'; and adults 'have power over a child ...

abuse of power can be … the issue' (13 yrs). Children readily perceive inconsistency and double standards in contexts where adults command respect from children, and are granted greater societal respect. Those same adults, however, can justify and condone assaulting small and dependent children.

The importance of language

Words are powerful in both perpetuating and changing attitudes and behaviour. This is particularly true in relation to words used to describe children and physical punishment of children. Replacing words such as 'smack' and 'spank' with words such as 'hit' and 'assault' may challenge perceptions that physically hurting a child as discipline is normal and reasonable. Recognizing each child's humanity and individuality through language is also important. Objectification of the child through language, referring to the child as 'it', and reference to children as 'kids', reflects perceptions of the child as less than an adult. Changes in language have motivated greater respect for other groups of people. It is time for children to receive similar consideration.

The rights of the child

> I'd also like to say to the parents, not only the government, to the parents, this is not the way to discipline, by hitting a child. Why? Think about it for a minute, any hitting, you can see a bruise but you can't see how it mentally affects someone and they'll carry that right through their childhood, right through their adulthood. (12 yrs)

Children are a vulnerable group of people in society. Physical punishment may threaten their health and safety. Any resultant injuries may simply be 'a matter of chance' (Gonzalez *et al.*, 2008, p. 763). Many parents and children described physical punishment as painful, frightening, disrespectful and degrading. Professionals interviewed in the course of this research had seen injuries that resulted from excessive physical punishment, and they had heard children talk about their distress and damaged relationships with their parents.

Children's rights are embedded in human rights documents and stated explicitly in the United Nations Convention on the Rights of the Child (1989). However, children's rights are only granted to the extent that adults will accommodate them, and the rights of the child are often pitted against the rights of the adult. The Convention legitimizes, and indeed compels, comment and action in response to adults' treatment of children. It thus motivates a climate for constructive change in which the state is required to intervene to safeguard children's interests (Lansdown, 1994). Positive changes in children's status were evident in this research:

> Children are more heard and valued and recognized ... as individuals rather than just being somebody's kid that you can do what you like with. (social worker)

However, evidence for positive change was not common in the comments of either children or adults. Change that involves modification of entrenched attitudes and behaviours is slow and incremental.

The way forward

There is an oft-cited proverb commonly attributed to African cultures: 'It takes a whole village to raise a child'. Our variation is: 'It takes a whole community to raise children without physical punishment'. We suggest this for a number of reasons. Firstly, children will continue to be physically punished by adults until whole communities recognize children as individuals with the same rights to physical integrity and protection from assault as adults. Secondly, this recognition of children as individuals in their own right needs to be reflected in the language that everyone in the community uses to refer to children and to physical actions directed at children. Thirdly, communities need to recognize children as active participants who make valuable contributions to society. Finally, those communities need to recognize the important and difficult role that parents play in nurturing and contributing to the development of children. Governments must be compelled to provide all parents and children with non-stigmatized support and education that will enhance every parent's parenting practices. Whole communities may then have less hesitation about endorsing a statement in law that children deserve the same protection from assault as adults. Violence directed at children will then be perceived to be as wrong as violence directed at adults.

Children silenced no longer

> I'd like the adults to ... actually listen instead of ignoring the children's thinking. (11 yrs)

The insights and wisdom apparent in children's comments demonstrate that there is much that adults can learn when children are valued as persons, consulted and accorded dignity and respect. As one eight-year-old commented, adults do not 'have to smack because you can choose'. The definition of child abuse has broadened since professional interest in the problem was finally awakened in the early 1960s. Physical punishment, nearly 50 years later, is still not included in that definition. Children's voices are still silenced.

Tolerance of physical punishment and its subsequent intergenerational transmission are unlikely to change until it is acknowledged that:

Children are our future so they have got to be important. (13 yrs)

If adults allow children and young people to speak, and pay attention to what they say, we 'may see things in a different way' (16 yrs). We may even come to recognize that 'there's a better way ... than hurting someone' (12 yrs).

References

Agathonos-Georgopoulou, H. (1997) Child maltreatment in Greece: a review of research. *Child Abuse Review*, **6**, 257–71.

Alanen, L. (2003) Childhoods: the generational ordering of social relations, in *Childhood in Generational Perspective* (eds B. Mayall and H. Zeiher), London: University of London, pp. 27–45.

Alcorn, B. (2000) 'Safety-valve' effect of spanking. *British Medical Journal* – Rapid responses. Available at http://bmj.bmjjournals.com/cgi/eletters/320/7230/261, **320**, 261–2 [Accessed 16 June 2009].

Alderson, P. (2004) Ethics, in *Doing Research with Children and Young People* (eds S. Fraser, V. Lewis, S. Ding, M. Kellet and C. Robinson), London: Sage, pp. 97–112.

Alizadeh, H., Applequist, K. and Coolidge, F.L. (2007) Parental self-confidence, parenting styles, and corporal punishment in families of ADHD children in Iran. *Child Abuse & Neglect*, **31**, 567–72.

Alston, M. and Bowles, W. (2003) *Research for Social Workers: An Introduction to Method*, 2nd edn, New South Wales: Allen & Unwin.

Ambikapathy, P. (2003) *Law Reform Advocacy on the Proposal to Repeal Provocation – Similarities with the Defence of Domestic Discipline of Children*. Tasmania: Office of the Commissioner for Children.

American Humane Association (2008) Children's Services Position Statements, p. 10. Available at http://www.americanhumane.org/about-us/who-we-are/position-statements/ [Accessed 21 June 2009]

Physical Punishment in Childhood: The Rights of the Child, by Bernadette J. Saunders and Chris Goddard
Copyright © 2010 John Wiley & Sons, Ltd.

Annerback, E.-M., Lindell, C., Svedin, C. and Gustafsson, P. (2007) Severe child abuse: a study of cases reported to the police. *Acta Paediatrica*, **96**, 1760–64.

Archard, D. (1993) *Children: Rights and Childhood*. London: Routledge.

Argles, P. (1980) Attachment and Child Abuse. *British Journal of Child Abuse*, **10**, 33–42.

The Argus Index (2005) Available at www.nla.gov.au/apps/argus?action= Menu&type=home [Accessed 16 June 2009].

Ariès, P. (1962) *Centuries of Childhood*. London: Jonathan Cape.

Arminio, J.L. and Hultgren, F.H. (2002) Breaking out from the shadow: the question of criteria in qualitative research. *Journal of College Student Development*, **43**, 446–60.

Ashton, V. (2001) The relationship between attitudes toward corporal punishment and the perception and reporting of child maltreatment. *Child Abuse & Neglect*, **25**, 389–99.

Australian Law Reform Commission (1997) *'Seen and Heard': Priority for Children in the Legal Process*. Canberra: Australian Government Publishing Service.

Bagaric, M. (2009) When is a smack just a smack? *Courier-Mail*, 5 January.

Bailey, M. (2003) Child protection in the 21st century: the corporal punishment debate in Canada. *Family Court Review*, **41**, 508.

Bainham, A. (1999) Corporal punishment of children: a caning for the United Kingdom. *The Cambridge Law Journal*, **2**, 291–3.

Ball, J. (2009) Intergenerational transmission of abuse of incarcerated fathers: a study of the measurement of abuse. *Journal of Family Issues*, **30**, 371–90.

Bandura, A. (1973) *Aggression: A Social Learning Perspective*. Englewood Cliffs, CA: Prentice Hall.

Barbour, R. (2001) Checklists for improving rigour in qualitative research: a case of the tail wagging the dog? *British Medical Journal*, **322**, 1115–17.

Barnes, J. (1984) *The Complete Works of Aristotle*. Princeton: Princeton University Press.

Barnombudsmannen. (2008) The Swedish Corporal Punishment Ban. Available at http://www.bo.se/Adfinity.aspx?pageid=90 [Accessed 21 June 2009].

Bartkowski, J. (1995) Spare the rod …, or spare the child? Divergent perspectives on conservative protestant child discipline. *Review of Religion Research*, **37**, 97–116.

Bauman, L. (1996) Assessing the causal effect of childhood corporal punishment on adult violent behavior. *Pediatrics*, **98**, 842–4.

Baumrind, D. (1966) Effects of authoritative parental control on child behavior. *Child Development*, **37**, 887–907.

Baumrind, D. (1996) A blanket injunction against disciplinary use of spanking is not warranted by the data. *Pediatrics*, **98**, 828–31.

Baumrind, D., Larzelere, R. and Cowan, P. (2002) Ordinary physical punishment: is it harmful? Comment on Gershoff (2002) *Psychological Bulletin*, **128**, 580–89.

Bayer, J., Hiscock, H., Ukoumunne, A. and Wake, M. (2008) Early childhood aetiology of mental health problems: a longitudinal population-based study. *Child Psychology and Psychiatry*, **49**, 1166–74.

Beauchamp, T.L. and Walters, L. (eds) (1989) *Contemporary Issues in Bioethics.* Belmont, CA: Wadsworth.

Beckett, C. (2005) The Swedish myth: the corporal punishment ban and child death statistics. *British Journal of Social Work*, **35**, 125–38.

Bedi, G. and Goddard, C. (2007) Intimate partner violence: what are the impacts on children? *Australian Psychologist*, **42**, 66–77.

Belsky, J. (1980) Child maltreatment: an ecological integration. *American Psychologist*, **35**, 320–35.

Belsky, J. and Vondra, J. (1989) Lessons from child abuse: the determinants of parenting, in *Child Maltreatment: Theory and Research on the Causes and Consequences of Child Abuse and Neglect* (eds D. Cicchetti and V. Carlson), Cambridge: Cambridge University Press, pp. 153–203.

Benjet, C. and Kazdin, A. (2003) Spanking children: the controversies, findings and new directions. *Clinical Psychology Review*, **23**, 197–24.

Berg, B.L. (2004) *Qualitative Research Methods for the Social Sciences.* Boston: Allyn and Bacon.

Birrell, R.G. and Birrell, J.H.W. (1966) The 'maltreatment syndrome' in children. *The Medical Journal of Australia*, **2**, 1134–8.

Bitensky, S. (2006) *Corporal Punishment of Children: A Human Rights Violation.* Ardsley: Transnational Publishers, Inc.

Blackstone, W. (1979) *Commentaries on the Laws of England – A Facsimile of the First Edition of 1765–1769.* Chicago: University of Chicago Press.

Blanchard, A. (1993) Violence in families: the effect on children. *Family Matters*, **34**, 31–6.

Bloor, M., Frankland, J., Thomas, M. and Robson, K. (2001) *Focus Groups in Social Research.* London: Sage.

Boen, J. (2008) Ruling blurs line on abuse: difference between discipline and abuse just got grayer. *The News Sentinel*, 21 July.

Boreham, G. (1996) Child-death review attacks staff failings. *The Age*, 31 October.

Boss, P. (1994) *Physical Punishment in Child Rearing.* South Melbourne: Oz Child.

Bower-Russa, M., Knutson, J. and Wineburger, A. (2001) Disciplinary history, adult disciplinary attitudes, and risk for abusive parenting. *Journal of Community Psychology*, **29**, 219–40.

Bower, M. and Knutson, J. (1996) Attitudes toward physical discipline as a function of disciplinary history and self-labelling as physically abused. *Child Abuse & Neglect*, **20**, 689–99.

Boyson, R. (2002) *Equal Protection for Children.* London: NSPCC.

Bradwell v. Illinois 83 US (16 Wall.) 130 (1872). Available at http://supreme.justia.com/us/83/130/case.html [Accessed 21 June 2009].

Bronitt, S. and McSherry, B. (2001) *Principles of Criminal Law.* Sydney: LBC Information Services.

Browne, K. (1995) Predicting maltreatment, in *Assessment of Parenting* (eds P. Reder and C. Lucey), London: Routledge, pp. 118–30.

Bullock, R. (1989) Social research, in *Child Care Research: Policy and Practice* (ed B. Kahan), London: Hodder and Stoughton, pp. 14–29.

Buntain-Ricklefs, J., Kemper, K., Bell, M. and Babonis, T. (1994) Punishments: what predicts adult approval? *Child Abuse & Neglect*, **18**, 945–55.

Burdekin, B. (1994) Transforming the Convention into law and practice, in *Children's Rights: Issues for the Nineties* (Vol. 22), (ed K. Healey), Balmain, New South Wales: Spinney Press, pp. 8–12.

Burnette, A. (1997) Corporal punishment … Yes. *Children's Legal Rights Journal*, **17**, 5–6.

Burrell, B., Thompson, B. and Sexton, D. (1994) Spotlight on practice: predicting child abuse potential across family types. *Child Abuse & Neglect*, **18**, 1039–49.

Bussmann, K.D. (2004) Evaluating the subtle impact of a ban on corporal punishment of children in Germany. *Child Abuse Review*, **13**, 292–311.

Butchart, A., Harvey, A., Mian, M. and Furniss, T. (2006) *Preventing Child Maltreatment: A Guide to Taking Action and Generating Evidence*. Geneva: World Health Organization and International Society for the Prevention of Child Abuse and Neglect.

Byng-Hall, J. (1995) *Rewriting Family Scripts: Improvisations and Systems Change*. New York: The Guilford Press.

Cameron, D. (1985) *Feminism and Linguistic Theory*. London: Macmillan Press.

Cane, P. (2002) *Responsibility in Law and Morality*. Oxford: Hart.

Capaldi, D., Pears, K., Patterson, G. and Owen, L. (2003) Continuity of parenting practices across generations in an at-risk sample: a prospective comparison of direct and mediated associations. *Journal of Abnormal Child Psychology*, **31**, 127–42.

Carey, T. (1994) Spare the rod and spoil the child. Is this a sensible justification for the use of physical punishment in child rearing? *Child Abuse & Neglect*, **18**, 1005–10.

Carpenter v. Commonwealth, 186 Va. 851, 44 S.E.2d 419, 424 (Va. 1947)).

Carter, M. (2004) Corporal punishment and prosecutorial discretion in Canada. *The International Journal of Children's Rights*, **12**, 41–70.

Carvel, J. (2008) Teen smacking surprises NSPCC. *The Guardian*, 8 October.

Cashmore, J., and de Haas, N. (1995) *Legal and Social Aspects of the Physical Punishment of Children*. Canberra: Australian Govt. Publishing Service.

Castan, N. (1976) Divers aspects de la contrainte maritale, d'après lesdocuments judiciaries du XV111 è siècle. Translated by K. Ryal. Paper presented to the American Sociological Association Convention, August, New York.

Cavanagh, K., Dobash, R.E. and Dobash, P. (2007) The murder of children by fathers in the context of child abuse. *Child Abuse & Neglect*, **31**, 731–746.

Chan, J., Elliot, J., Chow, Y. and Thomas, J. (2002) Does professional and public opinion in child abuse differ? An issue of cross-cultural concern. *Child Abuse Review*, **11**, 359–79.

Chen, Z. and Kaplan, H. (2001) Intergenerational transmission of constructive parenting. *Journal of Marriage and the Family*, **63**, 17–31.

Children Act (2004). Available at http://www.opsi.gov.uk/acts/acts2004/20040031. htm [Accessed 21 June 2009].

Children, Youth and Families Act 2005 (Vic) Available at http://www.austlii.edu. au/au/legis/vic/consol_act/cyafa2005252/ [Accessed 4 September 2009].

Chisholm, R. (2005) Post-Separation Parenting: Public Debates, Reports, and Policies. Paper presented at Australian Institute of Family Studies Conference, Melbourne, 9 February. Available at http://www.aifs.gov.au/institute/afrc9/chisholm.pdf [Accessed 23 June 2009].

Clarke, J. (2004) Histories of childhood, in *Childhood Studies: An Introduction* (ed D. Wyse), Malden: Blackwell, pp. 3–12.

Claussen, A. and Crittendon, P. (1991) Physical and psychological maltreatment: relations among types of maltreatment. *Child Abuse & Neglect*, **15**, 5–18.

Clement, M. and Cumberland, C. (2007) Physical violence and psychological aggression towards children: five year trends in practices and attitudes from two population surveys. *Child Abuse & Neglect*, **31**, 1001–11.

Clément, M.-è., Bouchard, C., Jetté, M. and Laferrière, S. (2000) La violence familiale dans la vie des enfants du Québec, 1999 [Family violence in the lives of children in Quebec]. Québec, Canada: Institut de la Statistique du Québec.

Cleverley, J., and Philips, D.C. (1987) *Visions of Childhood: Influential Models from Locke to Spock*. New South Wales: Allen & Unwin.

Cobley, C. (1995) *Child Abuse and the Law*. London: Cavendish Publishing.

Cobley, C. and Sanders, T. (2006) *Non-Accidental Head Injury in Young Children*. London: Jessica Kingsley.

Cohen, P. (1996) How can generative theories of the effects of punishment be tested? *Pediatrics*, **98**, 834–6.

Coleman, W. and Howard, B. (1996) Family-focused behavioral pediatrics: clinical techniques for primary care. *Pediatrics Review*, **16**, 448–55.

Combs-Orme, T. and Cain, D. (2008) Predictors of mothers' use of spanking with their infants. *Child Abuse & Neglect*, **32**, 649–57.

Committee on the Rights of the Child (2006) *GENERAL COMMENT No. 8 (2006)*. Available at http://www.unhchr.ch/tbs/doc.nsf/(Symbol)/CRC.C.GC.8. En?OpenDocument [Accessed 21 June 2009].

Concluding Observations CRC – Australia – September 2005. Available at http://www.bayefsky.com/docs.php/area/conclobs/treaty/crc/opt/0/state/9/node/3/filename/australia_t4_crc_40) [Accessed 21 June 2009].

Conger, R., Neppl, T., Kim, K. and Scaramella, L. (2003) Angry and aggressive behavior across three generations: a prospective, longitudinal study of parents and children. *Journal of Abnormal Child Psychology*, **31**, 143–60.

Connelly, C.D. and Straus, M.A. (1992) Mother's age and risk for physical abuse. *Child Abuse & Neglect*, **16**, 709–18.

Conway-Turner, K. and Cherrin, S. (1998) *Women, Families, and Feminist Politics: A Global Exploration*. New York: Harrington Park Press.

Cooper, D. (1993) *Child Abuse Revisited: Children, Society and Social Work*. Buckingham: Open University Press.

Corbett, A. (Australia, House of Representatives, 2001) Debates, 14063. Available at http://www.parliament.nsw.gov.au/prod/PARLMENT/hansArt.nsf/V3Key/LC20010531006 [Accessed 21 June 2009].

Corby, B. (2006) *Child Abuse: Towards a Knowledge Base*, 3rd edn, Maidenhead: Open University Press.

Council of Europe (2008) *Off the Books! Guidance for Europe's Parliaments on Law Reform to Eliminate Corporal Punishment of Children*. France: Council of Europe.

Crimes Act 1900 (NSW) S.61AA (2) (b) Available at http://www.austlii.edu.au/ [Accessed 21 June 2009].

Crimes Act (Vic) 1958. Available at http://www.austlii.edu.au [Accessed 21 June 2009].

Criminal Justice (Scotland) Act (2003) Available at http://www.opsi.gov.uk/ legislation/scotland/acts2003/20030007.htm [Accessed 21 June 2009].

Crittendon, P. and Craig, S. (1990) Developmental trends in the nature of child homicide. *Journal of Interpersonal Violence*, **5**, 202–16.

Crown Prosecution Service (2007) *Reasonable Chastisement Research Report*. Available at http://www.cps.gov.uk/Publications/research/chastisement.html [Accessed 20 February 2009].

Cunningham, H. (1995) *Children and Childhood in Western Society since 1500*. London: Longman.

Daly, M. and Wilson, M. (1991) A reply to Gelles: stepchildren are disproportionately abused, and diverse forms of violence can share causal factors. *Human Nature*, **2**, 419–26.

Daro, D. (ed) (2006) *World Perspectives on Child Abuse*, 7th edn, West Chicago: The International Society for Prevention of Child Abuse and Neglect.

Daro, D. and Gelles, R. (1992) Public attitudes and behaviors with respect to child abuse prevention. *Journal of Interpersonal Violence*, **7**, 517–31.

Darragh, D. (2005) Son thrashed over pocket money. *The West Australian*, 24 September.

Davies, J. (1996) How the state failed to save Baby Dillion. *The Age*, 20 October.

Davis, P. (1991) Stranger intervention into child punishment in public places. *Social Problems*, **38**, 227–46.

Davis, P.W. (1996) Threats of corporal punishment as verbal aggression: a naturalistic study. *Child Abuse & Neglect*, **20**, 289–304.

Dawkins, R. (1976) *The Selfish Gene*. Oxford: Oxford University Press.

Deater-Deckard, K. and Dodge, K. (1997) Externalising behaviour problems and discipline revisited: non-linear effects and variation by culture, context and gender. *Psychological Inquiry*, **8**, 161–75.

Deater-Deckard, K., Dodge, K., Bates, J. and Pettit, G. (1996) Physical discipline among African American and European American mothers: links to children's externalizing behaviors. *Developmental Psychology*, **32**, 1065–72.

Deater-Deckard, K., Lansford, J.E., Dodge, K., Pettit, G. and Bates, J. (2003) The development of attitudes about physical punishment: an 8-year longitudinal study. *Journal of Family Psychology*, **17**, 351–60.

Deater-Deckard, K. and Starr, S. (1996) Parenting stress among dual-earner mothers and fathers: are there gender differences? *Journal of Family Psychology*, **10**, 45–59.

Deitz, T. (2000) Disciplining children: characteristics associated with the use of corporal punishment. *Child Abuse & Neglect*, **24**, 1529–42.

De Mause, L. (ed) (1976) *The History of Childhood*. London: Souvenir Press.

Department of Health (2000) *Protecting Children, Supporting Parents: A Consultation Document on the Physical Punishment of Children*. London: Department of Health.

Detrick, S. (1998) European Court of Human Rights: Judgement in the Case of A v. the United Kingdom. *The International Journal of Human Rights*, **6**, 335–6.

Di Lalla, L. and Gottsman, I. (1991) Biological and genetic contributors to violence: wisdom's untold tale. *Psychological Bulletin*, **109**, 125–9.

Dobash, R.E. and Dobash, R. (1979) *Violence against Wives: A Case against the Patriarchy*. New York: The Free Press.

Dobbs, T., Smith, A. and Taylor, N. (2006) No, we don't get a say, children just suffer the consequences: children talk about family discipline. *The International Journal of Children's Rights*, **14**, 137–56.

Dobbs, T. and Wood, B. (2004) *The Views of Children in Aotearoa New Zealand on Physical Punishment*. Paper presented at the 15th International Congress on Child Abuse and Neglect, Brisbane, Australia.

Dobson, J. (1992) *The New Dare To Discipline*. Wheaton, IL: Tyndale House.

Durkheim, E. (1979). Childhood, in *Durkheim: Essays on Morals and Education* (ed W.F. Pickering), London: Routledge, pp. 27–32.

Durrant, J. (1994) The abolition of corporal punishment in Canada: parents' vs children's rights. *The International Journal of Children's Rights*, **2**, 129–36.

Durrant, J. (1999) Evaluating the success of Sweden's corporal punishment ban. *Child Abuse & Neglect*, **21**, 435–48.

Durrant, J. (2004) Whose body is it anyway? Physical punishment, children's rights and parental responsibility. *Childrenz Issues*, **8**, 23–6.

Durrant, J. (2006) From mopping up the damage to preventing the flood: the role of social policy in preventing violence against children. *Social Policy Journal of New Zealand*, **28**, 1–17.

Durrant, J. (2007) *Positive Discipline: What it is and How to Do it*. Sweden: Save the Children.

Durrant, J. (2008) Physical punishment, culture, and rights: current issues for professionals. *Journal of Development and Behavioral Pediatrics*, **29**, 55–66.

Durrant, J. and Olsen, G.M. (1997) Parenting and public policy: contextualising the Swedish corporal punishment ban. *Journal of Social Welfare and Family Law*, **19**, 443–61.

Durrant, J., Rose-Krasnor, L. and Broberg, A. (2003) Physical punishment and maternal beliefs in Sweden and Canada. *Journal of Comparative Family Studies*, **34**, 585–611.

Durrant, J., Sigvaldason, N. and Bednar, L. (2008) What did the Canadian public learn from the 2004 Supreme Court decision on physical punishment? *International Journal of Children's Rights*, **16**, 229–47.

Edelson, J.L. (1999) Children's witnessing of adult domestic violence. *Journal of Interpersonal Violence*, **14**, 839–70.

Edgar, P. (1994) Do children have rights?, in *Children's Rights: Issues for the Nineties* (Vol. 22) (ed K. Healey), New South Wales: Spinney Press, pp. 5–7.

Egeland, B. (1993) A history of abuse is a major risk factor for abusing the next generation, in *Current Controversies on Family Violence* (eds R. Gelles and D. Loseke), Newbury Park, CA: Sage, pp. 197–208.

Elliman, D. and Lynch, M. (2000) The physical punishment of children. *Archives of Disease in Childhood*, **83**, 196–8.

Ellison, C. and Bradshaw, M. (2009) Religious beliefs, sociopolitical ideology, and attitudes toward corporal punishment. *Journal of Family Issues*, **30**, 320–40.

Else, J.F. and Sanford, M.J. (1987) Nonsexist language in social work journals: not a trivial pursuit. *Social Work*, January/February, 52–9.

End All Corporal Punishment of Children. (2009) Global Initiative e-newsletter Issue 6 (January) and website. Available at http://www.endcorporalpunishment. org/ [Accessed 21 June 2009].

Engfer, A. and Schneewind, K. (1982) Causes and consequences of harsh physical punishment. *Child Abuse & Neglect*, **6**, 129–39.

Ezzy, D. (2002) *Qualitative Analysis: Practice and Innovation*. St Leonards, New South Wales: Allen & Unwin.

Fagan v. Metropolitan Police Commissioner (1969) *Law Reports, Queens Bench Division, 439*. London: Incorporated Council of Law Reporting for England and Wales.

Family Law Amendment (Shared Parent Responsibility) Act 2006 (Cth) Available at http://www.austlii.edu.au/ [Accessed 21 June 2009].

Family Law Reform Act 1995 (Cth) Available at http://www.austlii.edu.au/ [Accessed 21 June 2009].

Ferguson, S. and Webber, N. (1996) They got it wrong, says Gran. *Herald Sun*, 31 October.

Fergusson, D. and Lynskey, M. (1997) Physical punishment/maltreatment during childhood and adjusting in young adulthood. *Child Abuse & Neglect*, **21**, 617–30.

Fine, G.A. and Sandstrom, K.L. (1988) *Knowing Children: Participant Observation with Minors*. Newbury Park, CA: Sage.

Flynn, C. (1996) Normative support for corporal punishment: attitudes, correlates and implications. *Aggression and Violent Behavior*, **1**, 47–55.

Ford, K., Sankey, J. and Crisp, J. (2007) Development of children's assent documents using a child-centred approach. *Journal of Child Health Care*, **11**, 19–28.

Forrester, D. and Harwin, J. (2000) Monitoring children's rights globally: can child abuse be measured internationally? *Child Abuse Review*, **9**, 427–38.

Foster, S., and Gingell, B. (1999) Parental chastisement and Article 3 of the European Convention. *The Journal of Social Welfare and Family Law*, **21**, 187–93.

Foxley, B. (1974) *Emile/Jean Jacques Rousseau: translated* [from the French] *by Barbara Foxley*. London: Dent.

Freeman, J. (2007) Why it remains important to take children's rights seriously. *International Journal of Children's Rights*, **15**, 5–23.

Freeman, M. (1983) *The Rights and Wrongs of Children*. London: Frances Pinter.

Freeman, M. (1994) Legislating for child abuse, in *Reforms on Child Abuse* (ed A. Levy), London: Hawksmere, pp. 18–41.

Freeman, M. (1998) The sociology of children and children's rights. *The International Journal of Children's Rights*, **6**, 433–44.

Freeman, M. (1999) Children are unbeatable. *Children & Society*, **13**, 130–41.

Freeman, M. (2008) *Can we Conquer Child Abuse if we don't Outlaw Physical Chastisement of Children?* Paper presented at ISPCAN Congress, Hong Kong, 9 September.

Futterman, M. (2003) Seeking a standard: reconciling child abuse and condoned child rearing practices among different cultures. *The University of Miami Inter-American Law Review*, **34**, 491–514.

Gagne, M., Tourigny, M., Joly, J. and Pouliot-Lapointe, J. (2007) Predictors of adult attitudes toward corporal physical punishment of children. *Journal of Interpersonal Violence*, **22**, 1285–1304.

Gandevia, B. (1978) *Tears often Shed: Child Health and Welfare in Australia from 1788*. New South Wales: Charter Books.

Garbarino, J. (1994) Can most maltreatment be prevented? in *Controversial Issues in Child Welfare* (eds E. Gambrill and T.J. Stein), Boston: Allen & Unwin, pp. 49–52.

Garbarino, J. (1996) CAN Reflections on 20 years of searching. *Child Abuse & Neglect*, **20**, 157–60.

Garner, R. (1998) Fundamentally Speaking: application of Ohio's violence laws in parental discipline cases. *University of Toledo Law Review*, **30**, 1–29.

Garvey, C., Gross, D., Delaney, K. and Fogg, L. (2000) Discipline across generations. *Nurse Practitioner Forum*, **11**, 132–40.

Gelles, R. (1991) Physical violence, child abuse, and child homicide: a continuum of violence, or distinct behaviors. *Human Nature*, **2**, 59–72.

Gelles, R. (1996) *The Book of David*. New York: Basic Books.

Gelles, R. and Cornell, C.P. (1990) *Intimate Violence in Families*. Beverly Hills: Sage.

Gelles, R. and Straus, M. (1988) *Intimate Violence: The Causes and Consequences of Abuse in the American Family*. New York: Touchstone.

Gelzinis, P. (2007) Spanking law won't hit where it really hurts. *Boston Herald*, 28 November.

Gershoff, E. (2002a) Corporal punishment by parents and associated child behaviors and experience: a meta-analytic and theoretical review. *Psychological Bulletin*, **128**, 539–79.

Gershoff, E. (2002b) Corporal punishment, physical abuse, and the burden of proof: reply to Baumrind, Larzelere and Cowan (2002), Holden (2002), and Parke (2002). *Psychological Bulletin*, **128**, 602–11.

Gershoff, E. and Bitensky, S. (2007) The case against corporal punishment of children. *Psychology, Public Policy and Law*, **13**, 231–72.

Ghate, D., Hazel, N., Creighton, S., Finch, S. and Field, J. (2003) *The National Study of Parents, Children and Discipline in Britain: Summary of Key Findings*. London: Policy Research Bureau.

Gilchrist, I. (2002) Thrashing blamed on heritage. *Herald Sun*, 16 May.

Giles-Sims, J. and Lockhart, C. (2005) Culturally shaped patterns of disciplining children. *Journal of Family Issues*, **26**, 196–218.

Giles-Sims, J., Straus, M.A. and Sugarman, D.B. (1995) Child, maternal, and family characteristics associated with spanking. *Family Relations*, **44**, 170–76.

Gil, D. (1970) *Violence against Children: Physical Child Abuse in the United States*. Cambridge: Harvard University Press.

Gillick v. West Norfolk & Wisbech Area Health Authority and Department of Health & Social Security (1985). Available at http://www.hrcr.org/safrica/ childrens_rights/Gillick_WestNorfolk.htm [Accessed 21 June 2009].

Gillies, P. (1997) *Criminal Law*. New South Wales: LBC Information Services.

Ginn, D. (1996) *The Fence on the Cliff*. Ourimbah, Australia: Bookbound.

Giovannoni, J.M. and Beccera, R.M. (1979) *Defining Child Abuse*. New York: The Free Press.

Gittens, D. (1998) *The Child in Question*. New York: St Martin's Press.

Goddard, C. (1993) Daniel's day in court. *The Age*, 22 November.

Goddard, C. (1994). Lessons from the life and death of Daniel Valerio. *Montage*, June 12.

Goddard, C. (1995a) Kids deserve better. *Herald Sun*, 9 May.

Goddard, C. (1995b) Words, words, words: even the parliamentarians are the very models of post-modernists. *Children Australia*, **20**, 38–9.

Goddard, C. (1996) *Child Abuse and Child Protection: A Guide for Health, Education and Welfare Workers*. South Melbourne: Churchill Livingstone.

Goddard, C. (2000) A case of repeated abuse. *The Age*, 23 June.

Goddard, C. (2003) A role fit for Hollingworth. *The Age*, 6 May.

Goddard, C. (2007) Cody lived life short and died long. *Herald Sun*, 16 August.

Goddard, C. and Carew, R. (1993) *Responding to Children: Child Welfare Practice*. Melbourne: Longman Cheshire.

Goddard, C. and Liddell, M. (1995) Child abuse fatalities and the media: lessons from a case study. *Child Abuse Review*, **4**, 356–64.

Goddard, C. and Saunders, B.J. (2000) The gender neglect and textual abuse of children in the print media. *Child Abuse Review*, **9**, 37–48.

Goddard, C. and Saunders, B.J. (2001a) *Child Abuse and the Media 14*. Melbourne: Australian Institute of Family Studies.

Goddard, C. and Saunders, B.J. (2001b) Journalists as agents and language as an instrument of social control: a child protection case study. *Children Australia*, **26**, 26–30.

Goddard, C., Saunders, B.J., Stanley, J. and Tucci, J. (2002) *A Study in Confusion: Factors Which Affect the Decisions of Community Professionals When Reporting Child Abuse and Neglect*. Ringwood, Victoria: Australian Childhood Foundation.

Goddard, C., and Tucci, J. (2007) Tragedy to last a lifetime. *Herald Sun*, 5 April.

Goldner, V. and Taylor, Z. (2004) Helpless mum hit toddler. *Herald Sun*, 3 April.

Gonzalez, M., Durrant, J., Chabot, M., Trocme, N. and Brown, J. (2008) What predicts injury from physical punishment? A test of the typologies of violence hypothesis. *Child Abuse & Neglect*, **32**, 752–65.

Gough, B. and Reavey, P. (1997) Parental accounts regarding the physical punishment of children: discourses of dis/empowerment. *Child Abuse & Neglect*, **21**, 417–30.

Gough, D. (1996) Defining the problem. *Child Abuse & Neglect*, **20**, 993–1002.

Gracia, E. and Herrero, J. (2008) Beliefs in the necessity of corporal punishment of children and public perceptions of child abuse as a social problem. *Child Abuse & Neglect*, **32**, 1058–62.

Graziano, A. (1994) Why we should study sub-abusive violence against children. *Journal of Interpersonal Violence*, **9**, 412–19.

Graziano, A., Hamblen, J. and Plante, W. (1996) Sub-abusive violence in child-rearing in middle-class American families. *Pediatrics*, **98**, 845–8.

Graziano, A. and Namaste, K. (1990) Parental use of physical punishment in child discipline: a survey of 679 college students. *Journal of Interpersonal Violence*, **5**, 449–63.

Greig, A. and Taylor, J. (1999) *Doing Research with Children*. London: Sage.

Greven, P. (1990) *Spare the Rod: The Religious Roots of Punishment and the Psychological Impact of Abuse*. New York: Knopf.

Gulbenkian Foundation Commission (1995) *Children and Violence*. London: Gulbenkian Foundation.

Hall, S. and Ward, J. (2000) British get to the bottom of child discipline. *The Age*, 19 January.

Hamilton, E. and Cairns, H. (eds) (1961) *The Collected Dialogues of Plato*. Princeton: Princeton University Press.

Hammarberg, T. and Newell, P. (2000) *Corporal Punishment – Legalised Violence to Children: An Issue of Fundamental Importance to the Status of the Child and to the Prevention of All Forms of Abuse*. Paper presented at the Committee on the Rights of the Child Day of General Discussion 22 September, Geneva. Available at http://www.crin.org/docs/resources/treaties/crc.25/epoch.pdf [Accessed 21 June 2009].

Hammersley, M. (1992) Deconstructing the qualitative–quantitative divide, in *Mixing Methods: Qualitative and Quantitative Research* (ed J. Brannen), Aldershot: Avebury, pp. 39–56.

Hemenway, D., Solnick, S. and Carter, J. (1994) Child rearing violence. *Child Abuse & Neglect*, **18**, 1011–20.

Hendrick, H. (1997) *Children, Childhood and English Society 1880–1990*. Cambridge: Cambridge University Press.

Hengst, H. (2003) The role of the media and commercial culture in children's experiencing of collective identities, in *Children in Generational Perspective* (eds B. Mayall and H. Zeiher), London: University of London, pp. 111–32.

Herronkohl, R., Herronkohl, E. and Egolf, B. (1983) Circumstances surrounding the occurrence of child maltreatment. *Journal of Consulting and Clinical Psychology*, **51**, 424–31.

Herzberger, S. and Tennen, H. (1985) The effect of self-relevance on judgements of moderate and severe disciplinary encounters. *Journal of Marriage and the Family*, **47**, 311–18.

Hickley, M. (2001) Smacks take a beating in UK. *Herald Sun*, 8 September.

Hill, M. and Tisdall, K. (1997) *Children and Society*. London: Longman.

Hodgkin, R. (1997) Why the 'gentle smack' must go. *Children & Society*, **11**, 201–4.

Hodgson, S. (2007) Violent dad cares for shaken girl. *Herald Sun*, 3 April.

Hoff Sommers, C. (1994) *Who Stole Feminism?* New York: Simon & Schuster.

Holden, G.W. (2002) Perspectives on the effects of corporal punishment: comment on Gershoff (2002). *Psychological Bulletin*, **128**, 590–95.

Holden, G.W., Coleman, S.M. and Schmidt, K.L. (1995) Why 3-year-old children get spanked: parent and child determinants as reported by college-educated mothers. *Merrill-Palmer Quarterly*, **41**, 431–52.

Hood-Williams, J. (1990) Patriarchy for children: on the stability of power relations in children's lives, in *Childhood, Youth and Social Change: A Comparative Perspective* (eds L. Chisholm, P. Buchner, H. Kruger and P. Brown), London: The Farmer Press, pp. 155–71.

Hopkins, J. (2007) All this whipping to stop smacking is wasting time. *New Zealand Herald*, 16 March, p. 16.

Hops, H., Davis, B., Leve, C. and Sheeber, L. (2003) Cross-generational transmission of aggressive parent behavior: a prospective, mediational examination. *Journal of Abnormal Child Psychology*, **31**, 161–70.

Horin, A. (1995a) The door slammed on child discipline. *Sydney Morning Herald*, 10 June.

Horin, A. (1995b) Spare the rod. *Sydney Morning Herald*, 7 July.

House of Commons (2003) Health Committee Minutes, 27/3/03, Question 71. Available at http://www.publications.parliament.uk/pa/cm200203/cmselect/cmhealth/cmhealth.htm [Accessed 16 June 2009].

Howitt, D. (1993) *Child Abuse Errors: When Good Intentions Go Wrong*. New Brunswick, NJ: Rutgers University Press.

Huberman, A.M. and Miles, M.B. (eds) (2002) *The Qualitative Researcher's Companion*. Thousand Oaks: Sage.

Hughes, H. (1988) Psychological and behavioral correlates of family violence in child witnesses and victims. *American Journal of Orthopsychiatry*, **58**, 77–90.

Hughes, H., Parkinson, D. and Vargo, M. (1989) Witnessing spouse abuse and experiencing physical abuse: a double whammy. *Journal of Family Violence*, **4**, 197–209.

Human Rights Watch (2008) *A Violent Education: Corporal Punishment of Children in US Public Schools*. New York: Human Rights Watch.

Hume, M. (2003) Give the NSPCC a clip around the ear, somebody. *The Times*, 5 May.

Hunter, R. and Kilstrom, N. (1979) Breaking the cycle in abusive families. *American Journal of Orthopsychiatry*, **58**, 77–90.

Hyman, I. (1990) *Reading, Writing and the Hickory Stick*. Canada: Lexington Books.

Hyman, I. (1994) *Death and Discipline: A Study of the Justification for Beating a Child to Death, Unpublished study*: Temple University.

James, A., Jenks, C. and Prout, A. (1998) *Theorising Childhood*. Cambridge: Polity.

James, A. and Prout, A. (1997) *Constructing and Reconstructing Childhood: Contemporary Issues in the Sociological Study of Childhood*. London: Falmer Press.

Jaffee, S., Polo-Tomas, M., Caspi, A., Moffitt, T., Price, T. and Taylor, A. (2004) The limits of child effects: evidence for genetically mediated child effects on corporal punishment but not on physical maltreatment. *Developmental Psychology*, **40**(6), 1047–58.

Jamrozik, A. and Sweeney, T. (1996) *Children and Society*. South Melbourne: Macmillan.

Jenks, C. (1996) *Childhood*. London: Routledge.

Johnson, K. (1998) Crime or punishment: the parental corporal punishment defense – reasonable and necessary, or excused abuse? *University of Illinois Law Review*, **2**, 413–87.

Jones, D.N., Pickett, J., Oates, M.R. and Barbor, P. (1987) *Understanding Child Abuse*. London: Macmillan.

Jones, M. (1999) Myths and facts concerning the Convention on the Rights of the Child in Australia. *Australian Journal of Human Rights*, **5**, 126–49.

Jones, S. (2002) (Re)writing the word: methodological strategies and issues in qualitative research. *Journal of College Student Development*, **43**, 461–73.

Joseph, Y. (1995) Child protection rights: can an international declaration be an effective instrument for protecting children? in *Participation and Empowerment in Child Protection* (eds C. Cloke and M. Davies), London: Pitman, pp. 1–18.

Jouriles, E.N., Bourg, W. and Farris, A. (1991) Marital adjustment and child conduct problems: a comparison of the correlation across subsamples. *Journal of Consulting and Clinical Psychology*, **59**, 354–7.

Kadushin, A. and Martin, J. (1981) *Child Abuse – An Interactional Event*. New York: Columbia University Press.

Kaufman, J. and Zigler, E. (1989) The intergenerational transmission of child abuse, in *Child Maltreatment: Theory and Research on the Causes and Consequences of Child Abuse and Neglect* (eds D. Cicchetti and V. Carlson), Cambridge: Cambridge University Press, pp. 129–50.

Kazdin, A. and Benjet, C. (2003) Spanking children: evidence and issues. *American Psychological Society*, **12**, 99–103.

Kearney, M.K. (1995) Substantive due process and parental corporal punishment. *San Diego Law Review*, **32**, 1–51.

Keating, H. (2006) Protecting or punishing children: physical punishment, human rights and English law reform. *Legal Studies*, **26**, 394–413.

Keim, T. (2008) Mum jailed as court hears tot's injuries nearly killed him. *Courier Mail*, 15 December.

Keim, T. and Wenham, M. (2008) Smacking row reignited after mother thrashes her two children. *Courier Mail*, 6 August.

Kelder, L., McNamara, J., Carlson, B. and Lynn, S. (1991) Perceptions of physical punishment. *Journal of Interpersonal Violence*, **6**, 432–45.

Kempe, C.H., Denver, M.D., Silverman, F.N., Cincinnati, M., Steele, B.F., Droegemueller, M.D. *et al.* (1962) The battered-child syndrome. *Journal of the American Medical Association*, **181**, 17–24.

Knutson, J. and Selner, M. (1994) Punitive childhood experiences reported by young adults over a 10-year period. *Child Abuse & Neglect*, **18**, 155–66.

Kolar, V. and Soriano, G. (2000) *Parenting in Australian Families: A Comparative Study of Anglo, Torres Strait Islander, and Vietnamese Communities*. Melbourne: Australian Institute of Family Studies.

Kolko, D., Kazdin, A. and Day, B. (1996) Children's perspectives in the assessment of family violence: psychometric characteristics and comparison to parent groups. *Child Maltreatment*, **1**, 156–67.

Konstantareas, M. and Desbois, N. (2001) Preschoolers' perceptions of the unfairness of maternal disciplinary practices. *Child Abuse & Neglect*, **25**, 473–88.

Korbin, J. (1989) Fatal maltreatment by mothers: a proposed frame-work. *Child Abuse & Neglect*, **13**, 481–9.

Korbin, J. (1991) *'Good Mothers', 'Baby Killers' and Fatal Child Abuse*. Paper presented at the Annual Meeting of the American Anthropological Association, Chicago.

Korbin, J. (ed) (1981) *Child Abuse and Neglect: Cross-Cultural Perspectives*. California: University of California Press.

Korrel, K., Ulku-Steiner, B., Cox, M. and Burchinal, M. (2003) Marital relationship and individual psychological characteristics that predict physical punishment of children. *Journal of Family Psychology*, **17**, 20–28.

Kuzel, A.J. (1999) Sampling in qualitative inquiry, in *Doing Qualitative Research* (eds B.F. Crabtree and W.L. Miller), Thousand Oaks, CA: Sage, pp. 33–45.

Lansdown, G. (1994) Children's rights. In *Children's Childhoods: Observed and Experienced* (ed B. Mayall), London: Falmer Press, pp. 33–44.

Lansdown, G. (1995) Children's rights to participation and protection: a critique, in *Participation and Empowerment in Child Protection* (eds C. Cloke and M. Davies), London: Pitman Publishing, pp. 19–38.

Lansdown, G. (2000) Children's rights and domestic violence. *Child Abuse Review*, **9**, 416–26.

Lansford, J.E., Deater-Deckard, K., Dodge, K., Bates, J. and Pettit, G. (2004) Ethnic differences in the link between physical discipline and later adolescent externalizing behaviors. *Journal of Child Psychology and Psychiatry*, **45**, 801–12.

Larzelere, R. (1994) Corporal punishment by parents: Debate 12, in *Debating Children's Lives: Current Controversies on Children and Adolescents* (eds A. Mason and E. Gambrill), Thousand Oaks, CA: Sage, pp. 204–9.

Larzelere, R. (1996) A review of the outcomes of parental use of non-abusive and customary physical punishment. *Pediatrics*, **98**, 824–7.

Larzelere, R., Sather, P., Schneider, W., Larson, D. and Pike, P. (1998) Punishment enhances reasoning's effectiveness as a disciplinary response to toddlers. *Journal of Marriage and the Family*, **60**, 388–403.

Larzelere, R., Silver, C. and Polite, K. (1997) Nonabusive spanking: parental liberty or child abuse? *Children's Legal Rights Journal*, **17**, 7–16.

Larzelere, R.E. (2000) Child outcomes of non-abusive and customary physical punishment. *Clinical Child and Family Psychology Review*, **3**, 199–221.

Leach, P. (1979) *Baby and Child from Birth to Age Five*. London: Penguin.

Leach, P. (1992) *What's Wrong with Hitting Children? Ending Physical Punishment of European Children, Final Report from Two-Day Seminar*. London: EPOCH.

Leach, P. (1994) *Children First*. London: Penguin.

Leach, P. (1999) *The Physical Punishment of Children: Some Input from Research*. London: NSPCC.

Lee, N. (2001) *Childhood and Society: Growing Up in an Age of Uncertainty*. Buckingham: Open University Press.

Limber, S.P. and Flekkoy, M.G. (1995) The UN Convention on the Rights of the Child: its relevance to social scientists, in *Social Policy Report: Society for Research in Child Development*, Vol. IX, No 2. (ed N. Thomas), Ann Arbor: University of Michigan.

Lincoln, Y.S. and Guba, E.G. (1985) *Naturalistic Inquiry*. Thousand Oaks, CA: Sage.

Little, M. (1995) Child protection or family support? Finding a balance. *Family Matters*, **40**, 18–21.

Lloyd-Smith, M. and Tarr, J. (2000) Researching children's perspectives: sociological issues, in *Researching Children's Perspectives* (eds A. Lewis and G. Lindsay), Buckingham: Oxford University Press, pp. 59–69.

Ludbrook, R. (1995) The child's right to bodily integrity. *Current Issues in Criminal Justice*, **7**, 123–32.

Lynch, S., Turkheimer, E., D'Onofrio, B., Mendle, J., Emery, R., Slutske, W. and Martin, N. (2006) A genetically informed study of the association between harsh punishment and offspring behavioral problems. *Journal of Family Psychology*, **20**(2), 190–98.

Lyons, C. (2000) *Loving Smack or Lawful Assault: A Contradiction in Human Rights and Law*. London: Institute for Public Policy Research.

Margo, J. and Stevens, A. (2008) *Make Me a Criminal: Preventing Youth Crime*. London: Institute for Public Policy Research.

Mason, J. and Falloon, J. (1999) A children's perspective on child abuse. *Children Australia*, **24**, 9–13.

Mason, J. and Falloon, J. (2001) Some Sydney children define abuse: implications for agency in childhood, in *Conceptualizing Child–Adult Relations* (eds L. Alanen and B. Mayall), London: RoutledgeFalmer, pp. 99–113.

Masson, J. (2000) Researching children's perspectives: legal issues, in *Researching Children's Perspectives* (eds A. Lewis and G. Lindsay), Buckingham: Open University Press, pp. 34–45.

Mauthner, N. and Doucet, A. (2003) Reflexive accounts and accounts of reflexivity in qualitative analysis. *Sociology*, **37**, 413–31.

May-Chahal, C. and Cawson, P. (2005) Measuring child maltreatment in the United Kingdom: a study of the prevalence of child abuse and neglect. *Child Abuse & Neglect*, **29**, 969–84.

Mayall, B. (1994) *Children's Childhoods: Observed and Experienced*. London: Falmer Press.

Mayall, B. (2000) The sociology of childhood in relation to children's rights. *The International Journal of Children's Rights*, **8**, 243–59.

Mayall, B. (2002) *Towards a Sociology for Childhood: Thinking About Children's Lives.* Buckingham: Open University Press.

Mays, N. and Pope, C. (2000) Qualitative research in health care: assessing quality in qualitative research. *British Medical Journal,* **320,** 50–52.

McCord, J. (1996) Unintended consequences of punishment. *Pediatrics,* **98,** 832–4.

McGee, C. (1997) Children's experience of domestic violence. *Child and Family Social Work,* **2,** 13–23.

McGillivray, A. (1994) Why children do have equal rights: in reply to Laura Purdy. *The International Journal of Children's Rights,* **2,** 243–58.

McGillivray, A. (1997a) 'He'll learn it on his body': disciplining childhood in Canadian law. *International Journal of Children's Rights,* **5,** 193–242.

McGillivray, A. (ed) (1997b) *Governing Childhood.* Aldershot: Dartmouth Publishing Company.

Medley, A. and Sachs-Ericsson, N. (2009) Predictors of parental physical abuse: the contribution of internalizing and externalizing disorders and childhood experiences of abuse. *Journal of Affective Disorders,* **113,** 244–54.

Milfull, C., and Schetzer, L. (2000) *Sufficient Protection for Australian Children's Rights? Beyond the Corbett Bill.* Sydney: National Children's and Youth Law Centre.

Miller, W.L. and Crabtree, B.F. (1999) Clinical research: a multimethod typology and qualitative roadmap, in *Doing Qualitative Research* (eds B.F. Crabtree and W.L. Miller), Thousand Oaks, CA: Sage, pp. 3–30.

Miller-Perrin, C.L., Perrin, R.D. and Kocur, J.L. (2009) Parental physical and psychological aggression: psychological symptoms in young adults. *Child Abuse & Neglect,* **33,** 1–11.

Minow, M., and Rakoff, T. (1998) Is the 'reasonable person' a reasonable standard in a multicultural world? in *Fundamental Issues in Law and Society Research,* Vol. 2 (eds A. Sarat, M. Constable, D. Engel, V. Hans and S. Lawrence), pp. 40–68. Evanston, IL: Northwestern University Press.

Model Criminal Code Officers Committee (MCCOC) (1998) *Model Criminal Code Chapter 5 Non-Fatal Offences against the Person.* Barton, Sydney: Criminal Law Division, Attorney-General's Department.

Montague, A. (1978) *Learning Non-Aggression: the Experience of Non-Literate Societies.* New York: Oxford University Press.

Moore, B. (ed) (2002) *The Australian Pocket Oxford Dictionary.* Victoria: Oxford University Press.

Mount, S. (1995) Physical punishment in the home: a private prerogative? *Auckland University Law Review,* **7,** 985–1011.

Mudaly, N. and Goddard, C.R. (2006) *The Truth is Longer than a Lie: Children's Experiences of Abuse and Professional Interventions.* London: Jessica Kingsley.

Mudaly, N. and Goddard, C. (2009) The ethics of involving children who have been abused in child abuse research. *International Journal of Children's Rights,* **17,** 261–281.

Muir, H., Shaw, T. and Sylvester, R. (1996) Major vows to defend smacking – Tory anger as caned boy is given permission to challenge the law. *Daily Telegraph*, 10 September.

Mullender, A., Hague, G., Imam, U., Kelly, L., Malos, E. and Regan, L. (2002) *Children's Perspectives on Domestic Violence*. London: Sage.

Muller, R., Hunter, J. and Stollack, G. (1995) The intergenerational transmission of corporal punishment: a comparison of social learning and temperament models. *Child Abuse & Neglect*, **19**, 1323–35.

Murdoch, A. (1992) Smacking: why it doesn't help. *The Sydney Morning Herald*, 4 June.

Naylor, B. and Saunders, B.J. (2009) Whose rights? Children, parents and discipline. *Alternative Law Journal*, **34**, 2, 80–85.

Newell, P. (1989) *Children Are People Too: The Case against Physical Punishment*. London: Bedford Square.

News Nation (2007) Outrage at judge excusing mum for beating daughter. *The Cairns Post*, 30 March.

News Sentinel (2008) (editorial) The tricky line between discipline and child abuse: court's dismissal of battery conviction will add to the debate. *The News Sentinel*, 16 June.

Newsom, C., Favell, J.E. and Rincover, A. (1983) The side effects of punishment, in *The Effects of Punishment on Human Behavior* (eds S. Axelrod and J. Apsche), New York: Academic Press, pp. 285–97.

Ney, P., Fung, T. and Wickett, A.R. (1994) The worst combinations of child abuse and neglect. *Child Abuse & Neglect*, **18**, 705–14.

Nicholson, A. (2008) Choose to hug, not hit. *Family Court Review*, **46**, 11–36.

Nielsen Omnibus Survey (2008) *One Year On: Public Attitudes and New Zealand's Child Discipline Law*: Office of the Children's Commissioner.

Nielssen, O., Large, M., Westmore, B. and Lackersteen, S. (2009) Child homicide in New South Wales from 1991 to 2005. *Medical Journal of Australia*, **190**, 7–11.

Nilsson, M. (2003) *Global Initiative Handbook: Hitting People is Wrong – and Children are People Too*. Sweden: Save the Children.

Nobes, G. and Smith, M. (2000) The relative extent of physical punishment and abuse by mothers and fathers. *Trauma, Violence & Abuse*, **1**, 47–66.

Nofziger, S. (2008) The 'cause' of low self-control: the influence of maternal self-control. *Journal of Research in Crime and Delinquency*, **45**, 191–224.

Northern Ireland (Law Reform (Miscellaneous Provisions) Order (2006) Available from http://www.dfpni.gov.uk/uksi_20061945_en.pdf [Accessed 21 June 2009].

NSPCC (2002) *NSPCC Survey Shows Hitting Children Hurts Parents Too*. London: NSPCC.

NSPCC (2007) Press release, 10 April. Available at www.nspcc.org.uk [Accessed 22 June 2009].

NSPCC (2008) Equal Protection for Children under the Law on Assault (NSPCC Policy Summary). Available at http://www.nspcc.org.uk/ [Accessed 22 June 2009].

Oakley, A. (1994) Women and children first and last: parallels and differences between children's and women's studies, in *Children's Childhoods Observed and Experienced* (ed B. Mayall), London: Falmer Press, pp. 13–32.

Oldershaw, L. (2002) *A National Survey of Parents of Young Children*. Toronto: Invest in Kids.

Orb, A., Eisenhauer, L. and Wynaden, D. (2001) Ethics in qualitative research. *Journal of Nursing Scholarship*, **33**, 93–6.

O'Reilly, M. (2008) 'I didn't violent punch him': parental accounts of punishing children with mental health problems. *Journal of Family Therapy*, **30**, 272–95.

Palmerus, K. (1999) Self-reported discipline among Swedish parents of preschool children. *Infant and Child Development*, **8**, 155–71.

Parke, R.D. (2002) Punishment revisited – science, values, and the right question: comment on Gershoff (2002). *Psychological Bulletin*, **128**, 596–601.

Pears, K. and Capaldi, D. (2001) Intergenerational transmission of abuse: a two-generational prospective study of an at-risk sample. *Child Abuse & Neglect*, **25**, 1439–61.

Pearsall, J. (ed) (1998) *The New Oxford Dictionary of English*. Oxford: Clarendon Press.

Peterson, L., Ewigman, B. and Vandiver, T. (1994) Role of parental anger in low income women: discipline strategy, perceptions of behavior problems, and the need for control. *Journal of Clinical Child Psychology*, **23**, 435–43.

Philip, G. (1996) Violence in children: the scope for prevention. *Archives of Disease in Childhood*, **74**, 185–7.

Pinchbeck, I. and Hewitt, M. (1969) *Children in English Society*. London: Routledge & Kegan Paul.

Pinheiro, P. (2006) *World Report on Violence against Children*. Geneva, Switzerland: United Nations Secretary-General's Study on Violence Against Children.

Pollard, D. (2003) Banning child corporal punishment. *Tulane Law Review*, **77**, 575–656.

Pollock, L. (1983) *Forgotten Children: Parent–Child Relations from 1500 to 1900*. Cambridge: Cambridge University Press.

Pope, C., Ziebland, S. and Mays, N. (2000) Analysing qualitative data. *British Medical Journal*, **320**, 114–16.

Postman, N. (1982) *The Disappearance of Childhood*. New York: Delacorte Press.

Power, T. and Chiapeski, L. (1986) Childrearing and impulse control in toddlers: a naturalistic investigation. *Developmental Psychology*, **22**, 271–5.

Preston, N. (1990) 'Justice and security for our children': the rights of children and education. *Children Australia*, **15**, 10–13.

Price, J. (2000) Smacking and verbal abuse of children by parents. Available at *British Medical Journal*: Rapid Responses http://bmj.bmjjournals.com/cgi/eletters/320/7230/261, **320**, 261–262 [Accessed 16 June 2008].

QSR. Available at http://www.qsrinternational.com/ [Accessed 22 June 2009].

Qvortrup, J., Bardy, M., Sgritta, G. and Wintersberger, H. (eds) (1994) *Childhood Matters*. Aldershot: Avebury.

R. v. Hopley. (1860) *English Reports, 2 F and F 202.* Available at http://www.commonlii.org/int/cases/EngR/1860/ [Accessed 22 June 2009].

R. v. Terry (1955) *Victorian Law Reports*, 114. Melbourne: Butterworths.

Radbill, S. (1980) Children in a world of violence: a history of child abuse, in *The Battered Child* (eds C. Kempe and R. Helfer), Chicago: University of Chicago Press, pp. 3–20.

Rayner, M. (1992) Children's voices, adults' choices: children's rights to legal representation. *Family Matters*, **33**, 4–10.

Rayner, M. (1994a) Human rights, families, and community interests. *Family Matters*, **37**, 60–66.

Rayner, M. (1994b) The ugly truth about the hand that wields the power. *The Age*, 29 June.

Reder, P., Duncan, S. and Lacey, C. (2003) What principles guide parenting assessments? in *Studies in the Assessment of Parenting* (eds P. Reder, S. Duncan and C. Lacey), Hove: Brunner-Routledge, pp. 3–26.

Regalado, M., Sareen, H., Inkelas, M., Wissow, L. and Halfon, N. (2004) Parents' discipline of young children: results from the national survey of early childhood health. *Pediatrics*, **113**, 1952–8.

Rice, H. (2009a) Jurors rule quickly on Baby Grace. *Houston Chronicle*, 2 February.

Rice, H. (2009b) Baby Grace evidence: 'we need to break her'. *Houston Chronicle*, 28 January.

Roberts, H. and Roberts, I. (2000) Smacking. *Child: Care, Health and Development*, **26**(4), 259–62.

Roberts, J. (2000) Changing public attitudes towards corporal punishment: the effects of statutory reform in Sweden. *Child Abuse & Neglect*, **24**, 1027–35.

Robertshaw, C. (1994) *Brief to: Minister of Justice and Attorney General, Solicitor General, Minister of Health et al. re: Section 43 of the Criminal Code and the Corporal Punishment of Children.* Canada: The Institute for the Prevention of Child Abuse.

Rodriguez, C. and Green, A. (1997) Parenting stress and anger expression as predictors of child abuse potential. *Child Abuse & Neglect*, **21**, 367–77.

Rodriguez, C. and Richardson, M. (2007) Stress and anger as contextual factors and preexisting cognitive schemas: predicting parental child maltreatment risk. *Child Maltreatment*, **12**, 325–37.

Rodriguez, C. and Sutherland, D. (1999) Predictors of parents' physical disciplinary practices. *Child Abuse & Neglect*, **23**, 651–7.

Royal Commission on Human Relationships (1977) *Final Report*, Vol. 4. Canberra: Australian Government Publishing Service.

Ruane, J. (1993) Tolerating force: a contextual analysis of the meaning of tolerance. *Sociological Inquiry*, **63**, 293–304.

Saidla, D. (1992) Children's rights regarding physical abuse. *Journal of Humanistic Education and Development*, **31**, 73–83.

Salt, H. (1905) The ethics of corporal punishment. *International Journal of Ethics*, **16**, 77–88.

Sariola, H. and Utela, A. (1992) The prevalence and context of family violence against children in Finland. *Child Abuse & Neglect*, **16**, 823–32.

Saunders, B.J. (2005) *'Because There's a Better Way than Hurting Someone': An Exploratory Study of the Nature, Effect and Persistence of 'Physical Punishment' in Childhood*. Unpublished PhD, Monash University, Melbourne.

Saunders, B.J. and Goddard, C. (1999) *Why Do We Condone the Physical Assault of Children by Their Parents and Caregivers?* Ringwood, Victoria: Australian Childhood Foundation.

Saunders, B.J. and Goddard, C. (2001) The textual abuse of childhood in the English-speaking world – the contribution of language to the denial of children's rights. *Childhood*, **8**, 443–62.

Saunders, B.J. and Goddard, C. (2003) *The Role of the Mass Media in Facilitating Community Education and Child Abuse Prevention Strategies*, Melbourne: Australian Institute of Family Studies.

Saunders, B.J. and Goddard, C. (2005) The objectification of the child through 'physical discipline' and language: the debate on children's rights continues, in *Children Taken Seriously: In Theory, Policy and Practice* (eds J. Mason and T. Fattore), Birmingham: Jessica Kingsley, pp. 113–22.

Saunders, B.J. and Goddard, C. (2007) The importance of listening to children: a qualitative study on the use of parental physical punishment in childhood in Australia. *Social Development Issues*, **29**, 33–46.

Saunders, B.J. and Goddard, C. (2008) Some Australian children's perceptions of physical punishment in childhood. *Children & Society*, **22**, 405–17.

Save the Children (2001) *Ending Corporal Punishment of Children: Making it Happen*. London: Save the Children.

Scaramella, L. and Conger, R. (2003) Intergenerational continuity of hostile parenting and its consequences: the moderating influence of children's negative emotional reactivity. *Social Development*, **12**, 420–39.

Scarre, G. (ed) (1989) *Children, Parents and Politics*. Cambridge: Cambridge University Press.

Shay, N. and Knutson, J. (2008) Maternal depression and trait anger as risk factors for escalated physical discipline. *Child Maltreatment*, **13**(1), 39–49.

Silverman, D. (2000) *Doing Qualitative Research: A Practical Handbook*. London: Sage.

Silverstein, M., Augustyn, M., Young, R. and Zuckerman, B. (2009) The relationship between maternal depression, in-home violence and use of physical punishment: what is the role of child behaviour? *Archives of Disease in Childhood*, **94**, 138–43.

Simons, R., Whitbeck, L., Conger, R. and Chyi-lin, W. (1991) Intergenerational transmission of harsh parenting. *Developmental Psychology*, **27**, 159–71.

Simpson, B. (1996) 'Moderate and reasonable'? The early history of the administrative regulation of corporal punishment in Victorian schools. *History of Education Review*, **25**, 23–37.

Singh Narang, D. and Contreras, J. (2000) Disassociation as a mediator between child abuse history and adult abuse potential. *Child Abuse & Neglect*, **24**, 653–65.

Smart, C., Neale, B. and Wade, A. (2001) *The Changing Experience of Childhood: Families and Divorce.* Cambridge: Polity Press.

Smith, A. (2000) Introduction, in *Advocating for Children* (eds A. Smith, M. Gollop, K. Marshall and K. Nairn), Dunedin, NZ: University of Otago Press, pp. 13–18.

Smith, J. (1984) Nonaccidental injury to children: a review of behavioral intentions. *Behavior Research and Therapy*, **22**, 331–47.

Smith, M., Bee, P., Heverin, A. and Nobes, G. (1995) The nature and extent of parental violence to children, in *Child Protection: Messages from Research* (ed Dartington Social Research Unit (DSRU)), London: Department of Health.

Socolar, R. (1997) A classification scheme for discipline; type, mode of administration, context. *Aggression and Violent Behavior*, **2**, 355–64.

Socolar, R., Savage, E. and Hughes, E. (2007) A longitudinal study of parental discipline of young children. *Southern Medical Journal*, **100**, 472–7.

Socolar, R. and Stein, R. (1995) Spanking infants and toddlers: maternal belief and practice. *Pediatrics*, **95**, 105–11.

Solheim, J.S. (1982) A cross-cultural examination of use of corporal punishment on children: a focus on Sweden and the United States. *Child Abuse & Neglect*, **6**, 147–54.

Somander, L. and Rammer, L. (1991) Intra- and extra-familial child homicide in Sweden 1971–1980. *Child Abuse & Neglect*, **15**, 45–55.

Sommerville, C.J. (1990) *The Rise and Fall of Childhood.* New York: Vintage Books.

Sorbring, E., Rodholm-Funnemark, M. and Palmerus, K. (2003) Boys' and girls' perceptions of parental discipline in transgression situations. *Infant and Child Development*, **12**, 53–69.

South Wales Echo (2008) Smacking ban slapped down by Westminster. *South Wales Echo*, 18 January.

Spink, P. and Spink, S. (1999) What is reasonable chastisement? *Journal of the Law Society of Scotland*, **44**, 26–7.

Stacks, A., Oshio, T., Gerard, J. and Roe, J. (2009) The moderating effect of parental warmth on the association between spanking and child aggression: a longitudinal approach. *Infant and Child Development*, Online in Wiley Interscience. DOI: 10.1002/icd.596.

Standing Committee on Law and Justice. (2000). *Report of the Inquiry into the Crimes Amendment (Child Protection – Excessive Punishment) Bill 2000.* Sydney: Legislative Council, New South Wales Parliament.

Stanley, J. and Goddard, C. (1995) The abused child as hostage. *Children Australia*, **20**, 24–9.

Stanley, J. and Goddard, C. (1997) Failures in child protection: a case study. *Child Abuse Review*, **6**, 46–54.

Stanley, J. and Goddard, C. (2002) *In the Firing Line: Violence and Power in Child Protection Work.* West Sussex: Wiley.

Starling, S., Sirotnak, A.P., Heisler, K.W. and Barnes-Eley, M.L. (2007) Inflicted skeletal trauma: the relationship of perpetrators to their victims. *Child Abuse & Neglect*, **31**, 993–9.

Steinmetz, S. and Straus, M. (1973) The family as cradle of violence. *Society*, **10**, 50–56.

Stone, L. (1977) *The Family, Sex and Marriage in England 1500–1800*. London: Weidenfeld & Nicolson.

Strassberg, Z., Dodge, K., Pettit, G. and Bates, J. (1994) Spanking in the home and children's subsequent aggression toward kindergarten peers. *Development and Psychopathology*, **6**, 445–61.

Straus, M. (1983) Ordinary violence, child abuse and wife-beating: what do they have in common? in *The Dark Side of Families* (eds D. Finkelhor, R. Gelles, G. Hotaling and M. Straus), Beverley Hills: Sage, pp. 213–34.

Straus, M. (1994) *Beating the Devil Out of Them: Corporal Punishment in American Families*. New York: Lexton Books.

Straus, M. (1996) Spanking and the making of a violent society. *Pediatrics*, **98**, 837–4.

Straus, M. (2000) Corporal punishment and primary prevention of physical abuse. *Child Abuse & Neglect*, **24**, 1109–14.

Straus, M. (2009) The special issue on prevention of violence ignores the primordial violence. *Journal of Interpersonal Violence*, **23**, 1314–20.

Straus, M. and Gelles, R. (1990) *Physical Violence in American Families: Risk Factors and Adaptations to Violence in 8,145 families*. New Brunswick, NJ: Transaction Publishers.

Straus, M. and Mathur, A. (1996) Social change and change in approval of corporal punishment by parents from 1968 to 1994, in *Family Violence against Children: A Challenge for Society* (eds D. Frehsee, W. Horn and K.D. Bussmann), New York: Walter de Gruyter, pp. 91–105.

Straus, M. and Mouradian, V. (1998) Impulsive corporal punishment by mothers and antisocial behavior and impulsiveness of children. *Behavioral Sciences and the Law*, **16**, 353–74.

Straus, M. and Stewart, J. (1999) Corporal punishment by American parents: national data on prevalence, chronicity, duration, in relation to child and family characteristics. *Clinical Child and Family Psychology Review*, **2**, 55–70.

Strauss, A. (1987) *Qualitative Analysis for Social Scientists*. New York: Cambridge University Press.

Strauss, A. and Corbin, J. (1998) *Basics of Qualitative Research: Techniques and Procedures for Developing Grounded Theory*. Thousand Oaks, CA: Sage.

Stroud, J. and Pritchard, C. (2001) Child homicide, psychiatric disorder and dangerousness: a review and an empirical approach. *British Journal of Social Work*, **31**, 249–69.

Summary of the 404th Meeting: Australia 22/12/97. CRC/C/SR. 404 (Summary Record). Available at http://www.bayefsky.com/summary/australia_crc_c_sr. 4041997.php [Accessed 22 June 2009].

Sunday, S., Labruna, V., Kaplan, S., Pelcovitz, D., Newman, J. and Salzinger, S. (2008) Physical abuse during adolescence: gender differences in the adolescents' perceptions of family functioning and parenting. *Child Abuse & Neglect*, **32**, 5–18.

Swain, S. (1998) The State and the Child. *Australian Journal of Legal History*, **4**, 57–77.

Tasmanian Law Reform Institute (2003) *Physical Punishment of Children Final Report No 4*. Hobart: Tasmanian Law Reform Institute.

Taylor, A. (1998) Hostages to fortune: The abuse of children in care, in *Whistleblowing in the Social Services* (ed G. Hunt), London: Arnold, pp. 41–64.

Taylor, J. and Redman, S. (2004) The smacking controversy: what advice should we be giving parents? *Journal of Advanced Nursing*, **46**, 311–18.

Taylor, P., Moore, P., Pezzullo, L., Tucci, J., Goddard, C. and De Bortoli, L. (2008) *The Cost of Child Abuse in Australia*. Melbourne: Access Economics, Australian Childhood Foundation and Child Abuse Prevention Research Australia.

The Queen v. Damien Paul Ripper (County Court Victoria). Available at http://www.countycourt.vic.gov.au/CA256D90000479B3/Lookup/Judgments_R/$file/VCC0627.pdf [Accessed 6 September 2009].

Thomas, N. and O'Kane, C. (1998) The ethics of participatory research with children. *Children & Society*, **12**, 336–48.

Thompson, R.A. (1993) Developmental research and legal policy: toward a two-way street, in *Child Abuse, Child Development and Social Policy* (eds D. Cicchetti and S. L. Toth), Norwood, NJ: Ablex, pp. 75–115.

Thompson, R.A. (1995) *Preventing Child Maltreatment through Social Support: A Critical Analysis*. California: Sage.

Trumbach, R. (1978) *The Rise of the Egalitarian Family*. New York: Academic Press.

Tu, J. (2008) Advocate for spanking whips up furor in area. *Seattle Times*, 19 September.

Tucci, J., Goddard, C. and Mitchell, J. (2001) *More Action – Less Talk: Community Responses to Child Abuse Prevention*. Ringwood, Victoria: Australian Childhood Foundation.

Tucci, J., Mitchell, J. and Goddard, C. (2006a) *Crossing the Line: Making the Case for Changing Australian Laws about the Physical Punishment of Children*. Ringwood, Victoria: Australian Childhood Foundation.

Tucci, J., Mitchell, J. and Goddard, C. (2006b). *Out of Sight – Out of Mind: Community Attitudes about Child Abuse and Child Protection in Australia*. Ringwood, Victoria: Australian Childhood Foundation.

Tucci, J., Saunders, B.J. and Goddard, C. (2002) *Please Don't Hit Me! Community Attitudes towards the 'Physical Punishment' of Children*. Ringwood, Victoria: Australian Childhood Foundation.

Turner, M. (2004) Man beat son over breakfast. *The Cairns Post*, 29 January.

Turner, S. (2002) *Something to Cry About: An Argument against Corporal Punishment of Children in Canada*. Ontario: Wilfred Laurier University Press.

Turner, S. (2003) Justifying corporal punishment of children loses its appeal. *The International Journal of Children's Rights*, **11**, 219–33.

UNICEF (2001) *A League Table of Child Deaths by Injury in Rich Nations*, Innocenti Report Card 2. Florence: Innocenti Research Centre.

UNICEF (2007) *Child Poverty in Perspective: An Overview of Child Well-Being in Rich Countries*, Innocenti Report Card 7. Florence: Innocenti Research Centre.

United Nations Convention on the Rights of the Child (1989). Available at http://www.un.org/documents/ga/res/44/a44r025.htm [Accessed 22 June 2009].

US Advisory Board on Child Abuse and Neglect (1995) *A Nation's Shame: Fatal Child Abuse and Neglect in the United States*. Washington: US Department of Health and Human Services.

Vaidya, J.S. (2000) Re: 'safety-valve' effect of spanking. *British Medical Journal*: Rapid Responses. Available at http://bmj.bmjjournals.com/cgi/eletters/320/7230/261, **320**, 261–262 [Accessed 16 June 2008].

Vieth, V. (1994) Corporal punishment in the United States: a call for a new approach to the prosecution of disciplinarians. *Journal of Juvenile Law*, **15**, 22–56.

Virtrup, B., Holden, G. and Buck, J. (2006) Attitudes predict the use of physical punishment: a progressive study of the emergence of disciplinary practices. *Pediatrics*, **117**, 2055–64.

Vissing, Y., Straus, M., Gelles, R. and Harrop, J. (1991) Verbal aggression by parents and psychosocial problems of children. *Child Abuse & Neglect*, **15**, 223–38.

Vostanis, P., Meltzer, H., Goodman, R., Jenkins, R. and Brugha, T. (2006) Relationship between parental psychopathology, parenting strategies and child mental health. *Social Psychiatry and Psychiatric Epidemiology*, **41**, 509–14.

Waksler, F. (ed) (1991) *Studying the Social Worlds of Children: Sociological Readings*. London: Falmer Press.

Waldrop, D. (2004) Ethical issues in qualitative research with high risk populations, in *The Qualitative Research Experience* (ed D. Padgett), Belmont, CA: Wadsworth/Thompson Learning, pp. 236–49.

Waller, L., and Williams, C.R. (2001) *Criminal Law: Text and Cases*. New South Wales: Butterworths.

Walvin, J. (1982) *A Child's World: A Social History of English Childhood 1800–1914*. Harmondsworth, England: Penguin Books.

Ware, H. (1983) *Corporal Punishment in Schools and the Rights of the Child: Discussion Paper No.1*. Canberra: Human Rights Commission.

Watkins, D. and Cousins, J. (2005) Child physical punishment injury and abuse (part two). *Community Practitioner*, **78**, 318–21.

Watkinson, A. (2006) Supreme Court of Canada stands behind corporal punishment – sort of … *International Social Work*, **49**, 531–6.

Wauchope, B. and Straus, M. (1990) Physical punishment and physical abuse of American children: incidence rates by age, gender and occupational class, in *Physical Violence in American Families: Risk Factors and Adaptations to Violence in 8,145 Families* (eds M. Straus and R. Coellas), New Brunswick, NJ: Transaction, pp. 133–48.

Wells, D. (2008) 'Reasonable' assaults? *Proctor*, **June**, 25–6.

Wenham, M. (2008) Weapons used on children. *The Courier Mail*, 18 December.

Whipple, E. and Richey, C. (1997) Crossing the line from physical discipline to child abuse: how much is too much? *Child Abuse & Neglect*, **21**, 431–44.

Whitney, S., Tajima, E., Herrenkohl, T. and Huang, B. (2006) Defining child abuse: exploring variations in ratings of discipline severity among child welfare practitioners. *Child and Adolescent Social Work Journal*, **23**, 316–42.

Wilczynski, A. (1995) Child killing by parents: a motivational model. *Child Abuse Review*, **4**, 365–70.

Wilczynski, A. (1997a) *Child Homicide*. London: Greenwich Medical Media.

Wilczynski, A. (1997b) Prior agency contact and physical abuse in cases of child homicide. *British Journal of Social Work*, **27**, 241–53.

Willow, C. and Hyder, T. (1998) *It Hurts You Inside: Children Talking about Smacking*. London: National Children's Bureau Enterprises.

Winn, M. (1983) *Children without Childhood*. New York: Pantheon Books.

Wissow, L. (1996) What clinicians need to know about teaching families new disciplinary tools? *Pediatrics*, **98**, 815–17.

Wood, B., Hassall, I., Hook, G. and Ludbrook, R. (2008) *Unreasonable Force: New Zealand's Journey towards Banning the Physical Punishment of Children*. Wellington: Save the Children.

Woodward, L.J. and Fergusson, D. (2002) Parent, child and contextual predictors of childhood physical punishment. *Infant and Child Development*, **11**, 213–35.

Woodward, L.J., Taylor, E. and Dowdney, L. (1998) The parenting and family functioning of children with hyperactivity. *Journal of Child Psychology and Psychiatry*, **39**, 161–9.

Working Party on the Abolition of Corporal Punishment (1983) *Report of the Working Party on the Abolition of Corporal Punishment*. Victoria: Education Department.

Zeiher, H. (2003) Intergenerational relations and social change in childhood, in *Childhood in Generational Perspective* (eds B. Mayall and H. Zeiher), London: University of London, pp. 157–78.

Ziegert, K. (1983) The Swedish prohibition of corporal punishment: a preliminary report. *Journal of Marriage and the Family*, **45**, 917–26.

Zolotar, A., Theodore, A., Chang, J., Berkoff, M. and Runyan, D. (2008) Speak softly – and forget the stick. *American Journal of Preventive Medicine*, **35**, 364–9.

Zuravin, S.J., McMillen, C., DePanfilis, D. and Risley-Curtiss, C. (1996) The intergenerational cycle of maltreatment: continuity vs discontinuity. *Journal of Interpersonal Violence*, **11**, 315–34.

Index

Physical Punishment in Childhood: The Rights of the Child, by Bernadette J. Saunders and Chris Goddard
Copyright © 2010 John Wiley & Sons, Ltd.

4. Conclusion

272

Index